DECEIVE

By

The Phantom

RJ Publications, LLC

Newark, New Jersey

The characters and events in this book are fictitious. Any resemblance to actual persons, living or dead is purely coincidental.

RJ Publications
Thephantom_8182@yahoo.com
www.rjpublications.com
Copyright © 2011 by RJ Publications
All Rights Reserved
ISBN-10: 0981999859
ISBN-13: 978-0981999852

Printed in The United States

September 2011

1 2 3 4 5 6 7 8 9 10

Chapter One

Stink lounged comfortably in the passenger seat of the SL500 Mercedes Benz coupe, eyeing the passing trees that line interstate I-95. After being caged in the mountains of West Virginia for the last five years, freedom never felt better.

Peering to his left, Stink licked his lips in anticipation of the *lovin'* he planned on making to the beautiful specimen sitting next to him. Suddenly her freshly done French pedicured toes barely covered in 'Giuseppe Zanotti' stilettos, pressed down on the accelerator, causing the silver Mercedes to leap out in front of the traffic.

They were on a tight schedule that couldn't be hindered by the formalities of a traffic jam.

As stink continued his gratuitous glare of the exotic creature's body, her thick almond brown thighs glistened off the spring sun. The past five years hadn't aged her a bit; she was even more beautiful than when Stink first met her. More importantly, she remained loyal to him when everyone else fell by the wayside.

Stink attempted to look into the tint of Melody's 'Prada' shades, only to receive a heart melting smile.

While keeping her eyes on the crowded interstate, she asked "Boo, why are you looking at me like that?"

"I was just thinking," he replied coolly. "About What?" Melody asked slyly. Giving Melody a quick smirk, Stink leaned back and allowed her to tackle the road ahead. Once he was comfortable, he closed his eyes and allowed the last five years to replay through his mind.

December 1994

Breaking the monotonous silence that engulfed the courtroom, the judge firmly instructed, "Mr. Scott, answer the question!" Cross looked up to the judge briefly, and then turned his attention back to Mr. Hernandez who stood nervously awaiting a reply. With his features transforming into a contemptuous grin, Cross casually said, "Stink ain't know nothing about no drugs. Them drugs were all mines."

There was a loud sigh from the courtroom, causing the judge to bang his gravel, "Order! Order!" He yelled, and then added, "If I have to bring this courtroom to order once more, I won't hesitate to clear it!" He threatened.

In a daze, U.S. Attorney Hernandez stood in the middle of the courtroom dumbfounded. He couldn't believe his star witness had flipped on him in the middle of the trail. Desperately, he yelled, "I want this witness to be deemed a hostile witness!"

The judge looked to Mr. Hernandez pitifully, and then said, "Mr. Hernandez, the witness has complied with your questions. Now, are there any further questions for the witness?"

Stink watched the spectacle unfold through disbelieving eyes. Inwardly, he was smiling; he knew Cross couldn't 'cross' him in such a manner.

"Mr. Hernandez, if you have no further questions, I'm pretty sure the defense would like to cross-examine," the judge stated with a hint of sarcasm.

Frustrated and defeated, Mr. Hernandez flopped down in his seat.

Stink's lawyer, Mr. Clancy, stood and asked Cross a few questions reiterating his prior statement, which clearly exonerated Stink of all the government's accusations.

Once Mr. Clancy's questioning ended, Cross exited the stand. Looking toward Stink, Cross' eyes said a million things, yet the most important being, 'I Love you, Nigga.'

After four consecutive days of trail, it was coming to an end. The prosecution still had one unidentified witness to testify. "The government calls Damien Barnett," Mr. Hernandez announced. Stink was even more shocked than when Cross had been called to the stand. Seeing Dame walk freely from the door in the rear of the courtroom, Stink dropped his head in disbelief.

Unable to make eye contact with neither Stink nor Lil Man, Dame kept his eyes glued to the floor as he took a seat on the stand. While Dame was being sworn in, Stink and Lil Man looked to one another in unutterable shock.

"Could you state your name for the record?" Mr. Hernandez asked. "Um….yeah… Damien Barnett."

"Do you have a nickname?"

"Yeah…uh…Dame," he mumbled.

"Now, Dame, do you know defendants Kareem Little and Rahsaan Jones?" Hernandez asked, quickly receiving an affirmative nod from Dame, he continued, "What do you know them as?" Mr. Hernandez asked, careful not to repeat his earlier mistake.

"Uh…Lil Man and Stink," Dame replied in a dry tone.

"And which is, Stink?"

Dame pointed directly toward Stink.

"And which is Lil Man?" Hernandez asked cockily.

Attempting to avoid Lil Man's piercing gaze, he pointed to Lil Man. After positively identifying them both, Dame went along with the government script.

While Dame testified, Stink's attorney and Lil Man's attorney, frantically conferred amongst themselves. Once Dame was finished testifying to sordid tales of drugs and money, the defense was allowed to cross-examine.

Standing triumphantly, Mr. Clancy prepared to work his magic. ""Mr. Barnett, have you recently been charged with a crime?" Looking to Mr. Hernandez nervously, Dame stuttered, "Um…Um…yes."

Mr. Clancy raced his eyebrows in mock surprise, and then asked, "And what were you charged with, Mr. Barnett?"

Reluctantly, Dame said, "possession of cocaine with the intent to sale."

"And were you charged by the State, or by federal authorities?"

"Ah…I was ah…charged by the state," he revealed nervously.

"So, Mr. Barnett, why are you here today, in Federal court if your initial charges were state?" Mr. Clancy inquired slyly.

Dame looked totally helpless. Unable to extract an answer, he blurted, "They said if I ain't testify the 'feds' would pick up my case."

"I object! Your Honor, this witness clearly ~"

"Overruled!" The judge yelled, then added, "Mr. Clancy, please continue."

Quickly pouncing on Dame, Mr. Clancy asked, "Who said this, Mr. Barnett?"

Pointing directly at Mr. Hernandez and his assistants, Dame said, "them." Once again, the U.S. Attorney had been made a fool of. Bowing his head in defeat, Mr. Hernandez listened as Mr. Clancy made him look like the scheming, no good U.S. prosecutor that he was.

Despite all of the mishaps during the bizarre trial, Stink was still found guilty of money laundering count that stemmed from the money that the feds caught him and Lil Man with. However, Lil Man wasn't as favorable with the jury. He was sentenced to 15 years in the federal penitentiary.

As they were carted off, after being sentenced, Stink look Lil Man in the eye, and said, "Don't worry. That Nigga is going to pay. I promise." That would be the last time Stink and Lil Man would ever see each other.

New York City 1999

The city had a different feel to it, since Stink had seen it last. Glancing out of the window, he noticed all of the new construction underway along Lennox Avenue.

"Baby, we've got five minutes and he should be calling, "Melody informed, guiding the Benz through New York's mid-day traffic.

Stink looked to his moderately designed Robert Dubuis timepiece and noticed that it was already 12 noon, the planned time that he was supposed to be at Cross' mother house to receive the phone call. Years before, Stink and Cross had precisely planned this. Cross never divulged exactly what the phone call was about. However, Stink knew it had something to do with him meeting the Dominican girl that Cross had attempted to introduce him to years before. After many years, Stink would finally see what mystery this lady held.

While Melody double parked the Benz in front of Cross's mother's house on 116th Street, Stink hopped out and quickly made his way into the building. Bypassing the elevators, he took the steps four at a time to the 4th floor.

As Stink ascended the stairs, he noticed Mrs. Scott standing in front of her door with the phone glued to her ear. Seeing Stink headed her way, she announced," Here he is right here, Georgi!"

Giving Mrs. Scott a warm embrace, Stink retrieved the telephone from her, and in a voice filled with joy, he asked, "What up, Playboy?"

If one didn't know Carmella Bonillia personally, they would swear she was some Latin superstar. On the surface her beauty radiated like the sun. Her long flowing jet black mane, rested just above her waist. Her eyes, a tropical blue, set perfectly in her flawless tanned vanilla complexion. Her creamy thighs curved into a perfect pear shaped ass that would make any grown man cry. Yet, all this beauty hadn't been enough to help her escape the confines of her everyday hell.

Washington Heights, a section in Northern Manhattan, over populated by Latinos, was a ghetto within a ghetto. The neighborhood mostly known for its bustling cocaine market, than for the thousand exotic women it possessed, was nothing more than a living hell for Carmella.

Born in the Dominican Republic, Carmella's parents moved to the United States when she was 6 years old, along with her younger brother, Pepe.

Carmella's beauty enabled her to infiltrate certain circles, yet none stretched outside the confines of Washington Heights. For all practical purposes, Carmella had succumbed to the realization that she would be in Washington Heights, forever.

"Pepe! Mommies gonna fuck you up, if she finds out you got that shit in the house!" Carmella yelled.

"Don't worry mita Muchacha. I'm almost finished," Pepe replied nonchalantly, putting tiny pebbles of crack into plastic valves.

"Pepe, don't say shit when you're sleeping in Riverside Park with the rest of the vagos [bums]," she threatened, as she rushed to answer the ringing phone.

"Hello!" She answered in a snappy tone.

"Um, yeah… is a Carmella there?" Stink asked.

"Yes, this is she. Who is this? "She inquired in her deepest Latino accent.

"Damn, I hope my Nigga follows my directions precisely. I'd hate for that bitch to trick Stink out of all that paper," Cross thought as he hung up the phone.

Osining, New York, had become Cross' indefinite home. After being convicted of the double homicide years before, he had accepted his fate. Sing-Sing as it was commonly called had become home. Cross had been a regular prisoner up until that day. However, after five years of planning, his standings were about to change.

"What's up, God? What's got you so amped, dun?" Cross' cellmate, Shyborn asked.

"Hey yo, Shy, my nigga's home, B," Cross replied exuberantly.

"Oh, you talking about ya man from V.A.?" Shyborn asked, joining in on Cross' festive mood.

"Yeah. My Nigga, Stink, home, son," Cross said with a broad smile etched into his features. "It's about to be on," he added assuredly.

Although there was little to no chance that Cross would ever be released, he coexist through Stink. Giving Stink the keys to everything he owned was nothing to Cross. He knew Stink would never let him down, no matter what the circumstances held. They were brothers whose bond could never be broken.

Now, all Stink had to do was listed and they both would be filthy rich. Cross knew hooking Stink up with Carmella was a risky move, but it was his only shot.

Once the Feds got wind of Cross' whereabouts and kicked his aunt's door down, Carmella was the only person bold enough to grab the thousand dollars and the key that Cross urgently pushed into her lap just before he dove under a bed.

Now Cross's only hope was that Carmella still had the tiny key that went to the safety deposit box, which contained nearly 500 hundred thousand dollars.

"Yes, this is she. Who is this?" Carmella asked in her deepest Latino accent.

"This is Rahsaan, Cross' brother. He told me that you may have something of his for me," Stink said cutting through the bullshit.

"Cross!" She exclaimed, and then continued, "You must be talking about his precious key? Well, if that key means that much to him, I know you're going to look out for me," she stated, seizing the opportunity to get something out of the deal.

"I'll tell you what, mami, I'll do you one better than that. Not only will I lace your pockets with a few hundred, I'll also take you shopping," Stink replied.

"Um...OK   ... Do you know where I live?" She asked.

"Nah... not exactly."

"I live on 141st, between Broadway and Riverside. If you -----."

"I got you, Mami, just be outside in 15 minutes," Stink blurted.

"Ah...OK, 15 minutes," she replied, then quickly hung up to get ready.

Looking to Melody, Stink asked, "You ready?"

Melody nodded, and then quickly brought the conversation that she and Mrs. Scott were engrossed in to a close.

Heading the way to the door, Stink turned to Cross' mother. "Mrs. Scott, I'll be back to see you soon."

O.K., baby. You be careful out there. Oh yeah, don't call me Mrs. Scott no more, call me Momma. My son says you are his brother, so you must be my son," she stated sincerely, giving Stink a heartfelt hug.

"O.K., Momma. I'll be back soon," Stink replied, smiling broadly.

After dressing in her finest outfit, Carmella began to vigorously search for the small key that Cross had given her years before. Racking her brain, she finally remembered that she'd hidden it in her small jewelry box. Once she retrieved the key, she made her way to the door.

Quickly exiting her building, Carmella stepped into 141st Street just as the sun was setting over New York City's Westside. She stood on her stoop, eyeing the steady stream of cars coming down the steep block.

Suddenly a silver Mercedez-Benz convertible slowed down in front of her building, causing her jaw to nearly hit the pavement. "O' Mi Dios! [Oh my God!]," she exclaimed.

Stink pulled the Benz to a stop in front of the visibly striking Spanish girl. Cross had often expressed just how pretty she was; yet, seeing her standing there clutching her purse, Stink concluded that she was nothing short of beautiful.

He slowly exited the car and approached Carmella, "You must be Carmella," Stink said eyeing her with interest.

"Yes, and you must be, Rahsaan, or should I call you, Stink?" She asked slyly, extending her hand.

"Yeah. Either is cool with me," he replied smoothly, taking Carmella's hand in his.

Eyeing Stink approvingly, Carmella said," You don't look nothing like your brother.

Smiling, he replied, "Yeah, I've been told that." Breaking their flirtatious glares, he asked, "So are you ready to roll?"

"Uh…yeah, I'm ready. Oh, before we go, here's the key," she said holding the key out to Stink.

Placing it securely in the pocket of his 'Sean John' velour sweatpants, Stink led Carmella to the car.

Before opening the door to the sleek coupe, he asked, "Can you drive?"

"Yeah, I can drive, "She replied in a cocky fashion.

"Aight, you drive," he instructed, squeezing into the small back seat.

As soon as Carmella noticed Melody sitting comfortably in the passenger seat, a confused expression appeared across her face.

"Oh, hi, my name is Melody," Melody said smiling brightly.

Hesitantly taking Melody's outstretched hand, she said, "Oh… I'm Carmella."

Stink sat back and watched the interaction between the two vivaciously beautiful women with a smirk. "So, where you trying to go shopping, Carmella?" Stink asked.

"Um… I really don't know. What kind of shopping are we….um going to do?" She asked quizzically.

"Girl lets go to the 'Gucci' store downtown, then we can go to the 'Prada' boutique in Soho," Melody offered excitedly.

Carmella shot Melody a skeptical glance at the mentioning of such costly designers. She had never owned anything authentic by neither Gucci nor Prada. "Um…O.K. Which way?" She finally responded.

Stink had ten thousand in his pocket for Carmella. However, she saw fit to spend it, was up to her.

Melody was so happy that Stink was finally home. It had been five years four months and 16 days since he'd last touched her. She had methodically counted down to the exact hour. She had remained loyal to him in every aspect of the word. To suffice her sexual urges, she would pleasure herself which the many toys she'd purchased. She had religiously made the trip up into the mountains of West Virginia every week to visit him. Now that he was home, she would do whatever Stink desired of her.

"It's in the next block," Melody directed Carmella as she navigated the Benz through the Midtown Manhattan traffic.

Melody instantly liked the Spanish girl. Carmella's bright erotic features were comparable to her own.

Carmella found a parking spot, and then looked to Melody perplexed. Melody gathered her purse, and then announced, "Well, come on Carmella. Let's go shopping."

Stink casually walked around the boutique, inspecting the designer clothes, with acute eyes.

Melody led Carmella through the boutique, spending money recklessly. The broad smile that Carmella sported was evidence that she was having the time of her life.

Melody had picked out a few pieces for herself and Stink, but for the most part she assisted Carmella.

"How does she look in this, Boo?" Melody asked, presenting Carmella as if she were a prize.

Carmella turned around gracefully, showcasing the tight black, form fitting 'Prada' dress that accentuated her every curve.

Eyeing her hungrily, Stink's loins reminded him that he hadn't experienced the touch of a woman for many years." Looks good to me," he complimented effortlessly, as he attempted to readjust the positioning of his stiffening manhood in the flimsy velour sweatpants.

Looking at the time on his watch, he knew it was time to get the show on the road. The bank that held nearly 500 thousand closed in less than an hour, and Stink didn't plan on being late. He had to wrap this little game up and get moving fast. "Ladies! Ladies!" He yelled firmly, snapping them out of their giddiness as he looked down at his watch. "Let's wrap it up. I've gotta go see a man about a dog, so…" he concluded, using an adage that an old head told him in prison.

Instantly, Stink noticed the look of disappointment cover Carmella's face, as she realized her shopping spree was coming to an end.

Melody sensed the seriousness in Stink's tone, quickly ushered Carmella to the counter to make their purchases.

As they piled the shopping bags into the trunk, Stink knew that time wouldn't permit him to make the drive uptown, to drop Carmella off, before stopping by the bank. "Carmella, stop by 46th and 7th Avenue before you head uptown," he instructed.

Carmella and Melody sat in the car, waiting on Stink to exit the building in Midtown Manhattan. Carmella was still reeling from the exorbitant amount of money that Stink had just spent on her. No one had ever spent anywhere near the seven thousand that Stink had just blew on her for the flamboyant designer clothes. Breaking her thoughts, she looked at the Dooney & Bourke' pocketbook she held in awe, and then looked over to Melody.

The manner in which Melody embraced her, left Carmella perplexed. If it had been her man spending thousands of dollars on another woman, there was no way that she would be as jolly and friendly as Melody had been. This led her to believe that Melody could not have been his woman.

Stink abruptly appeared at the driver's door, snapping Carmella out of her contemplations. As he crawled into the back, Carmella noticed he now clutched a businessman type briefcase.

This automatically heightened her curiosity. "What could a pretty thug Nigga like him be carrying in a brief case, besides drugs or money?" She presumed logically.

Once Stink was comfortable in the small backseat, he said, "Carmella head uptown."

Carmella instinctively knew this demand was her inevitable dismissal. While she drove uptown, it was extremely quiet as they each delved into their own thoughts.

When Carmella pulled in front of her building, there was a trio of young Spanish guys lounging on her stoop.

Just as they noticed the 500 Benz stopping in front of them, their eyes grew wide in admiration.

"Yo, Pep. 'Who dat?" Chico asked.

Eyeing the car intently, Pep replied, "I don't know."

Soon as the words had escaped his mouth, he witnessed Carmella stepping out of the car. "Conyon! [What the Fuck]" Pepe exclaimed. "Pepe! Help me with these bags!" Carmella yelled in a commanding voice.

Stink eased from the backseat, holding the remainder of Carmella's purchases, passing them to the approaching Spanish guy.

"Yo, what up, fam?   Pepe said in his tick New York/Spanish accent. "I'm Pepe, Carma's brother," he announced extending his hand.

"Rahsaan," Stink replied, examining the young Dominican closely.   As Stink gripped the young man's hand, he immediately sensed that the young man wanted to be accepted, approved of and acknowledged.

"Hermanito! [little brother!]" Carmella snapped, handing Pepe another   hand full of bags, then shooed him off with the wave of a hand.

Turning her attention to Stink, Carmella's face held a mixture of happiness and disappointment. "Well, Stink, I guess this is it," she said sadly, adding, "Thanks for everything, though," as she turned to leave.

"Carmella!"   Melody yelled from the car.
Carmella abruptly stopped and turned to see
Melody's outstretched hand holding a piece of paper. "Call
me sometimes," Melody said.

Carmella accepted Melody's number, slightly
baffled. "Um…O.K., she managed. As she turned back
toward Stink, he was counting off a modest amount of bills.

Pushing the money toward Carmella, he said, "Here,
this is for you." Hesitantly, Carmella accepted the money,
and then looked to Stink in disbelief."   Thank you…so
much…I…. I," she stammered.

"Don't sweat it. If you need something, just call,"
Stink replied in a lackadaisical manner, then turned and
walked to the car. As he attempted to readjust the driver's
seat, he noticed Carmella's brother and his crew interact
with an approaching older Dominican in what looked to be a
drug deal in progress. Stink shook his head in despair, and
then sped off down the block.

Cross anxiously waited for one of the phones to
become available. He glared at the numerous prisoners
holding conversations with their loved ones and instantly
had the urge to revert back to his monstrous ways and just
take a phone.

He knew that Stink should have gotten the key from
Carmella by now. Just when his prior thoughts of violence
almost became a reality, one of the prisoners hung the phone
up. Cross moved stealth-like in the direction of the vacant
phone. Quickly snatching the receiver off the hook, he
began punching numbers. He knew that his mother had
forwarded the phone line specifically for him, to Stink's cell
phone.

"Hell-o," a woman answered in a sweet voice. 'This
call is from New York department of corrections. This call
is from…"Cross" To accept…' The automated recording
instructed. "Hello," the sweet voiced woman answered

quickly accepting the call. "Yeah, where Stink at?" Cross inquired hastily. "He's in the shower, but he should be out in just a second," Melody explained, asking "This is his brother Cross, right?" "Yeah. Who is this?" Cross replied. "Oh, I'm Melody. We met once, a looong time ago," Melody said, recalling the first night she met Stink vividly. "Oh yeah! I remember you," Cross concluded. "Really! H well, here's Rahsaan." "Cross!" Stink yelled into the receiver. "Wasup, Nigga?" "Ain't shit. Just chillin." "So, did shorty give you the keys to the car?" Cross asked slyly.

"Oh, definitely! And I went to 'Micky Dees' and got a value meal, you know 4 dollars and 85 cents," Stink replied, referring to the four-hundred and eighty-five thousand in his possession.

"That's what's up, Nigga!" Cross yelled excitedly.

"But yo, why you ain't put me on to how bad shorty was?" Stink inquired in a hushed tone.

"Nigga, I told you the bitch was bad, you just won't listen," Cross replied.

"Yo, shorty was jive fucked up at how I laced her, too" "If you was living in NYC broke and somebody laced you with ten g's, you'd be fucked up too," Cross explained chuckling. "Yeah. But what's up with her little brother?" "Oh, lil Pepe. He's a go hard lil Dominican Nigga, but he's young." Cross replied, then asked," So what you gonna do now? You gonna holla at Jose'?"

"I was thinking about it, but I really don't know what VA got in store for me. I've got a lot of unfinished business that I gotta handle before I can make any moves."

The mere thought of going back to Virginia filled Stink with mixed emotions. No longer were his grandparents living in Virginia. After his grandfather's long battle with heart disease took his life, Stink's grandmother moved back to North Carolina. In addition, the woman he was in love with was now just another woman. For five years, Bonni cared for his daughter the best she could, now all of that was about to change.

"Yo! Why don't you go holler at Jose', then go through VA and scope shit out.... Then BOOM; handle your B.I.," Cross advised.

"Yeah....yeah, I just might do that."

Chapter Two

Melody pulled the Benz into the familiar driveway and turned the engine off.

Stink glared at the house that he once called home through sad eyes. The manicured lawn that he remembered had gone astray. The wrought iron shutters hung aimlessly from the windows, as chips of the stucco siding had worn away over time.

Stink grabbed his cell phone and dialed his mother's phone number in North Carolina.

"Hello," his mother answered.

"Hey, Ma. I'm home," Stink announced casually.

"Boy! Where you at?" His mother yelled in astonishment.

"I'm home, baby," he repeated, eyeing his new residence. "Put Grandma on the telephone," he added before his mother could reply.

After speaking to his grandmother, she revealed that the house was in fact, his, according to his grandfather final wish.

Once he hung up the phone, he and Melody entered the dark creepy house. On a whim, Stink went into his old bedroom and checked the compartment in the floor that once contained his riches. As he opened it, his eyes became wide in bewilderment. Just as he'd left it years before, neatly stacked bricks of money lined the compartment. Stink pulled the money out and quickly noticed that not only had his grandfather not touched any of his money; he'd also added quite a few stacks of his own.

Inwardly smiling at his grandfather's humor, he pulled the remaining stacks of money out and passed them to Melody. As he and Melody descended the spiral stairs, Stink silently vowed to make the once lavish property into a dazzling estate.

While Melody backed the car out of the driveway, Stink was envisioning the beauty that the house would once again have.

Stink had been home for 24 hours and he hadn't touched Melody. She was beginning to experience anxiety from his lack of attention. She had accepted the cuddling they'd shared the night before, in the New York Hotel. However, tonight, in the confines of her seaside condominium she wanted to be made love to, fucked and simply ravished.

"Melody, pass me a towel!" Stink yelled from the bathroom. She quickly went to the closet to retrieve a towel, and then walked into the bathroom. Just as she entered, Stink stood inside the shower with beads of water covering his deliciously chiseled body.

Melody stood in a trance, eyeing his body hungrily as her gaze traveled down to his manhood.

"What's wrong with you?" Stink barked, snapping her out of her daze. "I... I... was just....," Melody stammered, quickly handing him the towel, then bolting from the bathroom.

Once she was out of his sight, her heartbeat returned to normal. She couldn't believe the effect that he had over her. Instinctively, she reached between her legs and felt her moisture.

When Melody returned to the bedroom, Stink was lying on the king-sized bed, partially covered. As she got closer to the bed, she noticed the devilish grin on his face. He peered at her intently.

"Come over here, baby girl," he taunted affectionately, then pulled the covers away, revealing his manhood.

Passively, Melody crawled between his outstretched legs, as her heart rate fluttered in anticipation.

Stink reached for her nightgown and pulled it over her head, uncovering her nakedness. Melody's pert titties sported a large, dark areola that surrounded her erect nipples.

"You miss me, baby?" Stink asked, teasing her as he planted soft kisses over her face.

"Yes, daddy," Melody replied almost child-like.

Stink cuddled her in his arms lovingly, allowing their bodies to mesh. Turning her onto her back, he stared deep into her eyes. "Melody, I want you to know that you have gone above and beyond the call of duty, and for that, I will forever be grateful."

"Rahsaan, I love you and I will do anything for you," she replied earnestly.

"I love you too, Melody," he said, then moved in close and slipped his tongue into her mouth.

The kiss, intense but short, lasted long enough for Stink to maneuver Melody's panties down her thighs. He then began to plant sensuous kisses down her body, spending just enough time to tantalize each part of her sensitive body.

Once he reached her bushy center, the exotic aroma caused Stink's manhood to throb. The first electrifying stroke of his tongue on her clitoris sent waves through her body.

Expertly, Stink's tongue licked, sucked and nibbled in what seemed like one motion, causing Melody's body to flounder with each touch.

"Hmmm….baby…..what are you doing….to me?" Melody inquired through spasms.

In response, Stink buried his face between her thighs. Interlocking her thighs with his forearms, he began to devour her pussy. "Oh shit! Oh….my…God! Baby, I'm cum….ming!" Melody hissed as her pussy spurted its sweet juices into his mouth. Stink continued to gently suck on her clit as her body continued to shiver uncontrollably.

"Hmmm…..daddy…please stop! I…..can't take it!" She whined. Stink obliged, but only long enough to say, "turn over." In a daze, Melody did as she was instructed. Eyeing her plump ass greedily, he spread her ass cheeks apart, and then ran his tongue from her oozing pussy to her tight asshole.

Once Stink's tongue made contact with the four-thousand or so nerve endings at her rectal entrance, she went berserk. Pounding her fist into the bed violently, she credit out, "Oh, fuck! Oh, my fucking, God! What the fuck are you doing to me!?"

Stink knew neither Melody nor the neighbors would be able to take much more of the freakish assault he was putting on her. Pulling back, he crawled onto a whimpering Melody and placed his shaft at the entrance of her soaked pussy.

Easily sliding into her well lubricated hole, Stink began to reacquaint himself with the tight channel that he'd missed for so many years.

"You miss this dick, baby?" Stink asked as he worked his dick into her core.

"Yess, daddy! Yes….I missed you! Oh, shit! Work your pussy!" Melody whimpered, leaning over her shoulder.

Stink gripped her firm ass cheeks and drove his dick in to the hilt.

"Oh, yess!   Daddy, get your pussy! Please... Oh yess... please don't cum yet!"   She yelled in a demonic voice.

Up until that point, cumming had been the furthest thing from Stink's mind.   Yet, just the mentioned of it, along with eyeing the glaze that escaped Melody's pussy and coated his manhood, were too much to bear." Oh...fuck! Why you.... Have to...Shit!" He grunted as his seed escaped his loins.

Collapsing on top of Melody breathlessly, Stink could feel her pussy pulsating around him.

After a brief recuperation period, they went back at it; rounds two and three followed, until their bodies were completely spent.

When they did finally fall asleep, Melody had a smile spread across her face as bright as the sun.

Carmella counted the money over and over.   She couldn't believe that Stink not only had taken her shopping, spending nearly seven thousand dollars, he'd also given her three thousand in cash.

Just as she was putting her money away, Pepe burst into her bedroom

"Why don't you fucking knock before you come in! Mierda! [Shit]," She yelled, attempting to cuff the wad of money.

"Oh, fuck!" Pepe exclaimed eyeing the roll of bills. "What the fuck you do, Carma? Rob somebody? "He asked in amazement.

"Fuck you, Pep!" Carmella spat.

"Nah, foreal. Lock out for me, Carma?" Pepe asked compassionately.

"Pepe, I'm not giving you nada, so you can go out there with that stupid shit. I'm going to open up a bank account," she revealed seriously.

Looking toward his sister with that look that only he possessed, all of Carmella's defenses disintegrated.

"How much, Pepe?" She asked defeated. "Give me a gee. I swear I'll pay it back," he stated earnestly. "Mmm-Hmm," she retorted, counting the bills-off.

Stink sat on Melody's bed and put the bills in neat stacks of twenty thousand. With 240 thousand dollars at his disposal, he was ready to put his plans into motion. After the meeting with Jose' in New York, he vowed to look out for Stink in a major way for not snitching on him to the feds. Stink further entrusted Jose by leaving the 400 thousand with him until he was ready to make his move.

There were some past scores that needed to be settled before Stink could implement his new rule. The city was unaware of his arrival, and that's how he wanted to keep it until he was ready to strike.

Although he desperately wanted to see his daughter even that would have to be put on hold until the time was right.

Stink quickly dressed, then headed out to the rental car that Melody had waiting for him.

Inconspicuously, Stink rode through the blocks that he once ruled. Newport News, or 'Bad Newz' as it was now commonly called, had the same grimy feel to it. The city was still deteriorating, more so now than when he left.

As he rode down the block that the infamous 'Friendship House' was located, Stink noticed that it too had succumbed to the city's deterioration. As he eyed the petty hustlers, running up to cars making crack deals, he couldn't help but to wonder which one of them knew where Dame was camped out in 'Bad Newz.'

Stink desperately wanted to give his longtime friend the rightful greeting that he had coming.

"Patience, Nigga. Patience," Stink reiterated to himself.

After aimlessly cruising the streets of downtown, Stink's cell phone rang. Knowing that it could only be one of two people, he answered, "Hello." "Hey daddy, I'm home," Melody announced joyously. Continuing, she said,"The company in charge of the house's restoration called and said they need... "Aight. I'll givem a call."

"So, will you be home for dinner?" She asked in a joking manner. "Melody chuckled at Stink's quip, then said, "Daddy, just be safe. I love you." Without any further response, she hung up.

Stink pulled into a convenience store just outside of the city's thrall. Before he could get out of the car, gold Mercedes 600 Sedan pulled up, sporting some of the biggest chrome wheels that he'd ever seen.

The driver is oblivious to his surrounding, with the cell phone glued to his ear.

Instinctively, Stink leaned back in the seat and peered in the direction of the driver of the Benz. Suddenly the driver's door swung open and there he was. Although he had gained a few pounds since Stink had last seen him, his features were oh so familiar. It was Dame.

Carmella sat in the third floor window and watched as Pepe and his crew vigorously sold the drugs that he felt were key to his success. True to his word, he'd given Carmella the thousand dollars that she'd let him borrow, plus an extra five hundred. It looked like Pepe was on his way to the top.

Just when Carmella's mind wondered off, there was a commotion down on the side walk that instantly drew her attention.

"What the fuck you mean, this all you got!" Pepe barked angrily. "Man, I... I only made that!" The object of Pepe's rage explained defensively.

Pepe, Chico and Manny had the man completely surrounded on the New York City street.

Without warning, Pepe pulled a gun from his waist and aimed it directly at the man's chest.

Carmella's scream was caught in her throat, as she attempted to stop her brother. Just when she found her voice, Pepe squeezed the trigger.

"Bop! Bop!" The two shots rang out, crashing into the man's chest, hurling him to the ground." Next time you'' keep my fucking paper straight, Maricon! [faggot!]" Pepe spat wickedly, standing over the dying man. Casually, Pepe, Chico and Manny disappeared through an alley.

Carmella sat in the window horrified at what she'd just witnessed. She quickly ran down the three flights of stairs and joined the other spectators, watching the helpless man choke on his own blood.

Once the paramedics and police arrived on the scene, all of the on lookers scattered except for Carmella.

Standing there, looking down at the dead man through disbelieving eyes, a fat New York City detective eased up to her, and asked "Man, did you see what happened here?"

Hesitantly, Carmella nodded her head, and then allowed the detective to lead her to the side.

The lovin' that Stink had put on Melody had her in a festive mood, as she strolled through her condo whistling love tunes. She could still feel the tingling in her center, at just the thought of Stink and the lovin' that he'd bestowed upon her.

For the last few days he had been frequenting his old stomping grounds, doing only God knows what. Nonetheless, Melody was content with having him cuddled up to her once she awoke.

Just as Melody had picked the phone up to call Stink, it rang in her hand.

"Yes, Hello," she answered in a joyous mood.

"Um...yes. Is Melody there?" A woman asked.

"Yes, this is she."

"Oh, hi Melody. This is Carmella from New York."

"Oh, hey girl! How are you doing?" Melody asked.

"Oh, I'm fine. Just a little stressed," Carmella replied accompanied by an exasperated sigh.

"Well, it sounds like you're a 'whole lot' stressed. What's going on with you?" Melody inquired.

"Same ole New York shit. Murder and mayhem," she said in a joking manner. Yet, she was 'dead' serious.

Chuckling, Melody said, "Girlfriend, it sounds like you could use a vacation. Maybe some fun in the sun would do you some justice."

"Yeah, that sounds good. But where would I go?"

"Shit, I've got a three bedroom condo on the ocean front. Why don't you come down here for a week or so?" Melody offered.

"Are you serious?" Carmella asked elated.

"As a heart attack," Melody replied.

After a meager amount of convincing, it was all set for Carmella to come to Virginia.

After packing her bags, Carmella sat in her family's tiny apartment, listening to her mother rant about Pepe's disappearance. It had been over a week since the man had been murdered on the block, and Pepe still hadn't surfaced. He'd called Carmella almost every day to let her know he was alright. Even though Carmella let him know that she had thrown the cops off of his trail by going to the police precinct and giving them three descriptions of assailants that looked nothing like him, Chico and Manny; Pepe still chose to play the underground, until he was absolutely sure that neither he nor any of his boys would be implemented in the meaningless murder.

Once the car horn blared down the street, signaling Carmella that it was time to go, she hugged her mother, and then quickly made her way down the stairs with her bags.

The driver of the battered Lincoln 'Gypsy' cab didn't move a muscle as the beautiful girl approached his car, struggling with her luggage.

Carmella stuffed her bags in the backseat, then hoped in and said," "Grand Central Station."

Once they were down Riverside drive and on the Westside Hwy., Carmella looked back and sighed in relief at her temporary escape from the confines of Washington Heights.

For three full days, Stink had stalked Dame's movements like an angry lover. The gated community that he lived in made it impossible to find out exactly where he laid his head. Besides, that's not how Stink wanted to handle him.

As he followed the big Benz up Jefferson Avenue, Stink knew exactly where Dame was headed.

"Yep," Stink said to himself, as he witnessed Dame pull into the parking lot of the strip club.

Unnoticed, Stink parked across the street and watched Dame wobble his heavy frame into the club.

"Blurrrp! Blurrrp!" Stink's two-way sounded.

"Blurrp! –Wazup, Melody?" He questioned into the walkie-talkie/phone.

"Blurrrp! – Hey, daddy," Melody whined.

"Blurrrp! – Melody! What's up? He snapped, as the loud chirping began to play on his nerves.

"Blurrp! – I just wanted to tell you that I've got a surprise for you when you get home," she quickly replied, sensing the irritation in his voice.

"Blurrrp! – Ahight! I'll see it when I get there! One," he said, quickly turning this phone completely off. Refocusing his attention on the club, he eyed the perimeter of the business, looking for anything that would alert him to a change in Dame's status.

Cross stood in the middle of his newly assembled crew, exuding a commanding presence. In the middle of the recreation yard, surrounded by the everyday activities of prison life, he held a round table of sorts.

Each man eyed Cross as if he was a military tactical leader giving his troops instructions for attack.

"Crook, we gonna make sure your girl gets the dope, twice a month, same time; same place, "Cross explained, then turned his focus to the next man. "Quan, I'm putting the coke in your girl's hands. Same arrangements as Crook," he instructed, receiving a nod from each man."

Looking back to Quan, Cross said, "Oh, one more thing, make sure your scary ass don't get knocked in the V.I. room."

Cross' comment received a round of laughter from everybody, including Quan. Quickly switching back to commander mode, Cross turned to his cellmate, Shyborn. "Ay yo, Shy, by your girl coming up every week, we're gonna put the smoke in her hands. We know most of those niggas smoke trees, so we gonna need a steady flow of weed," Cross explained.

"No question, dunn. You know my wiz gonna handle her BI. But what about the rest of these niggas?" Shyborn stated questionably, eyeing the other men in the circle.

There were a few incoherent mumbles, but no one spoke up. Cross seized the moment. "I'm pretty sure the rest of us have enough pull to uphold our end of the bargain, right?" He asked, eyeing everyone around him. Witnessing the defiant glares he received, he continued, "I thought so. Now, as for Kayso, Mont, and Flex, y'all niggas are the most important part to this shit. Y'all gonna make shit pop off. When the shit hits, y'all gonna be the ones making moves. Me, Shy, Crook and Quan gonna play the back."

None of the men knew it, but each one of them had been studied for years while Cross articulated his plan. Each man had been placed in their position like a game of chess by the master player. Cross had his pawns, rooks, knights..... And most importantly, he was the King. The only piece being more important than himself was Stink. Stink was the key to the entire scheme.

"So, when should I tell my girl to be on the look out for your man?" Quan asked.

"One week from tomorrow," Cross stated, sure that it would be done.

After hanging out with Carmella all day, Melody decided to eat in and enjoy a movie with her newfound friend. Carmella was easy to listen to, and even easier to talk to. One would automatically think that such a beautiful woman would have an adverse attitude. However, just as Melody carried her striking appearance, Carmella carried herself in the same manner.

Eyeing the screen intently, as rapper 'DMX' ground his penis into the actress aggressively in the movie 'Belly,' Carmella said," Girl, he is fucking the shit outta her chocha! [Pussy!]"

"Mmm Hmmm," Melody replied, slightly startled at the feeling she was experiencing from hearing such vulgar words come from Carmella. A sharp, electro spasm shot through her center, leaving behind a lingering chill.

They both lounged on Melody's King sized bed in over-sized T-shirts and panties, spooning scoops of 'Hagen Daaz ice cream.

Melody couldn't help herself from stealing a peek at Carmella's thick, vanilla thighs as the T-shirt she wore hiked further up her legs. Melody had never desired to be with another woman; yet, there was something about Carmella's beauty, which matched her own, that made her want to try.

It was nearly two o'clock and Stink still hadn't come home, which had become a common occurrence. Lately, the sun had beat him home nearly every night.

Reluctantly, Melody averted her attention back to the movie.

Carmella laid back on Melody's bed and allowed her T-shirt to advertently rise, exposing her lace, French cut panties. Slowly, she was seducing Melody with her alluring charm.

This was something that Carmella had been taught at a young age. When she was eleven years old, an older girl who'd been entrusted to look after her and Pepe, used these exact same tactics on her.

Tosca Menendez turned Carmella out to the taste of another woman before she'd leaned to jump rope. Tosca took complete advantage of Carmella's young body, taking her to heights she never knew existed. Tosca taught Carmella good, and at that very moment she was implementing those techniques on Melody.

Noticing how Melody continuously stole glances at her exposed thighs, Carmella asked, "Aren't you going to get comfortable?"

"Uh…yeah…I guess so," Melody, your thighs are soooo thick and smooth," "Oh….. um, thanks," Melody replied nervously.

Carmella knew that she was pretty; yet, the exotic looks Melody possessed countered her own in many ways. Melody's radiant, oriental eyes gave her a hypnotizing effect. Her long flowing hair rivaled Carmella's own. And although Carmella's body was curvaceous, Melody had ass and hips for days that fit perfectly onto her thunderous, pecan colored thighs.

While Carmella was caught up in her appraisal of Melody, her hand had subconsciously moved dangerously close to Melody's womanhood. Eyeing her lustfully, she noticed that Melody's breathing had quickened. With a dazed, far out look covering Melody's face, Carmella moved in for the kill.

"Melody, your body is so beautiful," she whispered, positioning her body between Melody's thighs.

"You.....are...too," Melody replied naively.

Moving closer, Carmella planted a soft kiss against Melody's lips. The strangeness of kissing another woman quickly faded, as Melody's tongue came to life in Carmella's mouth. Carmella reached under Melody's shirt and began to knead her already erect nipples. This sent shock through Melody's body as she gripped Carmella's body. Instantly their body shed their clothing as if they were on fire.

As their tongues reunited, Carmella could feel her juices oozing from her center at the thought of conquering the symbolic virgin.

As their kiss became more intense, Carmella glided her hand gently down Melody's body to her bushy entrance. Slowly, she inserted her forefinger into Melody's velvety funnel, and began to motion her finder as if she were beckoning someone to come to her.

Once Carmella's finger made contact with Melody sensitive G-spot, her body immediately responded, as she gyrated her hips to meet Carmella's probing finger. Carmella quickly pulled her tongue from Melody's mouth and focused her attention on Melody's pussy.

"Ahh....ahh!   Car...Carma....Carmella!" Melody panted breathlessly as soon as Carmella's tongue made contact with her womanhood.   Carmella took her time, licking Melody's lips as if they were a lollipop. Looking up into Melody's eyes, she said, "That's right, Mami....call my name." She then dove back between her thighs.

"Oh, my God! Car...Carmella, you're making me cum!" Melody announced as her body began to jerk uncontrollably.

Carmella didn't stop there; she continued to work her expert tongue on Melody's body, breaking her in just as she had been broken in years before.

Once Stink pulled up to Melody's condo, it was after 3 AM. His body was fatigued from being slouched in the car for the last 3 hours. He had gathered enough surveillance to take Dame's life that night, if he chose. However, it would have more than likely been sloppy, and sloppy wasn't on Stink's itinerary.

He slowly inserted his key into Melody's door and crept inside. Not wanting to wake her, he treaded lightly on the soft, plush carpet, As he approached Melody's partially opened door, the soft incoherent moans coming from within startled him. Instinctively, he reached for the .45 Heckler and Koch, nestled in his waist.

"Mmm....right there, Mami. Yeah... just like that. Mmm hmm," an unfamiliar woman's voice whined sexily, inside the dark room.

With the powerful handgun raised in preparation to inflict massive bodily damage, Stink flicked the infrared beam on with his trigger finger, and then slowly pushed the door open.

As the piercing red light steadied on one of the figures in the dark room, someone yelled, "Oh, God! Please don't shoot! Please!"

"Don't fucking move!" Stink barked, as he kept the well placed red dot on the head of the unsuspecting woman.

With his free hand, he turned the room light on.

As his eyes adjusted to the scene before him, he nearly fell into the floor laughing.

Melody's ass was cocked in the air as she rested on her knees, between Carmella's creamy yellow thighs.

Had Stink's nerves not been disoriented from being so close to inflicting damage, he would've joined the ladies. Nonetheless, he lowered the gun and walked away. Before he was out of ear shot, he could hear Melody whimpering.

As Stink entered the Kitchen and pulled the refrigerator door open, he could hear bare feet trotting behind him. Ignoring the sniffling figure, Stink pulled the orange juice container out and gulped the beverage down.

"It was all my fault, Stink. I swear it," Carmella said through tears. Continuing, she blurted," Melody didn't have a clue as to what was taking place."

Stink began to chuckle as the scene vividly played in his head. The more the thought about her statement, the more uncontrollable his laughter became.

"Stink, I swear it. I will do anything you ask of me, just don't blame Melody. Please, "she stated in a pleading tone.

Instantly, her tone caught Stink's ear. She actually thought that he was mad. If anything, he was more shocked than mad. What man in his right mind would be made at coming home to find two beautiful women enjoying themselves?

Reaffirming her offer, Stink asked, "Anything?"

Quickly closing the distance between them, Carmella dropped to her knees and looked up into Stink's eyes, exclaiming, "Anything?"

Chapter Three

Stink laid back in the bed totally spent from the two days of non-stop ménage a trois sex. This wasn't his initial plan but it happened. The free for all sex seemed to have built a bond between the three of them.

"Y'all is nasty," Melody joked eyeing Carmella as she took Stink's semi erect penis in her warm mouth.

Stink knew he couldn't lay between the two beautiful women another minute; he had to put his plan into action. "Melody, pass me the phone," he instructed. After punching in the number, he looked down at Carmella, and said, "Y'all get dressed. The party's over. It's time to handle business."

Quickly, they scampered off toward the bathroom, while Stink took care of his business on the phone.

After talking to the owner of the 'Platinum Pussycat' strip club, a meeting was set for later that afternoon. Once the strip club owner laid eyes on Carmella and Melody, he would undoubtedly snatch them up, making it possible for Stink to exact his revenge.

He had watched Dame on numerous nights leaving the strip club, with an array of women. However, when he chose either of Stink's dimes, his life would be over.

Melody followed Carmella closely through the dimly lit club, as the loud music played Juvenile's 'Back that Ass up?' Melody was petrified about getting up on stage and dancing in front of strangers. Carmella had coaxed her on how to sway her body on stage, and even schooled her on how to fraternize with the customers.

When Stink informed them that they would be dancing in a strip club for a few days, Melody began to open her mouth in protest. However, once she saw the wicked glare that he shot in her direction, she quickly recanted on the thought.

"Let's go chill by the bar until our set starts," Carmella said leading the way.

"Carm, is it cold in here to you?" Melody asked with her arms wrapped around herself.

"Look what we're wearing, Mami," Carmella replied with a tinge of sarcasm.

Both girls were clad in a G-sting, a matching bra, and a flimsy wrap that partially covered their bare asses.

"Melody, don't look now, but I think that's the guy that poppi showed us the picture of," Carmella whispered.

Slowly, Melody turned and looked in the direction that Carmella had motioned. Sure enough, it was Dame. Melody remembered him clearly from Stink's trial. Just as she was turning away, he lifted his drink in their direction, and winked his eye.

"Carm, that's him," Melody announced in a hushed tone, then blurted, "What are we gonna do?"

Carmella quickly seized control. "Don't worry, Mami. I got it. You just follow my lead. This will be our last night showing these Mother fuckers our chochas [Pussies]," Carmella stated in a matter of fact tone, then sexily slid off the bar stool and began to sashay in Dame's direction.

"You get all that?" Cross asked as he finished rattling off the numerous phone numbers.

"Yeah, I got it," Stink replied lackadaisically.

"You sure, B?"

"I got'em, man!" Stink repeated.

"Aight. So when you think you gonna holla at them?"

"Man, my lil shit down here is coming to a head, so give me like three days," Stink explained.

"Aight, that's cool. Now wasup with, Carmella? You ain't even put me on to what happened, yet. What's really good, B?" Cross inquired excitedly.

Sighing heavily, Stink gave Cross a vivid reenactment of the scene that played out a few days prior.

"Yo, B! Say, fucking, word!" Cross yelled in awe, then continued, "Ay yo, I know that shit was ill, B. You gotta put me down, Nigga!" Cross then pulled the phone from his ear and yelled to anybody who would listen in his pod, "My Nigga got two bitches! Manage a trois and the whole shit, B!"

"Chill out, Nigga! Hold on, my phone beeping," Stink said, and then click onto his other line.

Cross held the receiver, beaming. He couldn't believe what Stink had just told him. He'd actually had two bad bitches in the bed freakin. That's my fucking dream,' Cross thought to himself.

After holding on for nearly five minutes, Cross had begun to get salty.

Soon as Stink clicked back over, he yelled, "Cross! It's show time Nigga! I'm out!" Then hung up.

Without any other words being spoken, Cross knew that Stink had his man.

After calling Stink, Carmella made her way back to the table where Dame and Melody sat holding what looked to be a flirtatious conversation.

Taking her seat opposite Melody, Carmella fluttered her eyes lustfully, in Dame's direction, then said," I see you and my girl are getting along good."

"Yeah, we could be getting along a lot better if we all just blow this joint," Dame replied, licking his lips in anticipation.

"Well, as soon as we finish our set, we're down for whatever," Carmella said intentionally stalling, waiting on Stink's call.

"Aight, that's cool.   But when do y'all go on?" Dame inquired impatiently.

Just then, on que, the D.J. dropped Jay Z's 'Big Pimpin', signaling the start of Carmella and Melody's girl/girl set.

"Right now," Carmella stated standing up, closely followed by Melody. Winking an eye at Dame, they made their way to the stage.

Dame sat there eyeing both of the exotic women as they strolled their shapely asses toward the stage. Beads of sweat had formed on his forehead, as he envisioned what he'd be doing to them later that evening. Little did he know, things wouldn't pan out the way he'd planned.

Stink raced through the tunnel in the direction of the 'Platinum Pussycats.' He didn't think Dame would fall for his trap so easily.   Nonetheless, it goes without saying; when a man follows his smaller head, he's doomed.

Stink thought it was rather hilarious that after Carmella and Melody had only been in the club two nights, Dame had bitten.

He pulled into the parking lot across the street from the strip club, and pulled his cell phone out. He punched in Melody's cell number, and was met with a succession of rings. Stink repeatedly called the number, only to receive the same results. This caused an inferno to ignite inside of him. Eyeing the club's entrance, he scanned the parking lot and notice Dame's car was parked a few spaces from Melody's.

"Fuck!" He barked, banging his fist hard against the steering wheel. Just when he had thought of some real wicked ways to punish both Melody and Carmella, his phone rang.

Quickly snatching the phone up, he blurted, "Hello!"

"Baby, are you here yet?" Melody asked in a hushed tone.

"I've fucking been here! Why the Fuck y'all ain't answer the phone?" Stink barked.

"Uh….we were…..um, dancing, "She explained in an embarrassed tone.

"Oh. Well, I'm here. Listen; don't forget everything I told y'all to do. I'm a be right there with y'all," he explained in a comforting manner.

"O.K., we got it, daddy," Melody said, then hung up.

Five minutes later, Stink watched as Melody and Carmella exited the club, closely followed by Dame. After a brief exchange of words, Melody and Carmella hopped in Melody's car while Dame slid behind the wheel of his own.

As Melody's Benz pulled out of the parking lot, Dame's was close behind. At that moment, Stink knew that his promised revenge was at hand.

Stink steered the rental car out onto the street, keeping a safe distance, careful not to arouse any suspicions in his unsuspecting victim.   Revenge was now his.

Melody's stomach fluttered nervously as she pulled into the parking lot of the exclusive 1776 Holiday Inn hotel, in Colonial Williamsburg. She had never done anything remotely close to this before, yet for Stink she would do anything. The love she had for him was immeasurable.

Melody looked over to Carmella who seemed to be cool, calm, and collected, as she applied a fresh coat of lip gloss in the vanity mirror.

"You ready, Mami?" Carmella asked coolly.

"Yeah….I, um….guess so," Melody stammered.

"Let's go then, Mami," Carmella announced. Once they stepped out of the car, Dame was already walking towards them. "You got everything, Mami?" She asked

Melody in a hushed tone.

Melody nodded her head, and pushed the alarm on her key ring.

After the preliminaries of their "sexscapade" were taken care of, Carmella led Melody to the large bed in the back of the suite and began to grope her body sexily.

Both women, clad in nothing more than a G-string allowed their nipples to gently rub against one another's.

Under normal circumstances the act would've sent jolts of pleasure throughout their bodies. However, Dame's hulking presence eyeing them hungrily made the act somewhat fraudulent.

Carmella peered to him out of the corner of her eye, silently beckoning him to join. Laying Melody onto her back, Carmella hiked her firm ass in Dame's direction, giving him a clear view of her phat pussy from the rear. This view was too much for him to handle, prompting him to join the beautiful ladies.

As he was getting undressed, Carmella hopped from her position, and said, "Poppi, we want to try something new for you. Just lay back."

Once Stink's phone rang the one pre-planned time, signaling that it was clear for him to enter the hotel suite, he casually exited the car.

Just in case his plans had gone wrong, he gripped the Heckler and Kock .45 handgun inside his baggy jeans.

When he reached the door, he slowly turned the door knob and entered the room. There were sounds of giggles coming from the rear of the suite as Stink made his way through the room. Prepared for whatever, he held the gun high.

He felt a strong rush of adrenaline as he eased the cracked bedroom door open.

Once his eyes focused on the hideous spectacle, he allowed himself to relax. There he was, his long ago partner, sprawled across the bed naked; handcuffed and shackled.

Melody and Carmella were kneeling over his burly figure jiggling their titties in his face taunting him.

Unbeknownst to any of them, Stink stood in the doorway and watched them tease Dame until he'd seen enough. "Ugh! Ugh!" cleared his throat, garnering everyone's attention.

Melody and Carmella jumped from the bed and rushed over to him, planting kisses over his cheeks.

"Daddy, I missed you soooo much," Melody whined, clinging to Stink.

"Yeah, Poppi. What took you so long to come and save us?" Carmella joked.

Stink ignored their comments and eyed the figure stretched out before him with a menacing smile. "Well, well....looks like we meet again, Damien."

There was a look of complete horror plastered across Dame's face, as the raw irony of his situation came crashing into his realty. "Stin....Stink....yo, man. I ain't know man. I swear," he stuttered aimlessly.

"You ain't know what, Dame?" Stink asked through clenched teeth.

"Stink, man.... I'm sorry. I swear!" Dame pleaded, visibly shedding tears.

Dame, there's no need for apologies. What's done is done," he said nonchalantly, tossing Dame a patronizing smirk.

"Stink, man. I swear, I'll do whatever I gotta do to make it up to you," Dame pleaded, eyeing the powerful handgun in Stink's hand." Look, Stink, I've got a half a 'mill' at my spot. I swear I'll give it to you. Please! Please, just let me live...," he begged through sobs.

Stink looked to Dame without an inkling of compassion, then asked, "Where's the money, Dame?"

Dame quickly divulged the location of the money, along with the combination to the safe, in hopes that his life would be spared.

Carmella sat in the chair, gripping the .45 handgun with her eyes locked on Dame. Stink left her with specific instructions to shoot if he tried anything funny.

With her legs crossed, she looked to Dame with a slight tinge of compassion. "What did you really do to Stink?" Carmella asked inquisitively, breaking the silence.

"I ain't doing shit! He's just crazy! Fo real, shorty, if you let me go, I've got a lot more money than what they're going to get. I could make you a rich woman. You'd never have to strip again, "Dame offered, sensing some vulnerability in the pretty girl.

Carmella chuckled at his assumptions of her, and then decided to have a little fun. "Like how much money?" She asked, faking interest.

Dame struggled to lean up as far as the restraints would allow. "I've got over a million dollars put up, but only I can get to it," he revealed in a serious tone.

"And only you can get to it, huh?" She asked in a mocking fashion.

"Yeah. But if you let me go, half of it is yours, "Dame replied gaining hope.

Carmella couldn't help but to laugh at his remark. She knew there was no way he was going to part with one penny if she were to let him go. More than likely, he'd kill her immediately. Yet, with Stink and Melody, she had begun to feel like she was part of something special. She knew that better things were sure to come if she played her cards right." Gordito [Fat Boy], shut the fuck up!" She spat in a stink voice that dripped with sarcasm.

Melody steered Dame's big Benz into a parking space in the ritzy gated community, just outside the city limits.

"Stay here," Stink instructed, as he casually stepped from the car.

The entire evening had been one big rush for Melody. She couldn't help but wonder how the night would end.

Melody sat behind the wheel and watched as Stink eased up to the door of the dark house, then disappeared inside.

Stink walked up to the dark house and placed his ear to the door. Unable to hear any sounds coming from within, he carefully slide the key in the lock and eased the door open.

As he entered the house, it was totally dark, besides a light coming from the range over the stove. Not wanting to make any unnecessary noise, he left the door ajar and tiptoed through the house.

After checking the rooms downstairs, he lightly treaded up the flight of stairs to where Dame had informed him that the safe was located. Stink peaked into the bedroom, and then slid into the room. He quickly made his way to the large painting on the wall and pulled it down. Sure as Dame had said, the wall safe was right behind the picture. The darkness in the room made it nearly impossible to see the tiny digits. Stink carelessly cut the bed lamp on and pulled it as far as the cord would allow.

His first attempt at opening the safe was unsuccessful, causing a slight sigh of frustration to escape his lips. However, on the second attempt, the safe smoothly popped open, revealing neatly stacked bricks of money and five tightly wrapped packages.

Stink grabbed a pillowcase from the bed and emptied the contents of the safe.

After retrieving the loot and drugs, he snatched a towel from the adjoining bathroom, and then meticulously wiped everything that he touched.

Closing the door behind him, he was certain he hadn't left anything that would show that he'd been there.

Carmella quickly jumped to a standing position as she heard the door to the suite being opened. Aiming the gun carelessly at the bedroom's door, she was prepared to shoot it out.

Stink, closely followed by Melody, pushed the door open and eyed a visibly petrified Carmella, lowering the gun.

Rushing into Stink's arm, Carmella said, "Poppi, you scared me."

"Don't worry, Mami. I'll take it from here," he replied retrieving the gun from her.

Carmella and Melody embraced as if they had been separated for years.

"Were you all right?" Melody asked concerned.

"Yeah, I was O.K., other than him trying to bribe me with his secret million dollar stash," Carmella revealed, tossing Dame a snobbish smirk.

"Where he's going they won't be using our form of currency, "Stink stated, looking directly at Dame.

"Stink, man, please!" Dame bellowed fearfully in a pleading tone.

"Nigga, don't cry now!" Stink retorted, sporting a treacherous glare.

"Yo, man, we had a deal! You can't do this to me, man. You're my son's godfather!" Dame stated in a begging tone.

"I'll still be his godfather. You just won't be here to be his father…. Fah! fah! fha!" Stink replied, pulling the trigger on the powerful handgun, equipped with a suppression apparatus that muffled the otherwise loud gunshot.

Dame's body twisted and contorted as the three .45 caliber slugs tore into his right upper torso. Instantly, chunks of flesh splattered against the wall, leaving his crimson colored blood running down the white wall.

Stink coolly turned to Melody and Carmella. "Wipe everything down that y'all touched."

As they scampered off, Stink noticed the mixed emotions in them while witnessing his murderous act.

The manner in which Stink murdered Dame replayed in Carmella's mind, leaving her with a strong sense of reverence for him. She had witnessed men murdered before; even her little brother had taken a man's life right before her eyes. However, it was the power that he emulated and the calmness in which he showed that made Carmella's center moist, with just the thought of him.

She could tell that Melody was slightly horrified by the scene that played out just days before. Nonetheless, Carmella felt that Stink had solidified his bond between the three of them.

Stink jumped in Melody's Benz and quickly dropped the top. He had two stops to make, both of extreme importance.

As he cruised down the interstate with his hair neatly pulled into a ponytail, he enjoyed the warm air blowing through his hair, and the feeling of the morning sun on his face. Sliding the 'Fendi' sunglasses over his eyes, he pressed down harder on the accelerator, anxious to make his first stop.

Pulling up to Lil Man's mother's house, Stink grabbed the book bag containing half the money he'd taken from Dame and walked to the door. Lil Man's mother was shocked to see him after so many years, but she was even more shocked at the stacks of money he left behind.

His second stop, in downtown 'Bad Newz' crime

riddled 'Walker Village' apartments wouldn't be as easy. Stink parked the topless Benz in the project's parking lot and sat there for a moment to gather his thoughts. He quickly summoned the strength to face something that was so beautiful, so long ago.

He approached the building and located the address that had been given to him days before. With apprehension, he knocked on the door and instantly heard footsteps trampling down the hollow stairs.

As the door was flung open, there stood the little girl who once could only call him 'Wassan.' Tayvia had grown tremendously, acquiring the exact same features of her mother.

She eyed Stink curiously, allowing his once familiar face to register in her mid. Breaking out in a broad smile, she yelled, "Ma, Rahsann's here!" Pronouncing his name correctly for the first time in her short life.

Suddenly, there seemed to be a stampede of footsteps trampling down the hollow stairs. Quickly, Bonni came into view, looking every bit of her twenty-six years of age. Her beauty was still present, but the rigors of her life had taken their toll.

She eased her way in front of Tayvia with a confused look etched into her once flawless features. "Rah...Rahsaan, what are you doing here? I mean…. When did you get out?" She stammered.

"Today," he lied.

There was a tense silence between them, until a tiny voice asked,

"Mommy, is dat my daddy?"

Stink's heart melted as the little girl with his features fought her way into view. "Yeah. It's your daddy, Rahsaanique," he announced, reaching for her.

Rahsaanique fell into his arms, gripping him tight as her tiny arms would allow. "I miss you, daddy," she stated, causing emotions to rise in him that he thought were dormant.

"I missed you too, baby."

Bonni and Tayvia watched in silence, allowing the father and daughter to have their long awaited reunion. Throughout Stink's entire bid, Bonni had only brought Tayvia to see him once. After they had grown apart, Stink attempted to get Bonni to allow Melody to bring Rahsaanique to see him. However, Bonni quickly dismissed the request, by saying," Ain't no way I'm-a let some bitch I don't know bring my daughter up there! Bye!"

That was the last time he had talked to Bonni.

Interrupting their embrace, Bonni said, "Why don't y'all come in." Rahsaanique led Stink by the hand into the small, plainly furnished apartment. He immediately noticed a picture of him and Bonnie leaning on his Lexus, years before. They seemed so happy in the photo.

Stink skipped all the formalities and got down to business. "Bonni, I'm going to help you all that I can. But first and foremost, you gotta move up outta here," he said, motion to her apartment with the wave of a hand.

Noticing the defensive posture that she took, he quickly went into all for of his pockets and pulled out a total of thirty thousand dollars, then added, "This is for you to find a house. Now move," he stated in a somewhat commanding tone.

Before Bonni could protest, he gave Rahsaanique and Tayvia a quick peck, then headed for the door.

Halting him in his tracks, Bonni, "How will you know where I've moved too?" "Don't worry. I'll find you," he retorted confidently, then exited.

Melody and Carmella sat in Melody's car and waited on Stink to exit the dealership. He had just purchased a sixty thousand dollar Cadillac SUV with cash, and thought nothing of it.

"Mami, that fucking truck is sooo sexy," Carmella commented.

"Yeah, it is nice," she agreed unenthused.

Carmella quickly turned towards her, noticing the dry tone in which she responded. "Why you say it like that Mami? Is something wrong?" She asked. "Nah, I'm just … it's just that… that truck is in my name, and I haven't worked in a month. Where would I get sixty thousand to pay for that thing? I can barely pay for this," Melody sated referring to her own car.

"Mami, you love poppi, right?"

"Yes, But I –"

"But my ass!" Carmella blurted cutting her off, and then added. "Whatever he wants, you gotta be down for, Mami. I've only known him for a month and I'm down for whatever!" She concluded earnestly.

Melody nodded her head somberly, and then said, "Yeah, I guess you're right."

"Pssst, you'd better know, Mami" Carmella snapped, eyeing Stink as he walked out of the dealership. Hopping into the shiny, black Escalade, Stink motioned for them to follow him.

Carmella maneuvered the Escalade through the traffic on the interstate 95, while Melody bounced excitedly to the Mary J. Blige CD, playing through the state of the art 'Bang and Olufsen' sound system.

Stink lounged comfortably in the back, toying with the 'play station' video game, playing on the tiny screens in the headrest.

Carmella was elated about returning to the city, especially since it was only for a visit. She replayed the conversation she and Melody had earlier that day. She would have gladly signed for Stink to get the truck, but she'd never held a job paying enough money to account for such a luxurious vehicle.

"Hey ho, turn that shit down! Y'all fucking with my concentration!" Stink yelled over the loud crooning of Mary J. "As a matter of fact, take that shit out! Put Jay Z on or something."

Melody quickly pushed the number for Jay Z's CD as Stink had requested.

While the CD was loading, Carmella jokingly stated, "What's wrong, Papi? Is my girl, Mary, touching your sensitive side?"

"Nah. Ain't shit sensitive about me I'm tired of hearing that man bashing shit," Stink replied, and then added, "What? Y'all ain't happy or something?"

"Papi chulo, you know we happy, "Carmella quickly replied for the both of them. "Don't worry, I got something for y'all asses when we get to the city," he stated slyly, then laid back and allow JAY Z's rhythmic flow to ease his mind.

Cross was estatic. Stink had informed him that by 9'oclock that evening he would have already paid a visit to each one of his soldier's women. At some point, doubt had set in on each man in his crew. Even Slyborn had begun to second guess him. It became evident the day before that Slyborn didn't totally believe in Cross' plan.

"Yo, Cross, ya man's done put you off like three times already. What's the deal, god?" Slyborn stated full of inquisitiveness.

"Yeah, I know, high. I just hope he ain't playing you."

"Play me!" Cross exclaimed defensively. Jumping from his bunk, he began to pace the small cell. "Ay yo B. This Nigga like my brother! He would never play me! This Nigga broke bread when my own fam was shitting on me. Play me! Humph!" Cross concluded.

Attempting to calm Cross, Slyborn said, "Ahight, son. I feel you. I feel you."

Throughout their conversation, Cross intentionally withheld the fact that Stink was in route to NYC. More than likely, in the next few hours Stink would be filling Slyborn's girl's pussy with marijuana stuffed balloons.

Once they reached New York, Stink instructed Carmella to head straight to her mother's house uptown. As they pulled up to Carmella's building on 145 st, Stink noticed her brother, Pepe and his crew mingling on the stoop. They eyed the strange vehicle suspiciously, as each of them clutched the bulges in their pockets in preparation for any beef.

When Carmella hopped out of the driver's seat, dressed in a pink 'Baby Phat' velour sweat suit with matching Timberland hikers, Pepe's eyes lit up.

"Oh shit! Mi hermana [my sister], Carma!" Pepe exclaimed in astonishment. Quickly approaching, he continued, "Yo, Carma, to herear ona fortuna [you've come into a fortune]," he stated, eyeing the luxurious SUV in awe.

Nonchalantly, she replied, "Nah, Pepe, but I'm bueno [good]."

Just as Pepe was getting ready to inquire further, Stink stepped from the SUV. Dressed in his customary velour sweats and crispy construction Timberlands, Pepe and Carmella automatically turned there attention to him.

"Pepe, you remember Stink. He's familia," Carmella announced proudly.

Pepe stepped over to Stink and dapped him up, then asked, "Yo, what's the deal, fam?"

"Ain't shit. Just chillin. Wazup wit you?" Stink replied.

"Yo fam, just out here trying to get this money."

Pausing, Stink looked over to Pepe's crew, and then asked, "You think your crew can manage without you for a minute?"

Pepe shot his boys a quick glance, and then said,

"Yo fam, I'm trying to roll with you."

Stink smiled at Pepe's remark, and then turned to Melody sitting in the passenger seat." Melody, roll with Carmella for a few. Me and Pepe about to go handle some business."

Carmella quickly spoke up. "Papi, you just gonna leave us out here like this?" She asked in a voice laced with disappointment.

Displaying his best heart melting smile, Stink replied," Now would I leave my two favorite ladies out here like this?" Reaching into a bag sitting on the back seat, he pulled out a brick of money, and then said," Here, make sure y'all spend it wisely."

Melody and Carmella's eyes instantly lit up at the sight of a large stack of money. Nonetheless, it was the shock that registered on Pepe's face that caught Stink's attention.

Snapping Pepe out of his gaping stupor, Stink said," Come on, playboy, we've got moves to make."

As Stink made his way to the driver's side, Melody and Carmella hung onto him playfully, while planting kisses on both his cheeks.

Once Stink was behind the wheel, and Pepe in the passenger seat, Carmella asked in a pouting tone," Papi, how are we gonna get around if you're taking the truck?"

Stink eyed her with a disbelieving look on his face, then snapped in an irritated voice, "Mami, y'all got ten fucking gees a piece. Y'all will figure something out." Turning 'The life and times of Shawn Carter Vol 3' up to a level capable of shaking buildings, he pulled off.

Melody had taken Carmella to stores that she never knew existed. That in itself was strange; being that Carmella had lived in New York City her entire life.

Melody remembered the lovely time she and Stink had shared in the limo ride from New York years before, and decided to charter a limo. She could sense that Carmella had never ridden in a limousine from the way she looked around the spacious cabin in awe.

"Have you ever rode in one of these before?" Melody asked.

"Nah. Have you?"

"Yeah, one time, years ago. Rahsaan and I took one back to Virginia."

"Y'all rode in one, all the way to Virginia?" Carmella asked astounded.

"Mmm Hmm."

"Did y'all do it on the way back?" Carmella inquired.

With a smirk plastered across her face, she replied, "You know we did, girl." Immediately, Carmella wanted details. As Melody began to give her play by play details of the episode, Carmella moved in close and put her hand high on Melody's thigh. The more climatic her story became, the higher Carmella's hand eased up her thigh.

Near the end of Melody's rendition, Carmella looked deep into her eyes, and then in a husky animalistic tone, she said "Mami, I want to taste you while we ride around New York City."

Before Melody could protest, Carmella was already sliding between her thighs.

Pepe had taken Stink to buy everything he needed for Cross' little caper. From heroin; to cocaine; to balloons, Pepe knew where to get it.

As they'd finished packing the balloons with the assortment of drugs, they exited the hourly hotel on 145th, and made their way to Stink's Escalade on the opposite side of the street.

Initially, Stink didn't see anything out of place until Pepe casually advised, "keep walking, TNT on the block." There, right next to his truck was New York City's 'Tactical Narcotics Team', commonly called 'TNT.' Upon further inspection, Stink noticed the fashionably hip dressed police, shaking a group of guys down near his truck.

Pepe led the way into a clothing store on the corner of 145th and Broadway. Turning toward Stink, he blurted, "Give me the work, fam. I'm-a be on my block. Just come through and scoop me."

Without second guessing him, Stink handed over the brown bag containing the colorful balloons.

"Aight, lets bounce, fam," Pepe stated, calmly exiting the store, heading the direction of his block.

Stink casually walked over to his truck, ignoring the aggressive NYC detectives. Hitting the button on his key ring to deactivate the alarm, an ambitious cop yelled, "Hey you! You driving this truck?"

Stink abruptly stopped, and turned toward the Hispanic officer. In his best college educated voice, he replied, "Yes sir. And what seems to be the problem?"

Slightly baffled by Stinks tone, the officer asked, "Um, did you know that you are in a known drug area?"

"Sir, I'm not sure if this is a known drug area or not. However, I'm simply scouting the area for a video shoot. I'm executive director of operations with 'EX-Con ENTERTAINMENT." Stink stated proudly. Extending his hand, he added, "Rahssan Jones."

Taking Stink's hand in his own, the cop said, "Umm... I'm sorry, sir. Just be careful around here."

"I sure will, officer. And you have a nice day," Stink said, then hopped into his truck and pulled off.

Once he pulled up to Pepe's building, he breathed a sigh of relief.

Pepe quickly jumped in the passenger seat, and

asked, "You Aight, fam?"

"Nah, Pep. You drive man. Po-po got my nerves fucked up," He said opening the door.

As Pepe hopped in the driver's seat, he looked over to a visibly shaken Stink, and then called out to one of his boys.

"Yo, Chic! Let me get the rest of that 'Dutch' y'all just rolled?"

Chico jumped up, and came to the window, handing Pepe a freshly rolled cigar.

"Good looking, Chic. I got y'all when I get back," Pepe said pulling off. Once they got on Riverside Dr., he rolled the windows up and passed Stink the cigar, filled with hydroponically grown marijuana.

Carmella slowly pulled her pants up around her hips and fixed her disheveled locks. As the limousine pulled in front of the trendy 5th Avenue boutique, Melody's redden cheeks were just returning to their natural color. After experiencing the earth shattering orgasm from Carmella's tongue, her knees were like jello.

Once Carmella finished fixing her clothes and hair, she looked at Melody and asked," you ready, Mami?"

"Mmm hmm," Melody responded, just above a whisper.

As they exited the white Lincoln Navigator limousine, they were strutting their stuff as if they were two Hollywood divas.

Pedestrians eyed the pair suspiciously in an attempt to place the two seemingly famous women. Soaking the scene up like a sponge, they simply pranced into the boutique that specialized in shoes for women.

The boutique's proprietor instantly treated them as if they were royalty, showering them with champagne and hors' d' o evuvres'.

As Melody and Carmella enjoyed showings from

Manolo Blahnik to Vera Wang their pockets became thinner with each purchase.

After purchasing six pairs of the expensive shoes, they exited the boutique with a little over six thousand dollars between the two. Thanks to Stink's generosity, their day had been a blast.

Stink placed a call to each of the numbers Cross had given him and instructed the women to meet him at the world famous 'Juniors' restaurant on Fulton Street in Brooklyn.

The two women driving from Queens needed some encouragement to make the long drive to Brooklyn, prompting Stink to offer each of them a hundred dollars to meet him. The women nearly hung up in his ear, racing out of the door.

Meanwhile, he and Pepe sat in the Escalade battling one another in 'NBA LIVE 2K.' Occasionally, they'd press the pause button in order to take a bite of 'Juniors' world famous cheesecake.

It seemed as if the cakes delicious taste was magnified by the powerful hydroponically grown marijuana that they'd smoked.

Stink hadn't smoked marijuana since he'd been released from prison and the weed that they'd consumed earlier had him feeling as if he was on another planet.

"Damn, Pep, I bust yo ass again!" Stink taunted, looking at Pepe through eyes resembling those of a 'China - Man.'

"Run it back, fam. I'm taking L.A. this time," Pepe said.

As they restarted the game, Stink noticed a woman pull up, fitting the description of Quan's woman.

The thick red sister stepped out of the car and made her way straight toward Stink's Escalade.

Pepe, in a New York sate of mind, gripped the glock

in his lap.

As she approached the driver's side window, Pepe cautiously rolled the window down.

"Um, are you Stink?" She asked, staring at Pepe.

"Nah. I'm Stink. And who are you?" Stink chimed it.

"Oh, I'm Nichelle, Quan's baby mother," she stated.

"Aight, hop in, "Stink in instructed, hitting the button to unlock the door.

As she slid into the backseat, the paused video game reflected off of all of the monitors in the truck, prompting her to remark." DAMN! Y'all nigga's ballin foreal!" She said in awe, and then added. Y'all up in this bitch playing play station and the whole shit."

Her ghetto attitude reverberated throughout the truck, causing Stink to cringe. He quickly picked out the yellow balloons, and then turned to hand them to Nichelle. Once Stink had her in his sights, what he saw was sad. She had maneuvered her tight skirt up her thighs, revealing her red lace panties.

Stink shook his head in disgust, and quickly refocused his attention from her neck up. "Um... Nichelle, this shit is serious. Make sure your man gets this tomorrow. Now I'm-a hit you with two just for coming out here; however, you gotta keep your end of the deal. Aight?" Stink explained firmly.

"Yeah, I got you. But wouldn't it be best if I called you after I came from seeing Quantez, just to let you know I made it safely," she proposed, batting her eyelashes suggestively.

"I'll tell you what. How about I give you a call," Stink offered. In a defeated tone, she said," All right, that's cool." With that said, she exited the truck.

The next two meetings were just as eventful. They didn't go as far as flashing their pussies; yet the flirtatious

remarks were still the same.   Once Stink and Pepe had
discarded all of the balloons, they headed back uptown.

Chapter Four

Cross sat in his cell enjoying some of the potent marijuana that had made its way into his hands. Everyone in his crew was now a firm believer that he could make it happen.

One by One, each man's woman made the trip into the Adirondack Mountains and dropped the assortment of drugs from their vaginas.

The compound was flooded with every drug imaginable. True heroin addicts slumbered in their morphine induced haze. Cocaine users moved aimlessly, at twice their normal speed. And the weed heads were out in massive numbers. Everywhere you turned, you were met with bloodshot beads for eyes.

Cross felt like the King again as he inhaled deeply on the makeshift blunt, rolled in a 'Black & Mild.'

Passing Shyborn the cigar, Cross said, "I'm telling you B, this is just the beginning."

"Yo, I feel you, god. Word is bond, I was doubting ya man's crazily. But when my wiz told me that the God lace her wit two bills, on top of the balloons, I knew son was on some real shit," Shyborn explained in a sincere tone.

Cross just smiled. He'd already known about the two hundred dollars that Stink had given each woman. He also knew that each woman had attempted to throw themselves on Stink in one way or another.

If either of them ever attempted to show Cross any disloyalty, he wouldn't hesitate to have Stink sexually slay their girl. At that moment, Cross felt he had all of the keys, except the key to freedom.

"Yo, high, I'm about to hit my lil bro up. Finish that shit off, "Cross stated nonchalantly, and then exited the cell.

As Stink cell phone vibrated, he snatched it off his hip. Eyeing the caller identification, he quickly pressed the talk button. After bypassing the automated phone system, by pushing '1', Cross came onto the line.

"Yo, what's poppin, playboy?" Cross asked.

"Ain't shit. Just cruising the streets of New York," Stink replied coolly.

"You still up top?" Cross questioned, wondering why Stink hadn't left New York.

"Yeah, I'm trying to hook up with Jose, but he's out of town or some shit," Stink explained.

"Oh yeah. Well you know he's going to bless you whenever he pops up."

"Yeah, I know. That's why my ass still up here, paying 450.00 a night at the fucking Sheraton," Stink replied sarcastically.

"Nigga, you could've stayed at Ma Duke's spot," Cross stated.

"Yeah, with two fucking broads. Wonder how that would look?" Stink quipped slyly.

"Oh, I forgot about your 'murda mamis'. Where they at anyway?"

"Ah man, them bitches somewhere getting them toes done and they pussies waxed," Stink replied.

"Say word!"

"Word!"

"Yo, B, y'all doing it foreal," Cross concluded.

"Not like we about to," Stink sated seriously.

"I know that's right. So who you wit now" Cross inquired.

"Oh, just me and, Pep."

"Carma's Lil brother, Pep?" Cross asked.

"Yeah, Me and Pep been chillin for like three days. Shit, I'm falling in love with the lil Nigga," Stink said chuckling, and then added, "I might take him back to V.A. with me." His sudden revelation surprise both Cross and Pepe simultaneously. After a brief silence, Cross said, "Foreal B that might not be a bad idea."

This instantly came as a surprise to Stink. Usually, Cross didn't feel that anybody who was a descendant of NYC was trustworthy.

Slightly baffled, Stink asked, "You think so?"

"Yeah. Shorty could help you get shit poppin down there, but you gotta keep ya eye on that Nigga. You know how them fucking New Yorkers is," Cross stated.

Inwardly smiling at Cross final remark, he said," Yeah, I'm-a think about it. But yo, hit me back latter. I'm about to run up in 'Jimmy Jazz,' Aight."

"Aight, one!" Cross said then hung up.

Stink and Pepe made their way into the urban clothing store on 125th street for the third time in as many days. Every time Stink had bought himself an outfit for the day, he made sure that Pepe got whatever he wanted as well.

It was the least he could do for the youngster. Ever since Pepe had hopped into his truck, three days before, he hadn't left Stink's side.

While Melody and Carmella stayed in the hotel room all day enjoying room service and God knows what else, he and Pepe waited patiently for Jose's call.

Oh!! Oh, God! Melody.... I'm cumming," Carmella hissed as Melody worked her pussy with her tongue.

Carmella was spread eagle on the love seat in the hotel suite, with her Burberry skirt hiked up above her waist. Her panties had thrown to the side long ago. Melody continued to lap at Carmella's sensitive clitoris.

"You like that, Mami?" Melody asked in a submissive tone that instantly made Carmella's pussy cream.

"Ooh...Mel! I love it, Mami!" Carmella responded in a lust filled voice. Melody, who had been done the exact same way, only minutes before, gave Carmella's, lips one last kiss. Rising her from kneeling position, she flopped down on the couch beside a visibly shaken Carmella.

Starring at Melody with a serious look on her face, Carmella said, "Melody... I think I'm falling in love with you and papi." Returning her piercing stare, Melody whispered, "Me too."

Carmella couldn't believe she'd divulged her true feelings to Melody. With the exception of Pepe, she had never felt the emotional attachment that she now felt for Stink and Melody.

Pepe had always been her everything. He'd meant more to her than anything in the entire world, even herself.

She was happy to see the way he and Stink had been getting along. They were acting as if they had known each other for years, instead of days. Carmella just hoped Stink would still have interest in her and Melody now that he and Pepe had become so tight.

Ever since Pepe and Stink had hooked up, Stink hadn't so much as look at either of them. The night before, she and Melody had attempted to give Stink his own lingerie showing, yet he seemed more focused on the video game that he and Pepe were engrossed in.

However, tonight, they had devised a plan that would surely garner Stink's undivided attention.

Just as Stink and Pepe exited the store, Stink's cell phone vibrated. Unable to retrieve his phone from his hip while carrying the numerous bags, Pepe quickly retrieved the bulk of Stink's packages, freeing his hand.

Fumbling with the phone, Stink eyed the caller ID which read 'UNIDENTIFIED CALLER'. With precaution, he answered the phone.

"Speak pon it, bredren, "he announced in his fraudulent Jamaican dialect, instantly garnering a look of disbelief from Pepe.

"Oh, I'm sorry. I must have the wrong number."

Stink quickly recognized the voice, and blurted, "Jose! Yo, this is me. What's up?"

"How are you, my friend? I just received your messages. Are you alright?" Jose inquired concerned.

"Yeah, I'm good. But you had me worried about," Stink revealed.

"My friend, never worry. It only brings stress," Jose replied philosophically.

"Yeah, I feel you. But I'm trying to see you.

"Well, I should be in New York this afternoon. How important is it?" Jose asked.

"Um...you know, I'm uh...," Stink began, attempting to use his words carefully over the phone

Picking up on Stink's hesitancy, Jose said," Oh, is it about your property that you've left in my care?"

Inwardly smiling at Jose's quick-wit, Stink replied, "Yeah."

"Oh, well my friend, just say when and where and your property will be there."

Stink didn't quickly understand exactly what Jose was saying. "I'm in New York now. How about I just come and see you later."

"That's fine.   Teaneck, lets say around 5 o'clock,"
Jose said then hung up.

Pepe pulled the Escalade in front of Jose's elegant
house in Teaneck New Jersey. Turning to Pepe, Stink said,
"Pep, just chill for a second. I'll be right back." He then slid
from the truck.

Once Stink made it to the porch and pushed the
doorbell, he instantly heard a long succession of various
tones, chiming throughout the house.

Suddenly, a short, stout Hispanic woman appeared
dressed in a customary maid's uniform. "Si senor, poder yo
asistir tu? [Yes, sir, may I help you?]" She asked peering at
Stink suspiciously.

Unable to translate what she'd just said, Stink stood
there dumbfounded. The only reply he could muster was,
"Is Jose here?"

"Si, si. You must a be Stink-ah," she stated smiling
broadly. Motioning for Stink to enter, she led the way to a
small sitting room, decorated in an ancient Asian theme."
Have a seat. I get Mr. Rodriguez for you," she said, then
left the room.

Stink walked around the room, inspecting the
delicate artifacts curiously. The care taken in creating the
tiny treasures immediately made him think of his own
home.

"My friend, we meet again," Jose announced,
appearing out of nowhere. Startled, Stink turned and
instantly noticed that Jose's normal bright complexion was
now a tanned brown. He also noticed how refreshed and
well rested he looked.

"Hey, wasup, Jose," Stink said as he and Jose
embraced. "I've just returned from my home in Santa
Domingo," Jose revealed.

"You look good, man."

"Ahh, Stink, it's such a beautiful country. You must come one day."

"I will, man. I will," Stink replied earnestly.

"Remember my friend; you've given your word. You must come," Jose said, binding Stink to a promise. Motioning for him to sit in one of the delicate chairs, Jose took a seat opposite him, then asked," So are you ready to get back into your business?"

"Yeah, I'm ready," Stink replied.

"As I promised, I will do for you as I would do for my own familia. I am going to give you 80 Kilos for the money you've left in my care," Jose explained. Stink was absolutely shocked. He wasn't aware that Jose was going to extend such generosity.

"Is that fine with you?" Jose asked.

"Yeah. But, um, I'm going to need a few days to come up with a way to get the drugs to Virginia. I've got an i---," Stink explained, before being abruptly cut off by Jose.

Casually, Jose said, "Don't worry, it's already there."

"But…but … how – "

"You name the place and it is there. Anywhere you want it in the United States, it's there, "Jose stated in a matter of fact tone, and then continued. "Stink, you have been loyal to me when you didn't have to. For that, my gratitude will forever remain in your favor. Anything you ask of me, I will accommodate. Anything!" Jose revealed sincerely.

Stink couldn't believe his ears. Here was one of the most powerful drug lords in America, giving him his unadulterated loyalty. Returning Jose's sincere glare, Stink said, "Jose, thank you, man."

"No! Thank you, my friend. Now call me when you're ready to make the pick up," Jose replied, then stood, signaling that their meeting was over.

Once Stink hopped in his truck, he knew that it was about to be on and poppin.

Chapter Five

Stink laid back in the passenger seat of Pep's newly acquired Suburban equipped with every accessible gadget known to man. Not only did the inside resemble 'Circuit City', the exterior was done up in a major way. Sitting on a set of 22 inch chrome ' Mozzi's', the Suburban's blood red paint job instantly garnered attention.

It was strange just how much had been accomplished in only for short months. Pepe and his two man crew, of Chico and Manny, had miraculously put the city of Bad Newz on lock.

The low prices that Jose had given Stink, gave him room to undercut all the competition. It had taken Stink and his crew nearly the entire four months to finish the massive amount of drugs.

Pulling into his driveway, Stink inwardly beamed at the sprawling fortified estate that he'd built. As soon as the electronic gate swung open, Stink's well trained pit bulls, Fire and Ice, surrounded Pepe's truck.

Once they parked behind Stink's 2000 Porsche 911 Targa, Pepe turned to Stink, and said," Yo, fam, put them Motherfuckin animals up or I'm staying in my whip."

As Stink opened the door and greeted his man eaters, Melody appeared, coming from the makeshift beach that Stink had surgically installed on the property, instead of a pool.

He eyed her in a contemptuous manner. Since he'd caught her and Carmella enjoying each other's bodies, his compassion for her had begun to slowly deteriorate.

Somewhere along the way, Melody had become his bitch, along with Carmella.

In a sense, he had more respect for Carmella than he did Melody. Not only was Carmella witty, she also had a strong will, where Melody had neither.

"Melody! Put these fucking dogs up!" Stink barked, and then added." If yo ass wasn't so Fucking smart, you would've been listening when I told y'all not to let'em out until it gets dark!"

Melody quickly gathered the obedient dogs, then ushered them toward their cage.

"Stupid bitch!" Stink yelled before she was out of earshot.

"Yo, fam, don't let'em see you sweat," Pepe advised humorously.

"Nah, I'm good, Pep. But sometimes you gotta flip. Feel me?" Pepe nodded, and then followed Stink into the house. As they entered the house, their noses were instantly treated to an exotic smelling dish that filled the air.

"Pollo con hobichuelas! [Chick and beans]," Pepe exclaimed as the familiar smell invaded his senses.

Stink noticed Carmella standing over the oven, looking quite striking in her chef's apron with her long hair pulled into a ponytail.

Once Carmella turned to see them, she yelled, "Papi! Poco, Pepe!"

Enjoying Carmella hungrily, Stink quickly went into the den to handle his business with Pepe, and send him on his way.

Melody lounged on the lawn chair, as the machine-made waves, rushed onto the white sand. Tears flowed freely from her eyes as she racked her mind. She couldn't understand why Stink had been treating her the way he had. She had done nothing but love him.

Throughout the entire time he was incarcerated, she never once gave herself to anyone. The more she thought about it; he had been the only person she'd been with in nearly 7 years, except for…, "Carmella." She said aloud, allowing the name to slid off of her tongue.

Hearing the deep base from Pepe's system snapped Melody out of her thoughts. She stood and headed inside to face her dilemma. Once she'd entered the house, she could smell the concoction that Carmella had been cooking, yet there was no sign of Carmella or Stink.

Melody quickly headed upstairs, taking the steps two at a time. As she approached the partially open bedroom door, she could hear Carmella's moans of ecstasy coming from within.

"Oh! Yess, Papi! Ooh, yess, fuck your chocha, papi!" Carmella hissed. Melody eased into the room and watched as Stink pounded into Carmella's core furiously. Instantly, she felt helpless as everything that she ever dreamed of slipped from her grasp. She quickly exited the room, as tears cascaded down her cheeks.

Pepe parked his truck on the crowded downtown street corner, where Chico and Manny stood, directing drug sales, while talking to a group of females.

"Yo, fam, what's the deal?" Chico yelled as Pepe exited his truck.

"Ain't shit, Nigga," Pepe replied, eyeing a sexy, light skinned girl in the crowd who'd caught his attention. "Yo, Chico, who's the Chica?"

Shrugging his shoulders, he said," I don't know. Holla at her." Pepe, an extremely skinny young man, carried himself as if he was black. He kept his hair neatly trimmed into a fade. Even his walk, a slight bop with the swing of his arm, could be scrutinized as being a 'nigger' walk.

Pepe casually walked up to the pretty girl and said, "Wazup, Mami my name is Pep."

"Oh, hi. My name is Clarissa. But everyone calls me 'Rissa,'" she replied sporting a broad smile.

Pepe continued to spit his 'uptop' game to the girl, occasionally using his remote control to change CD's in his truck.

While Pepe's system played 'Big Pun's' CD at a moderate level, a thundering base that seemed to shake the concrete, totally drown out the music coming from Pepe's truck.

Everyone on the corner instinctively looked for the source of the ear shattering base. Pepe eyed the intersection of 23rd and Chestnut Avenue conspicuously, then suddenly saw the source of the loud music.

The Wild S 600 Benz crept at a snails pace down the Avenue. The two occupants of the vehicle peered into the crowd with profound ice grills etched into their faces. Both of them proudly showed their bright gold teeth as they slowly drove past Pep and his crew.

Pepe and the driver of the Benz locked eyes as they sized one another up mentally.

Once the car had disappeared down the block, Pepe gave Rissa his information, then jumped into his truck and sped off.

Pearl and Milk rolled through Chestnut Avenue just to see what was really going on. The last few months had been rough on Pearl's operations. Several of his customers had abruptly stopped doing business with him.

He couldn't understand how a quarter of a million

dollar operation could miraculously disappear over night. Pearl had a hunch that the Spanish dudes standing on the corner had something to do with it.

"My nucca, you see them fuck nuccas out there?" Milk asked in his deep southern drawl.

"Yeah, my nucca. I'm-a have to check dem 'squares out," Pearl replied.

"Fuck nuccas got da red 'Burb' on dubs and the whole shit," Milk point out.

"Yeah. I seen dat, "Pearl said, feeling the taste for war rising in his blood.

Pearl, originally from Miami's treacherous Liberty City, found hope in escaping his ghetto after visiting his cousin who played football for NNU. Once he visited Bear on Newport News University's campus, Pearl's choice was made. After finding his way back to the area, with his right hand man Milk, they quickly locked the city down with cheap prices. Miami, being the largest cocaine import in the United States, made their takeover that much easier.

Since Pearl was a teenager, murder and mayhem had been his forte. The two years that he'd resided in Virginia, his prior calling only had to be demonstrated on one occasion. However, once he got in 'Murder' mode, it was hard for him to snap out of it.

"Yeah, my nucca, I'm-a see bout dem," Pearl concluded, and then turned the thunderous system back up to earth shattering proportions.

Bonni carried a large box from her mini van to her newly obtained three bedroom house in Hampton.

On her final trip to the van, she heard a loud engine gunning down her street. She instantly hoped that she hadn't made a mistake in choosing her new living arrangements.

Once the sleek black sports car came into view, Bonni eyed it evilly, hoping to somehow deter the driver from speeding down her street again.

As the luxurious sports car got to Bonni, it abruptly stopped. Halting in her tracks, Bonni wondered what the driver could possibly want. Unable to get a clear view of the driver, sitting behind the dark tint, she stood frozen.

Once the driver stepped out of the car, she nearly broke out into a full sprint.

Stink slid from the car looking like a thugged out 'Shamar Moore'. He had lost a few pounds over the years, but his body was a chiseled as ever.

"Rahsaan! Boy, you had me scared!" Bonni yelled as she walked toward him.

"Scared. Not you," Stink replied, and then added. "I like your new spot. Now our daughters should be more comfortable," he said eyeing her reaction to his statement closely. "What? I can't call Tayvia my own no more?" He stated sarcastically.

"Boy, you know Tayvia still looks at you the same. I had to tell her the other night that …uh…why we …um…," She explained, her voice trailing off at the mentioning of them as a couple.

"So where are my princesses? " He asked, noticing her nervously fumble with her necklace.

"They're over my mother's house. But if they find out you came by and they weren't home, they'll have a fit."

"Well don't tell'em I came by. I'm-a come back later tonight, and I hope they'll be here," he stated coolly.

"Yeah, they'll be here," she replied in a submissive tone, eyeing him intently as he hopped in his car.

Stink turned the ignition, and was about to pull off when Bonni frantically waved her hand stopping him.

"Yeah. Waszup?" Stink asked.

"Rahsaan, how did you find out where I moved?" She inquired in a serious tone.

"Bonni, I know everything," he replied cockily, then sped off.

Stink cruised the streets in his hundred thousand dollar sports car, enjoying the prying eyes that attempted to get a look at the driver. He enjoyed the power that the Porsche possessed, and he tested it on every opportunity.

He was glad to see that Bonni had made the transition, without any further encouragement.

Time had changed, both he and Bonni. If she would have rode with him throughout his bid, he would've married her the day he was released. However, time was something she wasn't big on doing, and now she would have to pay.

Stink's cell phone abruptly rang, bringing his focus back to the present. "Yo, what up?" He answered.

"Fam, where you at?" Pepe asked in an impatient tone.

"I'm on the interstate. Why?"

"Nah, fam. I need to see you, "Pepe replied in a worried tone.

Noting Pepe's tone, Stink said, "Norfolk waterside. Thirty minutes." Then hung up.

Eyeing the newspaper's headline intently, Cross looked at the picture of the famed lawyer that he and Stink had hired to look into his case years before. 'Bruce Cotler Frees man on Death Row,' the headline read. Since Stink had been making the drop-offs, Cross' account had swollen to over fifty thousand dollars.

Cross had long ago let any hopes of miraculously being freed die; Yet, the article was arousing hopes in him that he didn't know existed.

He sighed heavily, and then grabbed a pen and pad. He knew it was a long shot, but it was his only hope of ever attaining his freedom.

Pearl sat behind his desk, in the exquisite home he'd built out in Colonial Williamsburg. His entire crew was in attendance. Pearl felt that this meeting was essential to him and his crew's reign.

Focusing his attention on his right hand man, Pearl firmly asked, "Milk, what you gathered on dem fuck nuccas?"

"My nucca, they supposed to be from New York. And word is, they got them birds for real cheap," Milk explained.

Rubbing his goatee in deep contemplation, Pearl looked to his cousin. "Bear, what about you? What you hear? "He asked hastily.

"My nucca, I heard the same thang as Milk. But I also heard that it's some local Fuck nucca named, Stank, Skimp, or Spank, or some shit," Bear revealed in a tongue tied manner.

Both, Bear and Milk nodded their heads in unison, then Bear added," He supposed to just come home from the feds."

Pearl shook his head in disbelief," Stank, huh?" He stated inquisitively to know one in particular.

Before either man could respond, Pearl's woman entered the office. "Pooh, I'm-a take Rah-Rah to my mother's, o.k.? I'll be back later," Tina blurted, sashaying her curvaceous figure across the room.

Once Pep arrived at the Norfolk waterside, Stink directed him to Jose's Crab shack where he was enjoying one of his favorite meals. Pepe entered the restaurant, closely followed by Chico and Manny. Eyeing the trio's cocky swaggers, Stink inwardly smiled. Pepe was undoubtedly the leader, and by far the smallest.

"Yo, what's the deal, fam?" Pepe asked, giving Stink a pound. Chico and Manny offered their greetings, and then the trio took their seats.

"So, what's up, Pep?" Stink questioned, tearing into the crab legs.

"Yo fam, today we was on the block, and the punto [faggot] comes through like he owns the fucking place. So, I'm looking at him like 'what?' But, fam, I think he may become a potential problema," Pepe explained in his customary spanglish.

After asking a barrage of questions, Stink knew he'd have to take a serious look into the matter before Pepe, or one of his henchment went off and did something crazy.

Once their business had been discussed, Pepe said," Oh yeah, fam, since we already here, lets check out one these clubs tonight."

Reluctantly, Stink nodded his head. "Aight, that's cool. But first, we gotta hit the mall and get fresh," Stink said, dropping a 'Benjamin' on the table.

"Yeah! That's what I'm talking about, Fam," Pepe stated in an exuberant tone.

"Same ole shit," Bonni muttered to herself, after putting Rahsaanique in bed. Bonnie had actually been fantasizing about getting back with Stink. Yet, the stunt that he'd pulled tonight nullified any thoughts of the aforementioned.

Bonni entered her bedroom and began to undress, removing the newly purchased skirt and blouse. She'd even had her hair and nails done earlier that afternoon.

Suddenly appearing in Bonni's doorway, Tayvia asked, "Mom, when is Rahsaan gonna come to see us? I mean he did tell you to get a house, and we still haven't seen him," she concluded in a sorrowful tone.

"Um, I don't know, Tayvia. But I'm pretty sure

we'll see him soon," Bonni explained, easing the diamond ring off her finger that Stink had given her years before.

"Mom, why were you so pretty today?" Tayvia pried, taking a seat next to her mom.

"What? Your mommy's not always pretty?" Bonnie retorted humorously.

"Yeah, you're pretty. But today you were really pretty," Tayvia replied in an animated tone.

"Oh, well, I just felt like putting some clothes on today."

"Mom, I hope Rahsaan comes to see us soon. I miss him," Tayvia revealed earnestly.

"He will, baby. He will."

'Shadows' Nightclub was packed. Several celebrities lined the V.I.P. area. Once Stink slid the bouncer three C-notes, he and his crew were allowed to enter the highly secured area.

Stink immediately ordered four bottles of 'Crystal,' and soaked up the festive scene.

If one didn't know Stink and his companions, they would swear that they were all of latin decent. Stink's bright complexion and long cornrows made him the object of Spanish-laced jokes while he was incarcerated. Even some Spanish guys mistook him for one of their own.

After their bottles of champagne were delivered, they all sat back on the cushiony leather couches and eyed the crowd.

The ladies were out in massive numbers, prancing by the V.I.P. section in an attempt to attract attention to themselves.

Amongst all of the famous people, Stink felt like a star himself. The platinum chain he sported, coupled with the 'Jesus' piece, contained over 40 carats of the finest diamond cut available. The sparkling piece of jewelry automatically put him in a league with the stars.

"Hey yo, fam, this spot is jumping!" Pepe yelled over the music. Standing, Pepe continued," I'm about to check some of these chicas out, fam." As Pepe stepped off, Chico and Manny followed closely.

Holding his bottle up in a mock toast, Stink said, Do y'all! I'm good!" Stink sat back and relaxed, sipping the sweet tasting champagne fashionably. As his mind began to wonder, he began to think about his daughter. Suddenly, he remembered that he was supposed to have stopped by to see her earlier that evening. Looking at his watch, he noticed it was almost 1 o'clock.

'Fuck it' he thought as he gathered himself and began to scan the crowd for Pepe, Chico and Manny. Unable to locate them in the sea of party goers, Stink reached for his cell phone/two way walkie talkie.

"Blurrp – Pep!" Stink said into the phone.

After a brief wait, Pepe answered "Blurrp – What up, fam?"

"Blurrp – I'm about to be out, Pep," Stink informed.

"Blurrp – Aight, we coming back right now. Hold up."

Stink put his phone back onto his hip and impatiently waited for Pepe and his crew.

Noticing the bouncer usher three guys into the V.I.P., Stink instantly knew the men weren't Pepe and his crew. However, once Pepe and his crew entered, Stink immediately picked up on the tense stare down that was taking place between Pepe's crew and the three men.

The tall dark-skinned guy, who sported dreadlocks and a mouth full of gold teeth, seemed to be glaring at Pepe menacingly.

Pepe broke the stare long enough to slide up to Stink

and whisper," That's the Nigga from earlier today."

Stink showed no emotion as the dreadlocked, gold toothed man kept his eyes focused in their direction.

"Come on, let's be out" Stink advised casually leading the way out of the club.

"My nucca, that's them suckers right there. And I bet that's that fuck nucca, Slank, or Spinks or whoever," Milk said eyeing the four men exit the club.

"Yeah, my nucca, that's him. I can feel it," Pearl stated deep in thought.

"That lil Spanish fuck Nigga think he tough, my nucca," Bear added.

"Don't worry my nucca. We gonna see how tough them fuck nuccas is real soon," Pearl vowed.

There was a tense silence between the three men, as each man brewed in their anger. Although there wouldn't be a war that night, bloodshed was destined.

Once Stink arrived at Bonni's house, it was almost two o'clock in the morning from his vantage point, behind the wheel of his Porsche, the house was completely dark. Nonetheless, he pulled himself together and made his way to the door and boldly rang the doorbell.

After a few minutes, Bonni appeared clutching her housecoat tightly around her body. "Rahsaan, what the hell are you doing here this late?" She asked in an irritated tone.

"What! You got company or something?" He quickly retorted.

"No, I don't have company. But the girls are sleep," she hissed angrily.

"So. I'll be here when they wake up," he said stepping past Bonni. Ignoring her look of frustration, he asked," Where's the couch?"

Bonni looked to Stink as if he was crazy, and then pointed toward the den.

After Stink found the couch and laid down, Bonni

appeared. "Rahsaan, what are you doing?" she asked.

"What it look like, Bonni," he snapped, then turned over to look at her, visibly fuming. He added, "get me a blanket.

Pearl pushed his Benz to the maximum." I don't believe them green ass fuck nuccas think I'm just sit back and let them take over my shit!" He canted.

"What we gon' do, my nucca?" Milk asked, purposely inciting Pearl's rage.

"We gon' handle them nuccas, that's what!" Pearl yelled, then added. "First I gotta find out wasup with that nucca Stank. Yo, Bear, get all the info' you can on that square."

"I'm on it as we speak, cuz," Bear responded, with his phone glued to his ear.

"And Milk! I want you to go downtown first thing tomorrow to get all the info on the rest of them nuccas."

Milk nodded his head. Beef was his thang. He loved the gun play just as much as Pearl. He knew it would come to a war, and he was ready.

"We gon' put these fuck nuccas out of business, then we gon' go back to handling ours," Pearl stated boisteriously.

Little did he know, Pepe, Chico, and Manny were having the same conversation on the other side of town.

Pepe paced back and forth across the living room of the luxurious condo. "Yo, that fucking punta [faggot] thinks we some pussies! I could see it in his eyes!" Pepe shouted with a grimace etched across his face.

"Fam, don't worry. We gonna 'Moke' them bitches," Manny said coolly.

"Yeah, Pep, just be cool. We gonna handle shit,"

Chico added.

'Manana [Tomorrow], I want to know where them niggas rest their heads. I want to know everything!" Pepe demanded.

Stink awoke in the unfamiliar room to the sweet scent of breakfast being cooked. The sweet smell invaded his senses as he pulled himself to a sitting position. Turning over, he noticed Tayvia and Rahsaanique sitting in the chair opposite him, eyeing him suspiciously.

"What?" Stink asked.

Simultaneously, they both presented wide eyed smiles as they hunched their shoulders.

"Well, don't just sit there, y'all come over here and give me a hug," Stink said holding his arms wide.

Tayvia and Rahsaanique rushed into his open arms, and hugged him tightly.

The lovable 'kodak' moment was short lived once Bonni appeared. "Girls! Y'all need to be getting ready for breakfast. Now go wash up," she commanded.

They reluctantly released their grasp from around Stink's neck and followed their mother's instructions.

Just as Rahsaanique was exiting the room, she turned to her father. "Daddy, you need to brush your teeth," she stated humorously, while squenching her nose.

Stink and Bonni shared a brief laugh at their daughter's comical remark. However, the joyous mood quickly faded as they were left standing there alone.

Breaking the silence, Bonni said, "There's an extra toothbrush in the bathroom for you." She then walked away.

Chapter Six

Cross, nervously opened the letter from 'Cotler and Associates' and read the neatly typed words.

'*Dear Mr. Scott,*

I am responding to your letter inquiring about my services in helping you to successfully defend you on your appeal to the New York Supreme Court of Appeals. For the sum of $40,000, my assistance will be rendered unto you, and I will fight diligently for a reversal of your sentence.

Sincerely,

Brown Cotler

Cross read the letter over and over, until he came to the conclusion that,"money without freedom was senseless."

Pearl and crew were once again assembled in the elaborately decorated office, inside of the luxurious home.

"So, what y'all got? " Pearl asked, eyeing Milk and Bear.

Milk was the first to speak. "My nucca, them suckers got a whole crew of green nuccas downtown, slangin they yola," Milk revealed

"Yeah, my peoples say they got birds for fifteen," Bear added.

Pearl sat in deep contemplation, allowing the

information that they'd just revealed to register in his sadistic mind, before he stated," Any nucca that's slangin' they shit, murder'em!"

With a sly grin, Milk looked to his longtime friend and said, "Say no more. It's done, my nucca."

Stink had begun to spend as much time as possible with his girls. Since his unexpected late night visit to Bonni's house, he hadn't attempted to repeat the act. However, the look Bonni gave him every time he exited her door was extremely reminiscent of the one she'd given him when she was his woman.

Stink pulled his Escalade into the elementary school's parking lot, and allowed Tayvia and Rahsaanique to exit. This had become his ritual for the last couple of weeks. He would drop them off every morning, then pick them up in the afternoon. This gave him a sense of reality, compared to the life he led outside of them.

As they crawled out of the truck, Rahsaanique turned to Stink and said," I love you, daddy."

"I love you to, Nique-Nique," he replied, noticing the uncomfortable expression that appeared on Tayvia's face.

Hesitating to close the door, Tayvia looked to him helplessly. Stink quickly took control, and in his most sincere tone said, "And I love you too, Tayvia."

A broad smile instantly appeared on her face, as she replied," I love you too, daddy."

Stink's heart melted as the reality of her words crashed into him. He sat there and watched them disappear through the school yard, with their little backpacks thrown over their shoulders.

As he pulled the SUV out of the crowded parking lot, with the rush of parents dropping their own children off, he nearly side swiped an Acura Legend.

The woman, behind the wheel of the car, glared toward Stink with accusing eyes.

Immediately, the woman's features became distinct to him.   The woman was his cousin's child's mother, Sharon.

Stink rolled down the tinted window, allowing her to get a clear view of who was driving the Escalade.

Soon as she got a good look at him, her glare became a defiant smile. "Stink!"   She yelled through disbelieving eyes.

He stepped from his truck and cordially greeted her.

After they covered the basis of their reunion, Sharon said," P.J. is going to be shocked when I tell him that I saw you."

Suddenly, the loud honking horns of the angry parents who were rushing to get to work cut the reunion short.

"Look Sharon, give P my number. It's 555-0123," Stink said, and then jumped into his truck.

Melody's sudden change of heart toward Carmella, had her somewhat perplexed.   Earlier that morning when she'd approached Melody exiting the shower; it was evident that something was wrong.

As Melody's body glistened from the beads of water, Carmella attempted to assist her in drying her body as usual.   However, as soon as Carmella made contact with Melody's skin, her body stiffened.

"I can dry myself, Carmella, Melody stated in a dry tone.   Slightly confused, Carmella watched as Melody sauntered off toward the master suite. Quickly catching up to her, Carmella asked," Mel, what's wrong with you? You've been acting strange lately, Mami," she stated with a hint of attitude.

"Nah. I'm alright, Carma. I just…I just have some things on my mind."

Eyeing Melody skeptically, Carmella asked," Things like what, Melody?"

"I'll be alright, Carmella," Melody concluded, pulling her panties up her thighs.

Carmella looked Melody up and down lustfully, then quickly covered the short distance separating them and grabbed her panties, halting them from covering her plump ass.

"Car…Carmella, please….please stop," Melody grasped in a contemptuous tone.

"Come on, Mami. I miss you sooo much," Carmella whined sexily, continuing to pull at Melody's panties.

"No!" Melody yelled, startling Carmella.

Melody had never used the forceful tone with Carmella; thus, she immediately caught her by surprise.

"Hold the fuck up, Punta! [Bitch!]" Carmella spat angrily. "Up until now, we have been sharing a bed, and a man!"

"I know! My man!" Melody retorted.

"Your man?" Carmella asked mockingly.

"Yes! My man!" Melody shot back defensively.

"So what, you having second thoughts now?" Carmella inquired.

"Look Carmella, ever since you came into the picture, Rahsaan has been treating me differently, and I want my man back," Melody stated calmly.

"Oh, so this is about, 'your man'?"

"Carmella, I've already said what I said, and that's that."

"Humph!" Carmella huffed, and then strutted from the room.

Chico, Manny, and Marquita, a loud hood chick, inconspicuously sat in the 'Mercury Marquise' eyeing the dark figure exiting the Lexus coupe.

"That's one of'em right there," Manny stated in a conspiratorial tone.

"Yeah, I can see his gold teeth shinning form here," Chico added.

Two of Chico and Manny's street soldiers had mysteriously been murdered in the last week. And coincidentally, on each occasion the person responsible was described as a Nigga with gold teeth.

It hadn't taken long for Pepe and his crew to realize that a war had been waged against them.

"Hey yo, Mami. All you gotta do is get his attention, and we got the rest," Chico instructed looking at Marquita." Can you handle that?"

"That shouldn't be too had, boo," she replied exiting the car.

Chico and Manny sat in the car and watched as Marquita sexily strutted her phat ass across the street.

The last minute stop at the liquor store would prove to be fatal for C-Lo, one of Pearls most trusted allies.

Pearl had brought C-Lo to VA in the hopes that his quick wit and even quicker trigger would prove to be essential to Pearl's rise. And did he assist in Pearl's rise to the top? C-Lo had hustled his way from a hired gun and package holder to running his own crew of hustlers from the M.I.A.

Chico and Manny quickly exited the Mercury, and made their way across the street where C-LO's Lexus was parked. They instantly mingled with the bums, who solicited money from customers exiting the liquor store.

Both Chico and Manny, Clad in hooded sweatshirts, eyed the front of the store awaiting their victim. Once they witnessed C-Lo coming from the store with Marquita in tow, each man inwardly smiled. Oblivious to any impending danger, C-Lo was intently putting his 'Mack' game down on Marquita. He was easy pray for Chico and Manny, as he rounded the corner to where his car was parked.

Their plan was to murder the man and leave his body amongst the bums. However, after seeing how easy it would be to kidnap him, then take him somewhere and torture him, they quickly changed their plans.

Chico staggered over to the couple, standing beside the Lexus, and slurred," A young blood, you got some change?"

C-Lo snapped his head in the begging man's direction, in preparation to unleash a barrage of venomous words. However, once he turned his head, he was met with the barrel of Chico's Glock 19, aimed directly at his head.

"A, my nucca, you can have everything. Just don't shoot," C-Lo begged.

"Shut the fuck up, bitch!" Chico snapped, forcefully pushing C-Lo across the hood of his car. He then turned to the girl. "Yo, Quita! Go get the car," he instructed while steadying his gun against C-Lo's head.

Chico frisked him, while Manny searches his car. Suddenly Marquita pulled the Mercury up beside the Lexus.

"Hold up, my nucca! Where we going?" C-Lo questioned, as he was being forcefully shoved towards the awaiting car. "Hold up! I –"he began to protest, before being abruptly cut off by a burning sensation, tearing through his buttocks and upper thigh.

Chico, not known for an over-abundance of talking, had aimed his pistol towards the struggling man's lower body and squeezed off two shots. "Bop! Bop!"

"Oh, my, fucking, God! You shot me!" C-Lo yelled as he was shoved into the backseat of the Mercury.

Manny looked at his childhood friend and laughed. Quickly hopping into C-Lo's Lexus, Manny followed the Mercury through the streets of 'BAD NEWZ."

All Bonni had on her mind was Rahsaan. She wanted him so badly she could literally taste it. His scent was omnipresent. Simply watching him when he was around her made her moist in her most sensitive places.

She couldn't hold her feelings any longer. She had to confess her feelings to him at once. She wanted him back in her life and nothing would stand in her way.

Eyeing the clock, she quickly grabbed her keys and exited the house.

Pepe laid across the bed with Clarissa sensuously rubbing his back. They were enjoying Chico and Manny's reenactment of the scene that played out earlier in the evening.

"Yo, fam, this Nigga fucking shoots the maricon [faggot] in the culo [ass] before he even gets in the car," Manny said chuckling.

"But, yo fam, after that, it was a wrap. Son gave up everything but his higado [liver]. And I tried to cut that out of his ass like he was a cerdo [pig]," Chico explained with a sadistic grin.

"So, he gave up the goods on this punta [punk], Pearl?" Pepe inquired in a serious manner.

"Todo! [Everything]" Chico quickly replied in a boastful tone.

"Bien, bien, [Good, good]," Pepe replied. Glaring at Clarissa sexily, he said," Now, if y'all would excuse me, I need to holla at my bonita mami."

Chico and Manny quickly exited the room, leaving Pepe and Clarissa alone.

The streets of Bad Newz weren't prepared for the violence it had been witnessing lately. Random murders were being committed everyday.

After Pearl had given Milk the green light, his appetite for murder had taken over from there. He implemented his murderous rage on anyone who was remotely connected to Pep, Chico or Manny.

The meaningless murders of Pepe's street soldiers was nothing compared to the gruesome mutilation of C-Lo, who was a major player in Pearl's organization.

C-Lo wasn't as close to Pearl as Milk or Bear, but he was still considered family.

"How the fuck they get my nucca, Lo?" Pearl asked in a somber tone. "Huh! Somebody up in this bitch got to know something!" He glared, looking around the room.

Milk quickly spoke up." I think a bitch set my nucca up," Milk offered.

"You think a bitch!" Pearl repeated in disbelief.

"Yeah. I think so, cause the way them square nuccas had it set up," Milk explained.

"O.K., nobody in our crew is to fuck wit them Skank ass hoes! You hear me!" Pearl yelled, banging his fist on the table for emphasis.

"Yeah, I got you, my nucca," Milk replied, then quickly exited the room.

Pearl was clearly upset. Stink and his crew had gotten one up on him with C-Lo's murder. He had to get one of theirs soon.

Carmella sat in the lawn chair relaxing, when she heard Stink pull through the gate. She refused to bow to him with Melody's insecurities. Instead, she planned to sit back and allow Melody's immaturity to play itself out, while she in turn showed Stink her unadulterated loyalty.

She quickly stood in her two piece bikini, profiling her flawless body and scampered over to him. "Hey, papi, how was your day?" She inquired, planting a soft kiss on his cheek.

"Everything's cool, Mami," he replied eyeing her hungrily.

"How are the girls doing?" She asked casually.

"They're good."

"I can't wait until you take us to meet them."

"Soon," Stink replied nonchalantly, allowing Carmella to lead him into the house.

As he entered the house, Melody who sat in the large den watching television on the 60 inch Bang and Olufsen flat screen, looked up to Stink with a gloomy expression, and said," Hey daddy."

Stink quickly picked up on her mood. "What's the long face for? You aight?"

"Yeah, I'm O.K." she replied joylessly.

Instantly, Stink felt a tinge of guilt for the way he'd been acting towards her. "Melody, come upstairs for a minute. I need to holla at you.

She quickly jumped up and followed him through the kitchen, tossing Carmella a piercing glare on the way.

Stink entered the master suite closely followed by Melody. Tossing his shirt onto the bed, he turned toward

Melody. "What's wrong with you?"

"Nothing. I'm fine," she said attempting to perk up.

"Melody, I'm not gonna ask you again. Now what the fuck is going on with you?" He asked firmly.

Melody allowed her tears to speak for her, as they cascaded down her cheeks.

Stink held his arms open, then said, "Come here, Melody."

She rushed into his arms child-like, allowing her tears to run freely.

"Talk to me baby. What's wrong?" He asked genuinely concerned.

"I...I don't want to lose...you," she revealed through sobs.

"How you gonna lose me, Melody?" Stink asked confused.

"Car......mella."

"Carmella?" Stink asked incredulously. Then added, "How is Carmella gonna make you loose me?"

"Cause, I know ...that you look at me ...different, since you...since you caught...us," she stated sobbing uncontrollably. Stink knew that if he had an ounce of love for her, he had to be honest with her. Taking a deep breath, he began, "Listen, Melody, I gotta be real with you because you've been real with me. When I caught you and Carmella in bed, I thought that's what you wanted. So I just – Abruptly cutting Stink off, Melody blurted, "Daddy, I'm sorry! I'll never do it again! I swear!"

Stink defiantly shook his head." Nah, Melody. Do whatever you feel makes you happy. If you want to keep fucking with Carmella, so be it," he concluded.

"But I don't want to no more daddy. I want you," she stated in a begging tone.

Lifting her chin, he planted a soft kiss on her lips, and then said, "Aight. You got me."

Pulling up to Stink's estate, Bonni couldn't believe what he had done to his grandparent's house. What was once a nice upper class home now was full fledge mansion. Bonni hopped out of her mini van and stepped over to the indigo screen and pushed the call button.

"Yes, may I help you? "A woman's voice asked from the intercom.

"Um…yes, is Rahsaan home?" She asked in a apprehensive manner.

"Who may I tell him is here to see him?"

"Tell him it's Bonnie; his child's mother," Bonni said proudly.

"Oh, I'm sorry. The gate is opening now."

Instantly, the gate began to open. Bonni jumped back into her mini van and pulled into the driveway behind a fleet of luxury automobiles.

Just as she was exiting her vehicle, a scantily dressed Puerto Rican looking girl appeared from the house." Hello Bonni. My name is Carmella. I've heard so much about you," Carmella said extending her hands towards Bonni." Papi should be coming down in a second. Why don't we go inside," she said leading Bonni into the once familiar house.

As Bonni entered the house, behind the visibly striking Spanish girl, she suddenly felt that maybe it was a mistake coming to see him.

"Have a seat and make yourself at home. Would you like something to drink?" Carmella offered, attempting to be as hospitable as possible.

"Um, no…I'm O.K. could you just tell Rahsaan I'm here," Bonni said clearly uncomfortable.

"O.K., I'll go and get him right now," Carmella replied, then rushed off.

As Bonni sat there, she began to look around at the elaborately decorated room in awe. A large redwood pool table sat in the corner, directly behind it was a fully stocked wet bar. The blood red carpet clashed against the rooms multi-colored suede furnishings. Eyeing the large canvas covered object, Bonni guessed it was the television.

Stink entered the room with a serious look etched into his face. "Bonni, wazup? Is everything Alright with the girls?"

"Uh…yeah…yeah, they're fine. I came to talk to you, but I think I may have come at the wrong time," she said standing to leave.

"Oh, nah. No time is a bad time when it comes to my daughter's mother. Carmella, Melody, take a ride or something," he said in a commanding tone.

Bonni looked on in shock as the two beautiful women quickly scurried out of the door.

Once Carmella and Melody were gone, Stink took a seat beside Bonni." Talk to me, Bonni," he stated in an earnest tone.

Bonni looked deep into his eyes. Unable to extract the words that she intended to say, she dropped her head and sighed in frustration.

Stink sat in the chair opposite, Pepe, Chico and Manny, listening intently to what they were revealing.

So, this Nigga was from Miami?" Stink asked.

"Yeah. Gold fronts and the whole shit, fam," Chico replied.

"And he told y'all where this Nigga, Pearl lives?" Stink asked, eyeing the trio closely.

"Yeah. His socio [partner] gave up all the info, in hopes that his life would be spared," Chico replied.

"He also gave us the layout of the crib. But it sounds like a fucking fortress," Manny added.

"Aight, look, this Nigga, Pearl, gonna be gunning at us hard. So, I want y'all niggas to go uptop. Besides ain't no more work to be moved so..." Stink explained eyeing their reactions closely. Leaning in closely, in a conspiratorial tone, he said, "Now tell me everything y'all got on this Nigga."

Chapter Seven

"Yo, what up son?" Cross voice boomed into the receiver.

"Ain't shit, man. Just living."

"Yeah, I can tell that. Wazup with your two ladies?"

"Man, these bitches out here jockeying for position. Then last week, my daughter's mom dropped some ole 'Arron Hall' shit on me, talking about 'I miss you.' Shit's crazy."

"Damn, Bro, sounds like you got major hoe problems."

"Nah. I can handle my end. Them hoes the ones with the problems," Stink replied coolly.

"Yeah! That's my Lil bro!" Cross announced emphatically.

As they continued to talk, Cross deliberately withheld the information that he'd hired Bruce Cotler to handle his appeal. If things didn't pan out for him, he didn't want anybody to know. However, if the famed attorney could work his magic, Cross would gladly reveal himself to the world.

Before hanging up, Stink informed him that Pepe should be making the next drop off to his boy's women any day.

With that said, Cross hung up. As he bounced in his customary walk out into the crowded yard, he silently prayed that his lawyer would somehow find a way to set him free. Soon.

Bonni cried for two days straight after her unexpected visit to Stink's house. It wasn't the soft rejection that he'd given her that saddened her, it was his reasoning for rejecting her that hurt her the most.

She knew that her inability to stand by him during his incarceration would undoubtedly hurt him deeply. However, she felt that what they had shared would somehow overcome that.

Nonetheless, Stink used her obscondment as the basis for not allowing her back into his heart. The abandonment that he felt during the five years he was incarcerated was something he could never forgive her for. Banging her fist into the bed in frustration, she sobbed, "It's all my fault!"

Had she known five years ago that turning her back on him would be the biggest mistake in her life, she would have done things differently.

Stink pulled in front of the single family home in Hampton and parked. It had been a long time since he'd seen the person who casually sauntered toward him.

"If it ain't my Nigga. What's up, cuz?" PJ said giving Stink a heartfelt hug.

"Just chillin, PJ. What's going on with you?"

"Man, the same ole bullshit. Trying to take care of my family, dawg," PJ replied.

"So what you doing? Working, hustling, what?" Stink grilled.

"Man, I ain't fucked with no 'coke' since back in the day. Right now, I just be slangin a lil herb," PJ divulged with a devilish smile."Oh, yeah. Like what kind of weed you be fucking with?"

PJ looked to him confused, then asked, "What you mean 'What Kind'?"

Stink inwardly smiled at his cousin's naivete concerning the new millennium marijuana game. Stink had learned through Pepe that there were some strains of marijuana that were just as expensive as cocaine.

"Check it out ,cuz. When I come back through, I'm-a bring you something."

"Something like what? Cuz, you know I ain't fucking with you on that –"

Cutting PJ off, Stink said, "P, I got you, man. It ain't what you think. Just be looking for me in a week or so," Stink said, then hopped in his Porsche.

Pulling away from the curb, Stink left a thick trail of smoke, as the rear tires of the Porches pinned feverishly, making it impossible to see the wide smile his cousin sported.

Pearl cruised the city in his customized candy painted 1973 Electra 225 Buick, sitting on dubs. The small war that started was already taking chunks of money from his pockets. There was absolutely no money being made on the streets, due to the fear that had been instilled on every block.

He had plan to bring all of his business back. It was dangerous, but that's what he thrived on; danger. Retrieving his cell phone, he turned the thundering base down and dialed Milk's number.

"Hell-o," a woman answered in a hushed tone.

"Where the fuck Milk at!" Pearl barked.

"I don' know who this is, but Milk is in the shower, and you -."

"Bitch! This is Pearl! Tell that nucca to get his ass on the phone!" He commanded.

Holding the phone to his ear, he heard the girl yelling for Milk to get the phone.

After a brief wait, Milk came onto the phone." What up, my nucca?"

"Oh, you got them square ass hoes answering your phone now?"

"Naw, my nucca. That bitch took it upon herself. Don't worry, I'm-a slap that bitch up, my nucca," Milk said.

"Fuck that bitch nucca! Get you vest and meet me on 23rd street. We about to take it back to 'Liberty City, my nucca!" Pearl yelled triumphantly, then hung up.

Pepe and Chico rode through the city, enjoying their new found celebrity status. The bright red Suburban stuck out in the sea of cars like a sore thumb.

Pepe pulled over on 149th and Amsterdam Avenue to pick Manny up. They were on their way to Brooklyn, and knew that their team needed to be assembled to make the drop. Although Pep's financial status had changed, he still was a New Yorker at heart.

Pepe slid out of the driver's seat and hopped in the back, allowing Manny to take the wheel. "Take the Brooklyn Bridge, Manny," he instructed, getting comfortable in the confines of his truck.

Milk stood defiantly beside Pearl on 23rd and Chestnut Avenue. Outwardly, both men wore the faces of fearless thugs. However, on the inside, both men were terrified.

"You Aight, my nucca?" Pearl asked eyeing every car suspiciously.

"Yeah, I'm straight," Milk replied in his deepest Macho tone. Milk actually felt like a sitting duck on the street corner, waiting on death.

Stink's crew had proven that they were some heartless killers, from the way they'd chopped up C-Lo's body.

Although Pearl had thought the bold move through, he was now beginning to second guess his rash decision.

At that same moment, Milk's doubt about standing on the known drug block began to show." My nucca, you think standing out here is such a good idea?"

Pearl quickly shot him a disbelieving look, then stated," Nucca, anything I do is a good idea."

Milk reached up and resituated the bulky bulletproof vest that snugly wrapped his torso. Nervously rubbing the crown of his bald head, he thought 'I hope they aiming for our chest.'

As Stink pulled into the driveway, he knew it was time to get away. Carmella and Melody's jockeying for position had begun to irk him. The combination of their nagging, Bonni's change of heart, and the street's murderous invitation, all called for a quick get away.

When Stink walked through the door, he quickly picked up on the somber mood in the house. As Melody sat in the den, lazily watching television, there was no sign of Carmella.

"Where's Carmella?" he asked, allowing his impatience to register into his tone.

Melody shrugged her shoulders nonchalantly, which instantly ignited his fury.

Covering the space that separated them in a nano-second, he quickly wrapped a handful of her hair in his fist. This caused Melody's face to immediately display her horror, as her screams seemed to be trapped in her throat.

"Bitch! How about you show me where the fuck she at!" Stink demanded in a demented tone, dragging Melody like a rag doll.

Melody's screams immediately got Carmella's attention, as she exited the bathroom. Stepping out into the hallway, Carmella eyed the spectacle through disbelieveing eyes.

Stink was dragging Melody's body up the stairs as she screamed uncontrollably.

Slinging Melody's body at Carmella's feet, Stink said, "I'm giving y'all bitches ten fucking minutes to get y'all shit together, or both you mufuckas is gone!" Taking a second to catch his breath, he added," I'm not the one who created this shit! Y'all did!" With that said, he turned and went back downstairs.

Pepe sat in the backseat of his truck, taking deep pulls of exotic weed. Parked in front of the familiar meeting spot on Fulton Avenue, Pepe eyed the traffic intently. Noticing that a car closely resembling one driven by Quan's woman, pulled in front of his own Suburban, Pepe grabbed the remaining balloons.

As the thick red sister approached the dark tinted SUV, the rear passenger door suddenly popped open.

"Damn, that shit smells good as a motherfucker," she commented, as the powerful aroma of the 'purple haze' invaded her senses.

"You trying to hit this shit, Mami," Pepe offered.

"Yeah. But ain't nothing in it, is it? "She asked cautiously. Pepe shot her an incredulous stare, then passed her the cigar. As she greedily ttoked the expensive marijuana, Pepe's mind began to think back to when Nichelle attempted to seduce Stink with the flash of her pussy.

When she passed the cigar back, Pepe had a devilish grin plastered across his face.

"Why you looking at me like that?" She asked suspiciously.

"It's nothing, Mami. I was just thinking," Pepe replied.

"Hmmm Mmmm. I bet you was," she said suggestively, licking her lips.

Throwing caution in the wind, Pepe put his hand high on Nichelle's thigh, and asked," What's really good, Mami?"

"You, Papi," Nichelle replied as sensuous as possible.

Easing his hand further up her skirt, Pepe instantly felt the blood rush to his loins. Once his hand reached her pantyless vagina, he breathed a short sigh of disbelief. Turning his attention to the front of the truck, he said, "Yo Manny. Pull around the block." Then guided Nichelle's head into his lap.

Once Stink entered the house from playing with his dogs, Fire and Ice, he went straight into the Master Suite, where he'd left Melody and Carmella.

Stepping into the room, he noticed that they were cuddled on the bed watching television. "Y'all got that bullshit together?" Stink asked, still seething from his earlier rage.

Immediately, both Melody and Carmella nodded in unison.

Stink walked over and took a seat on the bed, and looked into the eyes of both the strikingly beautiful ladies. "Look, both of y'all chose to make this shit how it is, not me. So for either of you to try and eliminate the other is simply eliminating yourself. But, if both of y'all do your part, everything will be aight," he explained in his most sincere tone.

In an upbeat manner, Melody replied, "O.K. daddy. We understand."

"Yeah, papi. We're straight now," Carmella added.

"Good!" Stink replied relieved, then added. "Y'all go and pack some clothes. We going uptop," he announced grabbing the bedside phone.

Pepe sat back enjoying the warmth of Nichelle's mouth, as she vigorously sucked his manhood. Throwing his head back in ecstasy, the sudden vibration of the cell phone located in his jeans, which were snugly around his ankles, jolted him from his dreamy state. "Hold up, Mami. Hold up," he mumbled, pulling her hungry mouth from his shaft.

Reaching down to retrieve his cell phone, Pepe quickly pushed the talk button, after noticing Stink's number. "Yo, what's the deal fam?" Pepe answered, looking on as Chico and Manny pounced on Nichelle.

"Yo, Pep. What's the deal? You handle that yet?" Stink asked

"As we speak, fam. AS we speak," Pepe stated assuredly, eyeing the spectacle taking place before him. Chico had climb in the backseat and was receiving a replay of the magnificent head job that Pep had just received. Nichelle's pantyless ass was hiked up, giving Manny a clear view of her pussy. Maneuvering himself between the seats in the front, Manny entered her from the rear.

"Yo, Pep! What the fuck y'all doing man?" Stink asked suspiciously, after hearing the sexual groans in the background.

"We, um, handling that B.I., fam," Pepe replied with a slight chuckle.

"Pep, I know y'all ain't fucking one of them broads?" Stink asked full of skepticism.

"Nah, not me. But Chico and Manny, now that's a

different story," Pepe confessed, ogling the scene being acted out in front of him.

"Man, y'all niggas better tighten up. I'll be up there later tonight. Okay" Stink said hanging up.

Pepe threw the phone to the side and joined the sexual melee.

Stink's next call was to Jose. Since his crew had been ensnared into the murderous game being played by Pearl and his crew, there was no money being made. Stink knew he couldn't allow the game to go on any further. His plan to annihilate Pearl and his entire crew was more business than personal. And that's how he was going to approach the situation, like business.

"Como estas, Stink? [How are you, Stink?]" Jose asked.

"Bien [Good]," Stink replied, showcasing his shallow Spanish vocabulary.

"Si, si, my friend. It's been a while since I last talked to you. I've been worried."

"Yeah, I know. I've been having a few problems," Stink revealed.

"Oye, maybe you are ready for the trip to my country. I am scheduled to depart in a week or so."

"I'm on my way to New York, and we'll talk when I see you."

"Fine my friend. Buenos tardes [Good Afternoon]," Jose said then hung up.

Pearl strolled through his home like the King he was. After successfully reclaiming his drug empire, he felt invincible. Bear and Milk were back to bringing in duffel bags of money. His adversaries had miraculously dropped out of sight.

Pearl eased into his bedroom suite, hoping to catch Trina in something sexy and put some of his expert loving on her. After creeping through the suite and unable to locate his woman, he quietly walked over to the partially open French doors.

Trina sat curled up on the chaise lounge chair, on the screened in porch, deeply engrossed in a phone conversation. Unbeknownst to her, Pearl entered the room, and watched her through appreciative eyes.

Trina was still a beautiful woman. After struggling as a single parent for a few years, it wasn't until she met Pearl did life take a turn for the better.

"Gurrl, when did he come home?" Trina inquired into the receiver.

"He still look the same?"

'Umph, umph, umph. Kesha, stop playing.'

As the conversation became more informative, Pearl slid down the wall into a seated position and listened intently.

"Gurrl, Stink will never fuck with me again"

Pearl's eyes nearly popped out of his head, at the mentioning of Stink.

'Oh, you saw him over PJ's house....Yeah, that's his cousin,' He's got a what!' She exclaimed then added. Rahsaan was always a flashy nigga,' she commented.

Pearl's mind was working overdrive. 'Was Stink, Rahsaan? Did Trina's son Rahsaan have anything to do with Stink's Rahsaan? Was Trina and Stink....'his mind questioned vigorously.

He quickly crawled back though the partially open doors, undetected by Trina.

As he stood, the pounding in his chest caught him by surprise. The one question that echoed in Pearl's mind, 'could Stink be Rah-Rah's father?

After Stink's rejection, Bonni desperately wanted to move on with her life, once and for all. Although she had her fair share of flings throughout his five year tenure in prison, she prided herself in never allowing any man around her girls. However, after blatantly being rejected by him, Bonni was anxious to get her groove back. Secretly, she hoped that the open display of her moving on with her life would somehow bring him back to her.

'Blurrrrrp! Blurrrrrp!' Bonni's cell phone rang. She quickly snatched the phone up. "Hello."

"Yeah. Can I speak to Bonni?" A man asked.

"This is she. Who's calling?"

"This is Rodney. I met you the other day," he explained.

Bonni immediately remembered giving the tall brown-skinned brother her cellular phone number, after he approached her in the super market.

"Oh, Rodney. How are you doing?" She asked jovially.

"I'm good. How about yourself?"

"Well, I guess I'm O.K., "she replied jokingly.

They talked for a short time, however, before hanging up they made plans to get together later that week for lunch.

Once Bonni hung the phone up, she assured herself that she was doing the right thing. Yet, only time would tell.

Melody, Carmella, and Stink was traveling 95 North with over 3 million dollars in case in the stash compartment of the Escalade. Stink had only received two shipments of drugs from Jose since he'd been home. However, the prices that Jose had given him for the drugs enabled him to boost his finances to the aforementioned amount, and quite a bit more in property and automobiles.

His plan was to give Jose the money, then slide back to Virginia and sow the seeds of havoc on his enemies. Immediately thereafter, he'd vanish from the U.S. of A, only to pop up in the clear blue waters of Santa Domingo.

He had everything planned out, now all he had to do was execute.

Cross sat on the bench, surrounded by his entire crew. They passed a 'Black & Mild' filled with some of the most potent marijuana that either man had ever smoked.

In Osinning Correctional Center, Cross and his crew were bona fide ballers. To some inside the prison, that would have been enough. However, for Cross, it was only a meager diversion of what he truly desired, freedom.

"Yo Cross, ya mans an'em came through like clock work, son. My wiz even says that they be hitting her with extras," Quann revealed, as the powerful marijuana loosened his tongue.

"Yeah. Extras like what?" Cross asked suspiciously.

"Nah, you know , like extra doe," Quan quickly cleared up, then continued. "She had the crazy-ill 'Coogi dress on in the V.I."

Inwardly grinning, Cross masked his humor from anyone present. He instantly understood why those extra 'ends' were being disbursed. Quan's girl was not only taking the balloons and a couple hundred from Stink and his crew, she was also taking some dick.

Nonetheless, Cross would never divulge this to the man, knowing that it would probably kill him. However, if he ever crossed the line, Cross wouldn't hesitate to destroy him and his bitch.

Chapter Eight

Every time Stink entered New York City a strange feeling would overcome him. It was a feeling close to exhilaration. No matter how many times he'd come to the city, the feeling was always the same.

"Carma, stop by the weed spot on 139th before you go uptown," he instructed. Carmella shot him a puzzled look in the rearview. They had already dropped the money off at Jose's Teaneck New Jersey residence. Stink usually chose to ride the streets of New York clean. Therefore, his request to stop at a marijuana spot left her perplexed.

Unbeknownst to her, Stink was going to the known weed spot to make good on his promise to PJ. He'd planned to buy 5 or 6 pounds of the exotic marijuana and give them to his cousin on G.P. (General Purposes).

Stink pulled his cell phone out and dialed Pepe's number, only to be quickly forwarded to his voicemail.

"Carma, call your mom's spot, and see if Pep an'em around there," Stink instructed in an agitated tone.

"Bien, papi," She replied, quickly dialing her mother's number. Stink turned his attention to Melody. "Melody, when we get to this spot, you coming with me, o.k?"

"O.k., daddy."

By then, Carmella had gotten a hold of Pepe. She passed the phone to Stink.

"Pep! Where the fuck you at?" Stink grilled.

"You here already?" Pepe asked.

"Nah, nigga! I just told your sister to make a prank call!" Stink stated sarcastically. "Hell yeah, I'm here!" His voice boomed.

"Aight, fam, aight. Where I need to be, or what I need to do. Damn!" Pepe replied, attempting to calm Stink's anger.   "130ᵗʰ!
The smoke spot!" Stink barked, then tossed Carmella's phone into her lap.

Eversince Pearl had been handed the earth shattering information about Stink, he hadn't been able to sleep a wink. He'd also made it his business to stay as far away from Trina as possible. He desperately wanted to confront her, yet to do that would have gone against his 'playerlistic' morals.

Nonetheless, he wanted Stink murdered. With him out of the picture, it would make everything else that much easier to accept. His presence alone stood as a mockery to his manhood. Stink had to go.

Pearl had an ace in the hole. He knew exactly who Stink's cousin PJ was. Over time, PJ and Pearl had built somewhat of a camaraderie. Pearl knew where PJ lived and where he hung out. If Stink reared his head anywhere near PJ, Pearl vowed to take it off. To bad the cool, skinny VA nigga that Pearl had come to like would ultimately be used as a pawn.

Pearl pulled is cell phone out and dialed Milk's number. "Hello."

"My nucca, you ain't seen shit yet?" Pearl asked.

"Nah, my nucca."

"Alright, my nucca. Just lay low, and hit me if you see anything," Pearl instructed then hung up.

Pearl sat behind his desk, and eyed the portrait of him, Trina, and Rah-Rah, down in Florida. He loved Trina dearly, and looked at Rah-Rah as if he was his own. He had to kill Stink.

Stink and Melody waited for the pounds of 'Hydro' to be delivered to the makeshift restaurant on 139th, while Pepe, Chico, and Manny sat outside prepared for anything.

Stink knew that the marijuana sellers weren't accustomed to people coming in dropping nearly twenty stacks for weed. Therefore, he called Pepe just in case.

A young Spanish man entered the store carrying a large shopping bag. Without saying a word, he handed the bag to Stink.

Instinctively, Stink poked his head in the bag and was met with the strong stench of the potent marijuana. He had already handed over the money for the weed, long before he was given the product. Quickly exiting the storefront, Stink walked hand in hand with Melody towards Pepe's truck.Soon as they reached the passenger side, the door popped open.

Stink handed the bag to Manny in the back seat, then said," Yo, y'all get this shit packaged for me. And don't smoke none!" He and Melody then walked over to his Escalade and hopped in. Turning his attention to Carmella, he said," Forty-third and 7th avenue. We going to the Grand Hyatt, Mami."

Melody cuddled under Stink's arm, while Carmella massaged his shoulder, as they lounged in relaxing waters of the Jacuzzi sitting in the hotel suite. Once Carmella had massaged Stink, she moved to Melody, working her magical hands into her shoulders. Melody allowed her body to relax under the wonderful pressure that Carmella's hands were causing.

Throwing her head back in enjoyment, Melody began to think about just how childish she had been.

Carmella wasn't the cause of any change that may have occurred between her and Stink. She now understood that he was just under an extreme amount of pressure.

Once Carmella's fingers had played Tic-Tac-Toe down her back, Melody suddenly wanted to reciprocate the feeling that Carmella had just bestowed upon her.

Standing in the bubbling hot water, she motioned for Carmella to sit between her thighs. Melody couldn't help but notice the devilish grin that spread across Stink's face. Suddenly Melody felt her center become moist. Instead of giving Carmella a massage, she decided to go a step further and reconsummate their union. Sliding sexily between Carmella's thighs, Melody pulled the string to her bikini top and allowed it to carelessly fall into the water.

Banging his fist against the steering wheel angrily, Pearl was livid. It had been almost a week and there was still no sign of Stink. He had Milk camped out across the street from PJ's house 24 hours a day, and there still wasn't a clue as to where he could be. Pearl had begun to believe that Stink had been personally annoying him the entire time.

Pulling into his long driveway, he noticed that Trina's M-class Mercedes was parked in the garage. It had been nearly two weeks since he'd held a conversation with her, without using two word responses.

As he exited the car, he decided that he couldn't go on treating the woman he loved that way any longer. As soon as he entered the house, the sound of Rah-Rah playing his play station on the large screen in the den invaded his ears.

"Hey dad!" Rah-Rah yelled exuberantly from his kneeling position on the floor of the exquisitely designed room.

"Hey, wasup, my lil nucca," Pearl replied as he made his way over to the young man.

As soon as Rah-Ray turned around and smiled his bright-smile, Pearl couldn't help but think if he was in fact Stink's son.Suddenly the anxiety of not knowing was too much for him to handle, he took off in the direction of their bedroom.

Cross frantically tore into the certified envelope from his lawyer and nervously read the words:

'Dear Mr. Scott, your payment of 40,000 has been received in my office. As stated before, I will diligently fight for a reversal of sentence. I have been given a date of 9/28/99 to argue your case in front of a three judge panel. Your attendance will not be required for this hearing. However, if your case should be remanded back to the original court, attendance is absolutely necessary.

Sincerely,

B Cotler

Once Cross finished reading the letter, he was astounded by how fast the famed lawyer was acting on his behalf. After nearly seven years of incarceration, he truly felt optimistic about his future.

Sitting comfortably on the deck of Jose's moderate New Jersey estate, Stink took a gulp from the glass that had just been handed to him.

"This is Louis the XIV aged cognac. It's to be sipped, not gulped, Jose stated, sitting opposite Stink. Leaning back on the lounge chair, he continued, "This stuff has been around since the early 1700's. Take your time my friend."

Stink relaxed and took small sips from the smooth tasting alcohol. He had never been much of a drinker; therefore sipping liquor had never been his forte.

Jose leaned up and looked at him in a serious manner. "Stink, tell me about this problem that you have? AS I told you before, any friend of yours is a friend of mine, and likewise any enemy is also my enemy."

Stink took his time and explained the entire situation to Jose. He really wanted to see what type of advice Jose would give him, so he was careful not to leave anything out. After he had filled Jose in on everything, he sat back and watched the older charismatic man, process the information he'd just divulged to him.

Once his short contemplation was complete, he looked to Stink as a father would look to his son, then said, "Stink, my friend, please have patience with this ....this situation. I want you to go away with me in three days, bring your lady friends also. Everything is on me. You won't have to raise a finger everything will be catered to you. However, once we return, I will personally see to it that this little problem is completely annihilated," he finished in a sincere tone.

Stink sat there in deep thought. What Jose was offering was self explanatory. All he had to do was comply. "O.k., Jose. I'll go away with you in three days, but I've got to go back to Virginia to fulfill an obligation. I promised you though, I won't attempt to do what I've told you I planned," Stink stated earnestly.

Jose shook his head disagreeably, but then said, "Since you have given your word to someone, I won't stop you. But for keepsake, leave me your two beautiful ladies and I know you'll be here when it's time to go," Jose concluded jokingly, eyeing Melody and Carmella sitting on the opposite side of the courtyard.

Calling Jose's bluff, Stink held his hand out, and said, "Deal!"

Bonni sat in front of the vanity mirror putting on the final touches of her make-up. Tayvia and Rahsaanique flanked both sides of her, asking questions after question.

"Mommy, who are you going on your date with?" Tayvia asked pryingly. "I told you. You don't know him," Bonni replied.

"Come on, mommy, tell us, is it our daddy?" Rahsaanique blurted. Slightly startled, Bonni hesitated, "Um..I...um...don't think that your father wants to go on a date with me," she revealed in a disappointing tone.

"Come on mommy, he didn't say that," Tayvia said.

"Yeah, mommy, daddy didn't say that," Rahsaanique added.

Bonni didn't know how to break it down to her kids. She didn't want to make him out to be the bad person in the kids' eyes.

On cue, the phone began to ring. Tayvia quickly took off, beating her younger sister to the phone. After a brief exchange of words, she passed the phone to her mother.

"Yes, hello," Bonni said into the receiver.

"Hey, Bonni. This is Rodney. I was just calling to make sure you were ready."

"Oh, yeah, I'm ready, but your not due to pick me up for another hour," Bonni replied.

"Yeah, I know. I was just checking up on you, "he said jokingly.

Bonni giggled at his sense of humor, then replied, "Rodney, I'll see you in an hour, bye.

Stink was traveling by himself, something he hadn't done in years. True to his word, he'd left Melody and Carmella with Jose. The two vacuum wrapped packages of weed sat on the passenger seat. He hadn't even bothered to put them in the stash compartment.

Stinks plan was simple. Drop the weed off with PJ, then have PJ to drop him off at the airport. He'd allow his cousin to keep his truck while he was in the Dominican Republic, enjoying the aqua-blue waters.

Stink unconsciouslessly allowed a wide smile to appear on his face just thinking about his vacation. Instinctively, he began to think of Bonni and the kids. Truthfully, he owed her a trip to a tropical island for what she'd endured years before. He knew he still loved Bonni, yet the pain that she'd caused was something he couldn't forgive.

For the remainder of the ride, Stink thought about the hurt and pain he'd caused, Bonni. As he began to compare some of things that she'd put up with, and what she'd done to him, he still couldn't bring himself any closer to forgiving her.

Even the R. Kelly cd that played couldn't change his heart. "What about when a man's fed up!" Stink asked himself.

Pearl stood in the door way for what seemed like an eternity, trying to articulate the right words to say. Trina was furiously following the Tae bo instructor's every demand that played on the T.V.

Eyeing the tight fitting spandex pants that Trina wore, Pearl could see every crevice in her body. Instantly, his body reminded him that he hadn't made love to his woman in nearly two weeks. Since he'd listened in on her phone conversation, the 'Platinum Pussycat' and 'Sugah Walls' had been his only sources of sexual relief.

Trina turned around and was slightly startled by him standing there rubbing his hardness.

"Oh! Hey boo. I didn't know you were standing there," she said, then grabbed her water bottle.

"Uh…yea…yeah. I wanted to holla at you," he stated, trying to get his words together.

"O.K., let me hop in the shower, then we can talk," she replied, biting her bottom lip nervously. Trina didn't know what it was, but from Pearl's tone and his recent actions, it had to be serious. She couldn't think of anything she'd done lately. The young lover she'd had a year ago was long gone. She hadn't cheated on Pearl since then. Her mind was racing with things, as Pearl quickly closed the distance between them.

"Trina Boo, you know I love you baby. But there's one thing I need to know," he stated, then paused to get his wording correctly. "But…um…is Stink Rah-Rah's daddy?"

The blood in Trina's face literally left her body at the mentioning of Stink. Now her mind was reeling with questions. How? Who? Why? She wanted to ask. Yet, when she attempted to speak, nothing came out.

Pearl eyed her reaction closely, then said, "Answer me, Trina." She attempted to open her mouth again and still, no words escaped.

Beginning to become frustrated, in a commanding tone, he said, "Trina you better tell me something!"

O.k., O.k." she began before taking a deep breath, then continuing," Long time ago, I used to go with Rahsaan. Then when….." Trina broke down their entire relationship for Pearl. Up until she received the blood test results disclaiming Stink as Rah-Rah[s father.

Once she was finished telling her heart wrenching story, Pearl was absolutely enraged. As she took a sobbing Trina into his arms, he silently vowed to murder Stink himself.

Sobs violently racked Trina's body as he held her tight, silently letting her know that everything was going to be taken care of.

Just as he laid down with Trina in his arms, his cell phone began to vibrate. Pearl initially chose to ignore the call. However, once the caller continuously called, he maneuvered the phone from his pocket.

"Hello," he answered in a hushed tone.

"My nucca! That sucka ass fuck nucca just pulled up! What you want me to do?" Milk asked in an exciting tone.

Pearl's body abruptly shot straight up, nearly tumbling Trina's tiny frame in the process. " Milk! Don't let him out of your sights, I'm on the way!" Pearl demanded, then bolted from the room. As he took the stairs in two leaps, he could hear Trina's screaming as he bolted from the door.

Chapter Nine

Bonni sat at the table in the restaurant that Stink took her to on their very first date. She couldn't decipher whether it was an omen, or just a coincidence on her date's part.   However, Rodney was playing the absolute gentlemen, opening doors, and holding chairs for her in the most courteous manner.

"Earth to Bonni," Rodney sang, snapping Bonni out of her thoughts.

"Oh, I'm sooo sorry. I was just thinking," she apologized.

"It's alright. But are you ready to order?" he asked.

"Um…yeah. I'll have the shrimp scampi in the butter sauce, baked potato and the seafood salad, with house dressing," she rattled off without even glancing at the menu.

Rodney instantly shot her a look of disbelief, then said," Damn! Is this restaurant a place you eat at everyday or something?"

Bonni's cheeks reddened in embarrassment. She hadn't even thought about her quick recital of the menu would affect her date. Thinking quickly, she replied, "Oh… I didn't tell you, this is my favorite restaurant." Rodney quickly soaked it up like a sponge, with a bright smile spread across his face.

Once Bonni saw the affect the statement had on Rodney, she relaxed and tried to put any thoughts of Stink out of her mind.

Stink pulled in front of PJ's house and parked. Noticing PJ's car wasn't there, he pulled his phone out and dialed PJ's cell number.

"Hello," PJ answered.

"Yo, P. Where you at fool?" Stink asked jokingly.

"I'm on my way to the crib. Why? Wazup?"

"Remember I told you I had something for you?" Stink asked, then added," well I'm at your crib right now. Hurry up," he said, then hung up.

Sitting in his truck, Stink decided to call the girls while he waited on PJ.

"Hello!" Rahsaanique answered breathlessly.

"Nique-Nique, what are you doing?" Stink asked curiously.

"Daddy!" She yelled in response, then turned her attention to whoever was close by, and announced, "My daddy's on the phone!"

Stink smiled broadly at the way his daughter was reacting. "Nique-Nique where's your sister?" He asked.

"Um…she right here, and she trying to take the phone from me…da…daddy!" Rahsaanique yelled.

"Hey, Daddy!" Tayvia yelled.

"Tayvia, what are y'all doing? And where is your momma at?" Stink asked suspiciously.

"Oh, mom's on a date," Tayvia blurted, then continued," Our babysitter is here with us, who's also our cousin." Tayvia divulged in a joking tone.

Stink held the phone to his ear, unable to respond to what Tayvia had disclosed. He didn't know that the realization of Bonni moving on with her life would affect him as it was.

"Um…Tayvia, when your momma comes in, make sure you tell her I called o.,. And I love y'all ok."

"We love you too, daddy," Tayvia crooned.

He quickly hung the phone up, as he noticed PJ's Acura pulling in front of him. Grabbing the two tightly wrapped packages, Stink hopped out of his truck.

"Wazup, cuz? What you got there?" PJ asked, eyeing the packages Stink held out to him.

"PJ, this is that new shit. 'Hydro'," Stink replied triumphantly, then added," This shit is five hundred dollars an ounce."

PJ shot Stink an incredulous look, then said," Come on, cuz, This shit is that good?"

"Look P, I've got a plane to catch right. But I want you to put this shit up, then come on and take me to the airport, Aight," Stink advised, eyeing his watch.

"Aight cuz, I got you. Just throw that super weed in my trunk, and I'm run in the house right quick," PJ said, tossing Stink his car keys. Stopping in his tracks, he turned back to Stink, and asked," What you going do with your truck?"

Smiling slyly, Stink replied, "you gonna keep it until I get back."

PJ smiled at his cousins cockiness then disappeared through the side door of his house.

Milk sat slouched in the late model Nissan Maxima, with his cell phone glued to his ear. "Yeah, PJ just went to his trunk. I think they about to roll. What you want me to do, my nucca? I could smoke both of these square ass fuck nuccas, right now!" Milk stated emphatically.

"Naw! My nucca, this one is on me. I gots to give this sucker ass nucca what he got coming, just stay on the phone," Pearl advised.

"Alright, my nucca. But it looks like PJ, hoping in the passenger seat of that fuck nucca, Stink's truck," Milk informed, eyeing the man as he climbed into the passenger seat.

Unbeknownst to Milk, PJ was just exiting the side door of his house. The only view that Milk had was of the passenger side of the Escalade.

As the truck began to pull off, Milk announced, "They moving, my nucca! They moving!"

"Follow'em! Follow'em!" Pearl commanded.

PJ hopped in Stink's Escalade, then looked over to him, and said "Damn cuz, I see you still ballin."

"Come on P, you taught me how to ball, nigga," Stink replied.

PJ pulled away from the curb and steered the SUV in the direction of the Newport News International Airport. "So where you on the way to, cuz?"

"Man, I'm about to go to the Dominican Republic."

"Damn! Who the fuck you know over there?" PJ inquired.

"You'd be surprised who I know," Stink replied.

Once again, PJ smiled at his cousin self-confidence.

Stink had only been gone for 24 hours, and Melody was already worried. She looked over to Carmella, who was stretched out on the lounge chair relaxed. Jose had truly been the perfect coutier. In just a short time he'd already spoiled the two beautiful women.

Earlier that afternoon, Jose had summoned a masseuse and a manicurist to pamper them.

Carmella rolled over to look at Melody, noticing the

far out look on Melody's face, she asked," Are you alright, mami? You look like you've seen a ghost."

Barely above a whisper, Melody said, "I'm worried about, Rahsaan."

"Come on, Mami. Papi's a big boy, he can handle himself," Carmella replied sarcastically.

Unable to find any humor in Carmella's remark, she stood up and made her way to the telephone.

As Rodney pulled up behind Bonni's mini-van and put his Honda in park, he looked over to Bonni with a dreamy glare in his eyes." Bonni, I really had a wonderful time with you this evening," he stated in an honest tone.

"I had a nice time too, Rodney," she replied.

"Well, when can I take you out again?"

"Soon, Rodney. Soon," she said.

Looking deep into Bonni's eyes, Rodney slowly moved in close towards Bonni's lips. Just before his lips made contact with hers, Bonni abruptly stopped him with her outstretched arm.

"I'm, um…sorry, Bonni," Rodney apologized.

"No, I apologize, Rodney. It was my fault," she explained quickly grabbing the door handle.

She didn't even bother to look back as she made a bee-line for the house. As she disappeared through the door, she heard Rodney yell," I'll call you o.k.!"

After tailing the black Cadillac Escalade for the past fifteen minutes, Milk had a good idea on where they were headed.

"Pearl! They gotta be going to the airport, my nucca," Milk surmised. Pearl was less than two minutes from the airport, coming from the opposite direction.

"Milk, I hope you're right, my nucca. I'm gonna head in that direction. If they come that way, I got'em. You just head up the rear," Pearl advised.

"My nucca, say no more! I got'em my nucca!" Milk replied in a boisterous tone.

With the intercom to his Nextel cell phone sitting in the passenger seat, Pearl gripped the 'Tec-9' in preparation to put in major work. "What they doing, my nucca!" Pearl barked.

"Yeah, they going to the airport, my nucca. They're turning onto airport road right--------."

"I see'em, my nucca!" Pearl yelled, cutting Milk off. "Listen, my nucca. When they pull to the light, I want you to cut them off, and I got the rest."

"I got you, my nucca!" Milk stated throwing the phone into the passenger seat. He could already see Pearl's old school up ahead at the intersection. Suddenly, his adrenaline began to pump as they drew closer to 'showtime."

PJ and Stink, were each engrossed in their own thoughts. The music being played at a moderate level caused the mood to be that much more relaxing . Stink laid back and thought about calling Bonni's cell phone, just to be nosy, but quickly thought against it.

Just as he was about to say something to PJ, he saw the front end of a car swerve in front of the truck. Leaning up to get a better view, Stink looked on in horror as another car to his right, had pinned the truck in. Opening his mouth to yell in protest, Stink saw the first flash of what proved to be many. "Pop! Pop! Pop! Pop! Pop! Pop!" The two gunmen unloaded their weapons into the Escalade.

Stink instinctively dove for cover. The shots seemed to be never ending as he tried to squeeze under the dashboard area. However, the gunmen continued to fire. "Pop! Pop! Pop! Pop!"

The assailant's bullets continuously sounded off inside the truck. Suddenly there was silence. Stink could hear footsteps as they stepped on the shattered glass. Just as he began to battle with the thought of staying alive, he heard two more shots. Shortly after, Stink couldn't hear, see nor feel anything. There was only peace and darkness surrounding him.

Melody dialed Stink's cell phone number, over and over. She had a dull pain in the center of her chest. She was almost certain something was desperately wrong.

"Did he answer yet, mami?" Carmella asked, now sharing Melody's worry.

Somberly, Melody shook her head. Frantically, she began to punch number after number. Unable to contain her composure any longer, she slammed her cell phone to the floor.Carmella rushed to Melody's side and embraced her." It's going to be o.k., mami," she said attempting soothe her.

"No, it's not, Carmella! We gotta go to Virginia, I know it!" Melody yelled on the verge of hysterics.

"Calm down, Melody. I'm going to call Pepe, he knows people in Virginia, he'll know what to do," Carmella said, reaching for her own phone. She didn't want to admit it, but Melody's paranoia was rubbing off on her.

After Bonni had undressed and gotten comfortable, she prepared to call Stink. Tayvia and Rahsaanique had been bugging her to call since she'd entered the house.

As she punched in his cell phone number, she silently prayed that he would somehow have a change of heart.

After a succession of rings, she was forwarded to his voicemail. Instead of leaving a message, she hung up and tried again. On this attempt, after only three rings, someone answered the phone, but only fumbled with it without speaking.

"Rahsaan," Bonni said into the receiver. As she listened intently to the silence on the other end, she heard a demented gurgle. The vile sound instantly heightened curiosity. "Rahsaan! Rahsaan!" She yelled. Pressing the phone painfully onto her ear, she heard the gurgle once more. This time she knew something was desperately wrong. She grabbed her cell phone and dialed '911'. "911, may I help you?" "Yes, I've got someone on my other phone…." She explained.

Emergency vehicles, paramedics and police rushed to the gruesome scene on Airport road. The Black Cadillac Escalade was riddled with bullets. The scene instantly looked like a fatal car accident as rescue workers began to pull the bodies from the vehicles.

Detectives instantly began their investigations, circling the SUV like a science project, looking for any clues.

The tall lanky, black detective walked over to the gurney, and pulled the sheet from over the corpse. Eyeing the revolting, bullet laced body, Detective Riley instantly recognized the man.

At the same time, the medical crew were feverishly working on the other victim of the gruesome attack.

Detective Riley walked over the paramedics, and asked, "How does this one look?"

A middle aged EMS worker replied, "Numerous flesh wounds, one average to medium caliber gunshot wound to the torso. If he's strong, he should make it."

The Detective looked at the helpless man as they carted him off, and shook his head in disbelief.

Cross laid back in the bed and thought about what Shyborn had just said. "What you mean what I'ma do if Bruce Cotler don't get my shit overturned?" Cross asked in an aggressive tone.

"I mean, what you gonna do, god?"   Shyborn repeated.

"Long as I got my lil brother, I can do whatever," Cross stated.

"Yo, god, you know ya man's gonna get tired of making them moves one day."   Suddenly, Cross cursed him self for telling his cellmate about his impending appeal. All he seemed to get from him was 'hate'. Put it this way Shy, if I don't get out, I'ma break the fuck out. Feel me?" This response must have been sufficient for Shyborn, because he didn't ask any more questions.

Pepe's Surburban was loaded down.   Melody, Carmella, Pepe, Manny, and Chico were all in the spacious SUV. Pepe intently pushed the trucks engine to its pinnacle. Each person's mind in the vehicle want to know one answer. Was Stink alive?

After Carmella had called Pepe, he quickly made a call to his girl Clarrisa in Virginia. Once Pepe put her on the case, she checked every news cast and called every hospital in the area. It wasn't until early that morning did she notice Stink's Escalade on the news. She was just about to call Pepe and tell him that his fears were confirmed, when the news reporter stated, "One man is confirmed dead, and another is currently battling for his life in I.C.U. Authorities haven't released any of the victim's names at this point. John Hughes reporting to you live from Newport News. Back to you, Ed."

Clarissa quickly called Pepe and transferred every word that she'd heard. Before she could finish, the line was dead.

Bonni awoke early the next morning in a state of

confusion. The 911 operator had really pissed her off. She felt that something was terribly wrong with Stink, yet there was absolutely nothing she could do.   Once she disconnected the call to Stink's cell phone, she attempted to call at least a hundred times, only to be continuously forwarded to his voicemail.

As she dragged herself from the bed, she could hear the girls' television blasting Saturday morning cartoons. To draw out their irksome television shows, she flipped on her own television and turned the volume up a few decibels. She then headed into her adjacent bathroom to take care of her morning essentials. As she brushed her teeth, something on the morning news caught her attention.

'Shooting in Newport News leaves one dead, and another struggling for his life,' the reporter began, causing Bonni to rush into the room. Starring at the television in horror, Bonni nearly fell to her knees. There on the television was Stink's truck mangled with bullet holes.

As the reporter continued to talk, Bonni broke down. 'The driver of this SUV was murdered last night in a gang style ambush. Authorities are being tight lipped about any leads in the case. However, the passenger in the vehicle is still alive and fighting for his life. Authorities say if anyone has any information, call 1-800-LOCK-U-UP.'

Bonni stared at the television through disbelieving eyes as the tears flowed freely down her cheeks.

In a voice unrecognizable, even to herself, she yelled, "Noooooooo!"

Pearl sat behind his desk with an eighty dollar cigar wedged between his lips. Milk and Bear followed suit as they toked on their victory cigars as well.

Pearl felt like he was back on top again, and absolutely nothing could bring him down. After Trina told him of how Stink treated her and lil Rah-Rah, he was furious. He never enjoyed putting slugs into human being as much as he did with Stink on the night before. Especially the final two he pumped into the slumped body.

"So, my nuccas, where we going to celebrate?" Pearl asked in a self assuring manner.

"You know what it is, my nucca. We going to 'Cobanna's out the beach," Milk announced.

Bear smiled in agreeance, enjoying the smooth taste of the Cuban cigar.

"O.K., my nuccas, 'Cobanna's' it is. Y'all niggas go jump clean and I'm a do the same. Tonight, we gon' show these square ass nuccas how real nuccas from the 'Yam' get down," Pearl stated triumphantly.

Milk and Bear promptly exited the office to go and get prepared for their evening. Pearl made his way up the stairs to his bedroom suite.

As he entered the room, Trina was just exiting the bathroom with a towel wrapped around her shapely body. Pearl eyed her hungrily, then made his way over to her.

Trina looked into Pearl's eyes timidly, then said, "Boo, please tell me you didn't have anything to do with what happened last night."

Pearl responded to her question by placing his mouth over hers. As their kiss became more intense, their bodies tumbled onto the large bed.

The towel that had been covering Trina's body was now carelessly thrown to the side. Eyeing her perky breasts lustfully, Pearl attacked her nipples, gnawing on them tenderly.

Trina's body instantly responded to the way he was tantalizing her. Pearl quickly disengaged his hold on her titties and stood up. In one smooth motion, he disrobed then dove back onto the bed.

"Pearl, I don't want to lose you, boo," Trina huffed sexily, gripping his head in her palms.

"Don't worry baby, you won't," he whispered, then slid down her body to her most sensitive areas.

"Is there a Rahsaan Jones here?" Carmella asked the receptionist, as everyone standing around stood attentive.

As the young woman behind the large desk began to tap on the keyboard of the computer, each person in their entourage silently prayed that Stink was there and not the morgue.

"Um, I'm sorry, but if neither of you is an immediate family member, I won't be able to give you any information," the receptionist stated eyeing the computer screen. Instantly, everyone looked to one another with confused expressions. Never having experiences such a situation, Melody looked on as a sense of helplessness filled her.

Suddenly, someone stepped through the small crowd, and said, "Yes, Rahsaan Abdul Jones is my husband and I want to know his status, immediately!" Melody, Carmella, Pepe, Manny, and Chico looked on in awe as the self assured woman waited for a reply from the receptionist.

Chapter Ten

As soon as Bonni heard the news reporter's condition of the incident concerning Stink's black Escalade, she went straight into wife mode. She quickly gathered the kids and dropped them off at her mother's house. Careful not to arouse any suspicions in the kids or her mother, she headed straight to Riverside Medical Center.

When she entered the hospital there was a crowd around the receptionist desk. Immediately she noticed the two pretty girls from Stink's house, standing around with hopeless looks spread across their faces.

Seizing control of the situation, Bonni walked straight through the crowd. AS she approached the information desk, she heard the receptionist say, "Um, I'm sorry, but if neither of you is an immediate family member, I won't be able to give you any information."

Without even a second thought, Bonni stepped to the counter, and said," Yes, Rahsaan Abdul Jones is my husband and I want to know his status, immediately!"

The receptionist quickly pryed her eyes off the screen, and looked to Bonni. "Yes maam, but is there ah....any type of documentation that you have to prove that?"

Casually, Bonni leaned in close, and said, "If you would check your computer records, it will show that I gave birth in this hospital to a Rahsaanique Tatiana Jones on June 6th of 1993 and Rahsaan Jones is listed as the father/husband. Thank you."

Dumbfounded, the receptionist vigorously tapped on the keys and until the information that Bonni had divulged was reiterated by the computer screen. "And you're Mrs. Bonita Lawson?" The receptionist asked.

"Yes, I'm Bonita Lawson," Bonni stated sarcastically, then slapped her I.d. onto the counter.

"I'm so sorry Mrs. Lawson. I can give you the information on Mr. Jones condition, But um...would you like to um...,"she stammered nervously, shooting contemptuous glares at the others in the crowd.

Thinking quickly, Bonni looked into the eyes of each person present, and noticed the distressing look covering their faces.

Turning back to the receptionist, she said, "yes, its fine. They're family also."

Hesitantly, the receptionist began, "Mr. Jones is currently in I.C.U."

Stink stood between his mother and father with a broad smile plastered across his face. This was the happiest day of his young life. His elementary school graduation ceremony seemed to be larger than life to him.

As him, his mother, and his father posed for the camera, Stink couldn't wait to get home to jump into his baseball shirt, Wranglers and 'fishhead' Nikes. At that very moment, life was what it was supposed to be for the bright ten year old. Being raised by both parents, in a single family home, in a lower middle class neighborhood, Stink's young mind couldn't ask for anything more.

Once they pulled into their driveway, Stink bolted from the car in the direction of his bedroom. He quickly shed his black pinstriped suit, and put on his favorite outfit. Before his mother and father could get comfortable into the house, Stink was on his way out.

"Boy, don't you come in this house all late," his

mother said to his tiny disappearing figure.

In Stink's neighborhood, he was a real-life 'Dennis The Menace.' There was nothing he couldn't get into, and there was nothing he hadn't already gotten into. AT that moment he was headed to Vicki Patterson's house, his neighborhood girlfriend.

Stink and Vicki had shared some very intimate moments to be such a young age. Vicki had introduced Stink to a lot of his first. His first sighting of a woman's genitalia, his first sighting of a female's breast, and of course his first tongue kiss. After staying over Vicki's house, until her mother's car pulled into the driveway, Stink made his way home.

As always, once he got home, his house was reminiscent of a twenty-four hour 'Juke Joint.' Music blasted from his father's prize component set, while numerous couples danced from the kitchen to the living room. Alcohol was consumed in high doses, as a thick layer of cigarette smoke hung in the air.

Once Stink appeared in the back door, he was immediately ushered into his room. He had become accustomed to being alone during these times. Going under the bed, he pulled out a 'Newport' and a cigarette lighter. Imitating what he'd seen his mother and father do, he lit the cigarette and inhaled deeply. Instantly, the strong tobacco smoke cause him to become lightheaded. After a few pulls from the cigarette, it wasn't long before Stink laid back on his tiny bed and went to sleep.

Soon after sleep had engulfed him, a crashing sound quickly jarred him from his slumber.

Sitting up in his bed, he could hear the curses being tossed between his parents. This also had become a regular occurrence in Stink's life. Suddenly, a loud crashing caused him to jump. It seemed as if a piece of furniture had been thrown into his bedroom wall.

'Motherfucker, I'm-a kill you!' his mother yelled.

'Birth! Not before I kill you and that Nigger!' his father retorted.

Stink had become immune to his parents fights, however, tonight seemed to be more than just one of their regular altercations.

After experiencing one final crashing sound, Stink quickly exited his room and ran down the hall to his parent's bedroom. Once he pushed their bedroom door open, he stood in shock, as his father straddled his mother with her arms pent under his knees, while his fist rained blows down onto her face.

Horrified, Stink closed his eyes and took off running towards the hideous scene. Just before he reached them, he threw his tiny body into his father's side, causing an extremely sharp pain to shoot through his chest.

Once Stink opened his eyes, a blinding light made it impossible to see anything. Desperately trying to focus his eyes through the piercing light, he looked around the room in a confused state. Nothing in the tiny room was recognizable. Even his own body was unfamiliar to him.

No longer was Stink a little boy trying to keep his parent's lives together, he was a grown man fighting for his own.

Cross continuously dialed Stink's cell phone, only to be quickly forwarded to his voicemail every time. He couldn't understand why he couldn't catch his man for the last few days. He had finally decided to tell Stink about his appeal. Mr. Cotler had gotten the three judge panel to remand his case back to the actual trial court. Cross was ecstatic about the news he'd received, and he couldn't even tell his man.

Although, Mr. Cotler had informed him that the case may take up to a year to be heard, Cross was still optimistic about his chances.

Pearl and Trina sat at the table of a cozy seaside restaurant in Virginia Beach. Ever since the murder of Stink, he'd been romancing his woman. In some strange way, he was trying to make up for all the pain and hurt that Stink had caused her. "Is everything alright, Boo?" He asked eyeing Trina closely. "Yeah, I guess so," she replied.

Quickly picking up on her somber mood, Pearl said, "What you mean, "I guess so?"

"I'm o.k. daddy. It's just I worry about you," she revealed, then added. Ever since that stuff out by the airport happened, you've been acting strange."

Pearl noticed the sincerity in Trina's eyes and instantly felt that he had to tell Trina exactly what had happened. Taking a deep breath, he looked into Trina's eyes, and said, "Trina, what happened out by the airport had to be done." Pausing to judge her reaction, he continued," Stink had to die."

Instantly, Trina's face turned stark white at the mentioning of Stink dying. Although Stink had totally cut all ties with her, she secretly dreamed of one day being with him. After the many years they'd been apart, she still loved Stink.

Bonni sat by Stink's bed for nearly twelve hours, until he abruptly stirred. Startled, she took off in the direction of the nurse's station. Once she returned with a team of doctors and nurses, Stink was painfully clutching his chest, as he struggled to see.

The hospital's staff quickly took their positions around the room. The doctor stood directly over Stink, attempting to shine his tiny flashlight into his eyes.

"Give me thirty cc's of sentient stabilizer! His pupils have dilated!" The doctor stated commandingly.

Suddenly, everyone began to frantically move about in the tiny hospital room.

Bonni stood by the door in shock. She didn't know what was taking place, but it didn't look good.

Melody and Carmella restlessly laid on the uncomfortable couches in the I.C.U. waiting room. They hadn't left the hospital since they'd arrived. They'd held a 24 hour vigil along with Bonni. Even though his condition hadn't changed up until that point, they were still hopeful.

Suddenly, Bonni entered the waiting room looking as if she'd seen a ghost.

"What happened, Bonni?" Carmella asked, eyeing her closely.

With her palms glued to her face, she shook her head violently.

"Noooo! Noooo!" Melody cried out, quickly jumping from the couch.

"What happened, Bonni?" Carmella repeated firmly.

Bonni removed her palms, only to reveal bloodshot eyes. Releasing a deep sigh, she began," I was just sitting there, when Rahsaan just started to mumble. Then he opened his eyes and began to grab at his chest. After that I ran to get the doctors and nurses. When they got to the room, he was still grabbing at his chest. After the doctor gave him a shot of something, they made me leave the room."

Melody listened intently to every word Bonni said. She had been a registered nurse for most of the time Stink was away. From what Bonni had explained, it sounded like Stink was coming out of his coma looking to Bonni, Melody asked," What did the doctor ask for when he gave him the shot?"

"I don't know!" Bonni stated in an irritated manner, then said, "Some kind of sea-sent or shen shon stabilizer of something," she concluded presumptuously.

Unbeknownst to either of women, Melody just smiled. She knew now that Stink was coming through.

Pepe, Chico, and Manny rode through the streets of 'Bad Newz' with one thing on their minds. Murder.

Anybody that so much as resembled a nigga from Miami was going to feel their wrath. Each of them carried a high powered. semi-automatic assault riffle, ready for action.

"Hey yo, Pep. Why don't you ride out to where that fucking maricon [faggot], Pearl lives? Maybe we can catch one of them coming or going," Chico stated.

"Yeah, that's cool. But first we gonna clean the fucking streets up. These mufuckas think they gonna get money, and our fucking familia is fucked up in the hospital? Nah, I don't think so," Pepe said in a demented tone.

Steering the Suburban in the direction of Chestnut Avenue, each man gripped their weapons, with the taste of war heavy on their minds.

Stink looked around at all the smiling faces in the room. Bonni, Melody, and Carmella were all looking down at him, as he laid helplessly in the bed.

Since he'd regained his consciousness, he'd racked his brain trying to figure out how he'd ended up in the hospital with numerous gunshot wounds to his body.

Fragments of the incident flashed in Stink's mind, but nothing came to him that would piece things together for him.

Opening his mouth to speak, Bonni, Melody and Carmella all attempted to 'shush' him.

Ignoring their pleas for him to be quiet, he managed to say, "wat...er"

Quickly, Melody filled a Styrofoam cup with water, then put a straw in the cup and put it to Stink's lips.

The ice cold water seemed to do a lot more than quench his thirst as he felt the water travel through his entire body.

Looking down at his heavily bandaged chest, Stink delved deep into his mind for answers. Closing his eyes tightly, vision began to come to him.

He could remember talking to Rahsaanique and Tayvia while he sat in his truck, yet everything after that was blurry.

Closing his eyes tighter, he tried to envision what happened after he talked to his daughters.

Suddenly, the image of a very familiar face came into his mid. Attempting to shake the gruesome scene before his eyes, he felt a warm tear roll down his cheek.

As Stink's emotions welled up inside of him, he whimpered, "P.J." Instantly, all of the women rushed to his side, hoping to somehow divert his mind from his current plight.

Looking into each woman's eyes, he repeated, "PJ. Where's PJ?" As he locked eyes with Bonni, he knew his cousin was dead. His mind instantly gave him a play by play of that night, as he laid helplessly in the hospital bed flocked by three of the most beautiful woman a man could dream of.

Instinctively, Stink grabbed for his heavy bandaged chest, just to see if he was in fact alive.

Pepe, Chico, and Manny casually exited the SUV with identical mini-14 assault riffles draped over their necks as if they were fashionable jewelry.

The dark streets and the many drug transactions being made on the corner, assisted in their undetected approach.

Each man's eyes held an evil glare as they drew closer to the street corner. Just as their planned mission was at hand, they each leveled their weapons and began to squeeze.

"Pow! Pow! Pow! Pow!!!!" The shots rang out in rapid succession.

Instantly, the block erupted into mayhem, as hustlers and friends alike ran for their lives.

The trio stood defiantly in the middle of the street, continuously firing their weapons at anything moving.

Bodies were dropping like flies, as Pepe, Chico, and Manny aimed their guns recklessly.

Once their murderous rage was executed, they quickly escaped the street.

Melody stood outside of the hospital with her cell phone glued to her ear. She was eagerly giving Jose directions to the hospital in Newport News. Jose and his two henchmen had just landed at the airport, and were in route.

"After you make a left turn onto Jefferson, drive down maybe four lights and you'll see Riverside drive, take that right. Riverside Regional is on the left side, you can't miss it. I'll be standing in front," Melody explained, then pressed 'end' on her cell phone. As she patiently waited for Jose to show up, her cell phone began to ring again. Eyeing the caller Identification suspiciously, she pushed 'talk.'

Cross had begun to get extremely worried about Stink. It had been almost a week and he still hadn't been able to contact Stink. He was nearly running his mother crazy, with request of somehow locating Stink. Finally, his mother remembered the cellular number of Stink's girlfriend.

Cross' mother was more relieved than him, once she called the number with Cross on the line and heard the girls familiar voice pick up.

"Hello," Melody answered.

"Yo! Where's Stink?" Cross blurted before his mother could even make an introduction.

"Um...who is this?" Melody asked perplexed.

"This Cross! Where my lil brother at?" He snapped inquisitively.

"Oh...um, Cross. Stink is, uh....Stink is in the hospital."

"For what!"

"He was shot, Cross," Melody revealed in a distressing tone, then added. "But he's doing much better now."

There was a tense silence on the opposite end of the phone. Melody held the phone in silence, until she heard a soft click on the other end. "Hello," she said.

"Yes Melody, I'm Cross' mother. Do you remember me?"

"Oh, yes maam."

"Well, it looks like we lost my son. But I want you to keep me informed on Stink's condition, if that's O.K.," Mrs. Scott said.

"O.K., maam. I sure will," Melody replied.

"Thank you so much, Melody. And have a nice day," With that said, she hung up.

Melody eyed the traffic pulling into the hospital's parking lot intently. It wasn't until she noticed the trio of black S-Class Mercedes Benz', parking in front of the hospital's entrance, did she realize who was behind the dark limousine tint.

The doors to the car in the middle, abruptly swung open, and two giant Latinos exited. The one on the passenger's side stepped to the rear door, while the other stood guard as if the president was exiting the Mercedes.

Melody stood there in awe, as she noticed Jose slide from the rear of the car and casually approached her.

"Melody, it's good to see you again," he said extending his hand. Continuing, Jose looked deep into Melody's eyes, then said," Melody, Stink has given me his word on something, and I'm sure he won't recant. Now my two constituents are going to make it possible for Stink to do as he promised," Jose explained motioning to the two men hovering over them.

Instantly, Melody was terrified. To her it sounded like Jose was making some type of threat toward Stink.

Noticing the horror register on Melody's face, Jose took her hand in his and said," My chica, I have come to take Stink away with me." Turning toward the two hulking figures, Jose strolled off.

Chapter Eleven

As the fire alarm began to sound off, Carmella and Bonni looked around with confused stares.

Stink laid in the hospital bed, looking around in hopes that the loud alarm would stop. The irritating buzzing sound somehow caused his wounds to ache.

As the sound persisted, Bonni and Carmella ignored it and went back to attending to Stink. Suddenly, the door burst opened and in walked two giants, dressed in long white doctor's smocks.

"I'm sorry ladies, but we must move the patient immediately. If you'd like to come along, come along," the smaller of the two giants said.

Once Stink focused his sights on the men, they both immediately looked familiar to him. Instinctively, he was uncertain about being led out of the room with the two men. The policed had ceased to give his room around the clock protection, for they had deemed his shooting to be random. Even though the two men looked familiar, Stink was still apprehensive about the pair.

As they roughly ushered his gurney onto the elevator, Stink groaned in pain. Carmella and Bonni tried to keep up with them, by quickly squeezing into the small elevator.

Slightly suspicious at the way in which they were handling Stink, Bonni look to the smaller of the two men, and asked," Exactly where are you transferring him to?"

With a slight smirk on his face, he said," Um, Saint Mary's Medical."

Before Bonni could launch a reply, the elevator

doors swung open, and there stood Melody accompanied by an older Spanish man, with a broad smile etched into his weathered features.

Pearl knew that Stink's crew would launch some type of retaliation. However, the many senseless murders that transpired on the eve before, were inhumane.

The formal body count hadn't even been released, but Pearl had been given a first-hand account of the damage. Nearly all of his street soldiers had been murdered. As Pearl had heard it, there were at least ten gunmen firing machine style guns.

Sitting in the passenger seat of his 'crayola' yellow Navigator, Pearl looked over to Milk, and asked, "My nucca, you think them square ass wetbacks was behind that shit?"

Milk smiled a devious smile, then said, "I'ont know. But I know that sucker ass nucca Stink won't."

Giggling, Pearl joined in on his man's festive mood, then replied," Yeah, I'm just glad we let his cousin live. I kind of like that lil nucca. Shit, I might buy a pound from that nucca in dimes just to look out, my nucca."

As Milk continued to navigate the bright colored Navigator through the city, Pearl leaned back and relaxed. He knew nothing or nobody could stop him. Especially a group of immigrants, this was his world.

For the last few days, Cross was a walking time bomb. He'd contemplated hitting the fence numerous times in the last few hours, let alone days. His little man was somewhere laid up fighting for his life, and there was absolutely nothing he could do about it. Cross had always prided himself on protecting Stink, but now he was helpless.

On the day before, his rage became evident, when Crook approached Cross and asked, "Yo B, when is ya mans gonna holla at my baby moms?"

It might be a minute, son," Cross replied somberly.

Apparently, Crook didn't pick up on Cross' mood, when he blurted, "Come on, B. I know ya mans ain't on no 'flam' shit now. The least he_____."

Crook was abruptly cut short by a sweeping right hand that landed square on his chin, instantly knocking him out. Cross rushed over to the unconscious man and stood over him. Quickly regaining his composure before anyone could restrain him, Cross casually walked away.

Pepe, Chico, and Manny casually drove through the upscale community in Williamsburg. They had parked Pepe's fire engine red Suburban and hopped in the 'Mercury Marquise.'

The houses in the neighborhood looked like churches with big gates around them. The information that they had gathered on Pearl had panned out to be correct, yet using the information would be nearly impossible.

Pepe had thought about parking near the exit on the interstate that Pearl would likely use, then follow him. However, that idea was quickly blotched once they noticed that a state trooper's car was parked at or near the exit of the prestigious section of the city, every time they'd come.

Pepe also knew that they couldn't continue to aimlessly drive around the neighborhood, or they would be pulled over. Directing his focus toward Manny, he said," Yo Manny, bounce fam, before we get knocked on some bullshit."

Immediately, Manny made the correct turns in order to exit the area, and put them on the interstate.

Stink couldn't believe his eyes when he saw Jose. Instantly he remembered where he knew the two hospital orderlies. They were two of Jose's most trusted men. Jose approached Stink grinning foolishly, then cheerfully stated," My friend, we meet again."

Stink could only smile and nod his head. The pain of being roughly moved around had him speechless.

Jose looked around at his men, then said, "Mi amigos, lets go, we have a plane to catch. Without further warning, the men quickly rolled Stink through the lobby and out of the sliding doors, where a small fleet of Mercedes Benzes awaited them.

Quickly, the rear door of the car parked in the back opened and the two giants placed all of the hospital contraptions onto Stink's torso. Then, in what seemed like one quick painful motion, they slid him into the spacious rear cabin of the Mercedes.

Stink didn't open his eyes until the pain had subsided. By then, the big Mercedes was rolling. Focusing his eyes on the middle aged woman hovering over him, Stink couldn't help but to look on in shock as she plucked a syringe. Once the woman had loaded what looked to be the longest needle Stink had ever seen, she smiled down at him, and said, "Don't worry, Stink. I am Dr. Juanna Lopez and I will be accompanying you on your flight to Santa Domingo."

Once the needle entered his flesh, and the substance released into his body, all pain quickly turned into euphoric bliss.

Bonni still wasn't fully aware of what was taking place, as she sat in the back of the car watching Melody and Carmella carry on with the older gentleman as if they were long lost friends.

She didn't know if they had been kidnapped, or if they had just kidnapped Stink. The manner in which they were quickly ushered out of the hospital and into the awaiting cars, had her perplexed.

Apparently picking up on her confused look, the older Spanish man turned his attention to her, and asked, "And who is this bonita chica? [Pretty girl]"

Quickly, Melody spoke up. "This is, Bonni. Stink's child's mother." "Si, si. Nice to meet you, Bonni. I am Jose, Stink's friend," he said, extending his hand to her. Clearing his throat, he continued, "If I may ask, does the name Bonni derive from Bonita?"

Smiling at his factual question, she replied, "Yes, my real name is Bonita." "Si, I will call you Bonita then. In my country, Bonita means pretty."

Blushing at his comments, Bonni quickly turned serious and asked, "Where are we going? And where are you taking, Rahsaan?"

Jose instantly shot her a confused look, then turned to the other two women in the car, and asked, "Neither of you have explained to Bonita where we are going?"

Both Carmella and Melody shook their head in response to his question. Turning his attention back to Bonni, he said, "Bonita, we are on our way to the Dominican Republic."

Trina sat around the house in a state of affliction. The man who had cared for her and her son for the last five years, had murdered the man that she'd been secretly harboring an undenying life long love. She didn't know what to do with herself. On the one hand she felt the pain of a grief stricken widow, and on the other, she felt the rage of a vengeful lover.

Ever since Pearl had revealed that he'd murdered Stink, she couldn't bare the feel of his touch. Every time he'd touch her, she would inwardly cringe.Trina knew she couldn't continue to live this way, something had to be done, fast.

Bonni stood and watched the sleek Lear jet soar into the sky, with a pained expression covering her face. She desperately wanted to accompany him to the foreign country, but her presence was needed more by her children. She couldn't just up and leave, traveling halfway across the ocean. That wouldn't have been motherly of her. And Bonni prided herself on being a good mother.Nonetheless, Melody and Carmella promised to call her and keep her informed on Stink's condition.

Once the plane had disappeared into the clear blue sky, she turned to the big black Mercedes and slid in the backseat. As the driver pulled off, Bonni laid her head against the plush leather seats and pondered the strange relationship between Stink, Melody, and Carmella. She knew it was possible for one of the women to be Stink's woman, yet they both acted as if they were his woman. What was really surprising to Bonni was that neither of them seems to get jealous of the attention the other one gave.

Shaking her head violently, she tried to erase the thought of him having both women.

Once Bonni came to her senses and looked around, the driver of the Mercedes was traveling through the tunnel toward Norfolk.

Clearing her throat, Bonni said, "Excuse me, sir. But I think your going the wrong way. I live in Hampton."

"Oh, I'm sorry Mrs. Bonita. But Mr. Rodriguez says to take you to his home," the driver explained.

"Well, I'm telling you that I've got two kids to pick up from my mother's house, then I'm going home," she retorted in a irritated tone.

"Mrs. Bonita, maybe you don't understand. Somebody tried to kill Oye Stink. Now as of this moment, nobody knows why or who, so until someone does, I must take you to Mr. Rodriguez' estate in Virginia Beach. Now I will turn around and pick your kids up. But as for you going to your house in Hampton?   It doesn't look to promising, if you get my drift," he concluded humorously, then swung the big Mercedes around in the direction they'd just come from.

Bonni dropped her head in frustration, and massaged her throbbing temples.

Once Stink came to, he looked around once again in a befuddled state. He was laid across an extremely soft bed, as the same woman from the car hovered over him, checking his vitals.

"Hello Stink. I'm glad to see you're back with us," Dr. Lopez said smiling.

"Where are we?" Stink asked confused.

"I'd say we're around twenty thousand feet over the Atlantic ocean," she remarked.

Before Stink could reply, Melody walked into the cabin with a glass of orange juice." I thought you might be thirsty when you awoke," she said cozying up to him in the tiny bed.

Stink allowed Melody to place the glass at his lips, while he greedily gulped the delicious tasting beverage down. Once he'd downed the juice, he turned to Dr. Lopez and asked again," now where did you say we where?"

Smiling, she nodded toward Melody, silently urging her to explain to him.

"Daddy, were on Jose's jet on our way to Santo Domingo, Dominican Republic," Melody quickly explained.

"What?" Stink asked just above a whisper.

Suddenly, a voice said," My friend, you heard the lady. We are on our way to Santo Domingo. Remember, you gave me your word," Jose said appearing inside the jet's rear cabin. Placing his hand over Stink's he continued," Don't worry, Stink. We are going to get you patched up, and back to your old self in no time."

Pep was in deep thought as Clarissa rubbed his shoulders. From what his sister had said, Stink wouldn't be back in the game for a minute. Not only was Stink out of the game, he was also out of the country. Pepe knew he had to come up with a plan quick. He had dismissed the thought of hustling in New York long ago. The big flip that Virginia offered was what he was after.

Quickly moving from under Clarissa, Pepe had made his mind up. He would not only have several blocks pumping whenever Stink decided to return, he'd also eliminate his enemies.

As Bonni exited her mother's house with Rahsaanique and Tayvia in tow, she instinctively had the urge to flee. Even though she was aware that what the driver had told her was serious threat, she still didn't want to feel like a prisoner in some house that wasn't her own. The driver of the car suddenly appeared from nowhere and quickly opened the door for her and the kids.

This seemed to be amusing to the girls." Oohwee, Mommy! We've got a chauffeur!" Tayvia squealed in delight.

"Mommy, does this mean we're rich?" Rahsaanique added inquisitively. Bonni shot her daughters an incredulous look as they got cozy in the back of the luxurious Mercedes. "Girls, we are going to a fried of your father's house for a few days," she explained. Instantly, this caused a barrage of questions to be launched from the two. "Where is our daddy? Is he going to be there? Does he have a dog? Can we go swimming? What about our toys?"

Instead of attempting to answer the many questions, Bonni responded only by laughing hysterically.

Cross had never felt as he was feeling at that moment. Even the letter he'd received from Mr. Cotler's office hadn't been able to pull him from his dejection.

The only bright spot was that in two months he'd be transferred back to Rikers Island, and if his captors failed to do their job to the fullest, his plans of freedom would be extracted one way or the other.

As Jose's twelve passenger Lear jet descended in the direction of Las America International Airport, Stink was fully awake. The flight had been smooth up until that point. Once the plane prepared to land, the ride immediately became rough. Stink braced himself on the tiny bed as the plane began to shake violently.

Dr. Lopez, the only person present in the tiny cabin

turned to Stink and said," Hold on, we should be on the ground any second." Stink gripped the bed as his wounds began to throb with every vibration of the aircraft.

There was one final jolt, and the plane was rolling smoothly on the tarmac. The pilot steered the plane toward the back of the large airport where there were two identical Mercedes Sedan waiting.

Once the plane came to a stop in between the two automobiles, a customized van pulled up next to it. Immediately, everyone converged on the plane and began to unload the baggage.

The driver of the van, along with his assistants made their way to Stink. Carefully, they lifted him from the small bed in the rear of the plane and carried him to the awaiting van. Leaving everyone else at the airport, the van quickly pulled off in the direction of Boca Chica.

At that very moment, Bonni, Tayvia, and Rahsaanique were being driven through the tall gates of Jose's seaside mansion in Virginia Beach.

Bonni couldn't believe her eyes, as the elaborated designed house of glass and red brick sprawl before her. She had never seen such a beautiful house in her life.

The circular driveway wrapped around a large statue of the virgin Mary as water bubbled at her feet. The large driveway, set off to the left housed a fleet of European luxury model cars.

As the driver stopped in front of the affluent home, the large double doors swung open and out walked a stout Hispanic woman in a customary maid's uniform, and a tall Hispanic man in a customary butler's uniform. Bonni eyed the pair through disbelieving eyes, as they approached the car.

Turning around to face Bonni, the driver said, "Mrs. Bonita, if there is anything that you should need, or if you may need to go out for anything, dial 4117 on the house line. My name is Miguel, maam." Suddenly, Bonni thought that maybe she was dreaming. In a matter of months, she had gone from living in a two bedroom apartment, to staying in a million dollar mansions.

Snapping her from her stupor, the door was opened by the maid. "Mrs. Bonita, it is so very nice to have you. Welcome to Casa Rojo," she said extending her hand to Bonni. Turning to the man, she said, "This is Pedro and I am Consuella. If you need absolutely anything, one of us will always be around."

Bonni nodded her head and allowed Consuella to lead them into the house. Once she stepped in the foyer of the mansion, she nearly fainted. There, in the middle of the room was an identical, yet smaller statue as the one that greeted her in the driveway, equipped with tropical fish swimming at Mary's feet. There were two staircases that whined up each wall and connected on the second floor. There was gleaming white tile laid out as far as the eye could see.

"Mrs. Bonita, please allow me to show you and your princesses to the wing of the house that has been prepared for you," Pedro announced, then led the way up the stairs on the far wall.

Pepe was sitting in the Dominican restaurant on 140th and Broadway, waiting on his man Mookie to return.

Pepe had decided to make moves on his on. He wasn't trying to go over Stink's head while he was in remission from the game, he was simply trying to survive while he made a name for himself and Stink.

On que, Mookie walked through the doors of the café with a shopping bag. Pepe eyed the bag that Mookie carried, and knew he'd followed directions to a tee. The black plastic bag, with the gold 'Broadway' lettering had come from the head cocaine distributors on Broadway, insuring it's potency.

"Yo fam, everything's there, "Mookie announced, passing Pepe the bag.

Pepe passed the bag to Chico, then turned back toward Mookie. "Yo fam, I'm a hit you off with a few gees when I get back, but until then," Pepe peeled off a few hundred then passed them to Mookie," this should hold you."

Trina sat in the chair beside Kesha in 'Exquisite's beauty salon', listening to the latest gossip. It had been almost two weeks since Pearl had divulged to her that he'd murdered Stink. Up until that moment, Trina hadn't heard anything of the situation.

"Girrrl, that was so sad what happened to PJ and Stink," Gloria, the woman standing over Kesha's mane said.

"Hmm Mmm, I heard about it Blo," Kesha replied, cutting her eye at Trina conspiratorially.

"Yeah, chile, but that shit was crazy how Stink just disappeared from the hospital," Gloria said.

Instantly, Kesha and Trina looked at one another perplexed. Slowly Kesha turned her head back, and asked," Uh Glo, how could, um Stink get out the, um hospital when um ___."

"I know gurrrl, I said the same thing. 'How could he leave the hospital after being shot in the chest?" But that nigga did it," Gloria blurted, cutting Kesha off.

"Glo, wasn't PJ shot in the chest?" Kesha asked

confused.

"Oh naw gurl. You must've got yo info off the news or something, cause PJ is the one who got killed. Stink is the one that lived," she explained.

At that moment, Trina felt the weight of the world being lifted from her shoulders. Now all she had to do was find Stink and tell him everything and undoubtedly he'd love her again.

Carmella exited the car behind Melody and was instantly hit with the sweet smell of the ocean. It had been nearly twenty years since she'd been to her homeland. In fact she didn't remember a thing about the beautiful country.

As she strolled up the stairs to Jose's seaside estate, the view that she was met with nearly took her breath. The aqua blue waters of the Caribbean crashed into a rocky wall on the back side of the house. Further down, the white sand beach traveled as far as the eye could see.

Jose's house was nothing short of immaculate. The cream and white color scheme seemed to have a serene feel to it.

Once Carmella and Melody were shown to their rooms, they began to search frantically for Stink.

After unsuccessfully being able to locate him, they found Jose. "Hello my lovely chicas. What can I do for you?" He inquired full of hospital glee.

"Jose, we we're looking for Stink and we could ---" Melody began, before Jose cut her off.

"Couldn't find him. Yes I know. Well, Stink is in good hands, don't worry my chicas." Jose replied then added, "You all should have some fun while you're here. As a matter of fact, why don't you two take a trip to plaza lamas and buy Stink a few things." Reaching into his pocket, he pulled out a wad of money and passed it to Carmella, then walked away.

Carmella and Melody eyed the ruffled bills in disbelief. Not only were there an colossal amount of bills, they each contained the face of Benjamin Franklin.

Bonni walked into the large bedroom in awe. The large colonial style bed sat high in the air. There was a small step encircling it's wide frame. The opposite side of the room was decorated like a den, equipped with a sectional couch, end tables and a large television mounted into a wooden chest.

The room in which Tayvia and Rahsaanique were taken to was nothing short of beautiful. The pink and white color scheme seemed to cover everything, from the plush carpeting to the furnishing. Once the girls entered the room filled with the soft hues, they instantly fell in love.

Bonni had nearly forgotten about Pedro standing there, until he cleared his throat, then said, "Mrs. Bonita, Mr. Rodriguez has left strict orders that you and your family be treated as family. If there's absolutely anything you need, just ring us."

Bonni turned to Pedro, and said, "Me and my kids are going to need a change of clothes. Were are we –"

Cutting Bonni off, Pedro held his hand up, then said, "We were expecting you, Mrs. Bonita. Please, check the closets and drawers, and if we have made any mistakes just let us know." Pedro then turned to leave. Just before he disappeared, he turned back to Bonni and said, "Please tell the two Princesses to do the same. Buenas noches [Good Night]." He then exited.

Bonni stood in the middle of the room completely

flabbergasted.

As the Grand Marquis pulled behind Pepe's Suburban, each gentleman breathed a sigh of relief. They had just successfully transported enough crack cocaine down Interstate 95 to get each of them life behind bars.

Pepe knew he'd made a risky move, yet the proceeds would ultimately outweigh the risk. The ten kilos of crack that he'd paid 150 thousand for would net him a return of well over 300 thousand. However, the slickest part of his move had yet been seen. Unbeknownst to the rest of his crew, their orders of operations were undergoing a chain of venue.

Stink lay in the tiny hut in a bed that seemed to be made of clouds. The medieval stove that sat in the middle of the floor held a single pot that contained a concoction derived from some deep dark secret on the island.

Stink had been made to drink the thick mushy fluid everyday, twice a day since he'd been there. Then Dr. Lopez would come in and rub a sticky substance from a large leaf on his chest.

In just three short days, Stink was feeling 100% better. On the forth day, Dr. Lopez took him out onto the white sands of the beach and cleansed his wounds in the sea water. Although the salt stung every wound tremendously, Dr. Lopez wouldn't allow him to get out of the water.

Miraculously, on the 6th day of Stink's recovery in the Dominican Republic, while he was ingesting the mushy concoction, a small disfigured piece of lead extracted from his chest wound. The tiny piece of metal, covered in blood was immediately placed in a small container and placed by the bed.

Dr. Lopez turned to Stink, and said, "Stink, if you had any more of those in you, they would have come out by now. As of today, you may begin your recovery," she explained.

Later that evening, Stink was given his first meal of solid food since he'd been shot.   A scantily dressed Dominican girl served him roasted chicken, vegetables, and rice, along with a foreign sauce poured over it. Once Stink had devoured the food, he was given an array of fruits and a glass of freshly squeezed mango juice.

From that night forth, Stink ate hearty. Not only was his appetite building, so was his strength.

He was so engrossed in his recovery; he'd nearly forgotten everybody and everything, besides Dr. Lopez and the lovely Dominican girl, who he'd find out later was actually Dr. Lopez' daughter, Ambria.

Chapter Twelve

Sweat poured from Cross' face as he slowly walked the ball up the court. Eyeing the defense intently, he made a quick move to the right of the court, then abruptly reversed his direction back to the left. There were 'oohs' and 'ahhs' heard from the crowd as Cross' defender stumbled on wobbly legs, while he elevated and smoothly dropped a 19 footer.

Basketball had actually been Cross' first love. However, once he was introduced to the love of money, all thoughts of basketball quickly diminished. Nonetheless, Cross had reverted to his first love as a means to exert some of his anger and aggression.

After nearly a month and still no word from Stink, Cross was distressed to say the least. Not only had his only real family, besides his mother disappeared, he'd also received a letter rescheduling his highly anticipated court date.

"Yo, Cross! Let's run it back, son," one of the players on the losing team said.

"Nah, B! I'm good," Cross replied heading for the side lines. There was a disappointing sigh heard from the crowd of onlookers as the prison superstar exited the court, content.

Pearl quickly disrobed and eased in the large bed behind Trina. As soon as Trina felt the mattress move she was awake. However it wasn't until she felt Pearl's throbbing member probing her from the rear did she tense up. It had been over a month since she'd had sex with Pearl, and she wasn't planning on doing it any time soon. Once she felt him tug at her panties, she sleepily mumbled, "No, Pearl."

Over the last few weeks, she had given Pearl every excuse imaginable, yet she was prepared to give him a million more, or however many it took for her to plan her revenge.

"Come on Trina, I want some," he whined into her ear.

"Pearl, I've told you that I have a yeast infection, and until it goes away I'm not doing shit," she explained in an irritated tone.

"Lil ma, I'ont give a fuck. I want some pussy." He stated roughly grabbing at her night gown.

Trina quickly snatched away from him and jumped from the bed." I said no, Pearl!" she exclaimed, then headed fro the door. Just before she exited, she turned to him, and said," I know you wasn't thinking about taking my pussy, cause I promise you that I will cut yo shit off."

Pearl laid in bed for a few more minutes with his rapidly deflating dick in his hand. Looking over to the bedside clock, which read 12:48 AM, he knew where to go and get himself a nice piece of pussy for the night.

Quickly, he grabbed the phone from the nightstand and dialed Milk's number.

After only a few rings, Milk picked up, "Hello."

"My nucca, I'm trying to go through 'The Drop'," Pearl announced.

This in itself was a strange request coming from Pearl. Lately he'd been preaching against hanging out in strip joints. However, no matter how strange the request, Milk replied, "Come scoop me, my nucca."

Bonni and the girls exited the MacArthur Center Mall at Norfolk's prestigious waterside. The last three weeks had been like a dream of sorts for her and the kids. They'd been waited on hand and foot in the luxurious house. Melody had called on several occasions to tell Bonni that she hadn't seen nor heard anything from Stink since they'd arrived in the Dominican Republic. Somehow in Bonni's heart, she knew that Stink was fine if her and the kids treatment was any type of testament as to how he was being treated.

There wasn't a thing that Bonni couldn't imagine doing that wasn't afforded to her and the children.

Daily, there were prepaid credit cards given to Bonni, with a minimum thousand dollar limit. Therefore on each day that she'd been there, her and the kids had been treated as if they were royalty.

"Mommy, I want to go to 'Jillians'," Tayvia whined, sporting her little 'Gucci' frames.

"Yeah Mom, I want to go too," Rahsaanique added. Bonni couldn't help but to smile at her two princesses. They had fallen into their temporary lifestyles with ease. Although Bonni knew that their dream lives would soon come to an end, she inwardly made the choice to have fun while it lasted. Turning toward the girls, she said, "Let's go."

Melody and Carmella were terribly worried about Stink. Every time they'd asked Jose about him, he'd beg them not to worry, then quickly switch the subject. They had done enough shopping for Stink to last him a lifetime, yet at that moment neither of them even knew if he was alive.

In a state of helplessness, Melody vowed to confront Jose the very next time he appeared. And if he didn't give her the answers she so desired, then she'd just try another tactic.

Stink extended his arms out, while using correct breathing techniques. As he continuously pumped his arms, his chest and shoulders began to burn feverishly. He had been doing calisthenics for almost two weeks, and his body had been responding.

Once he finished exerting his muscles, he ran on the white sandy beach for thirty minutes. After returning to the small makeshift village belonging to Dr. Lopez, and her daughter Ambria, Stink dove into the beautiful aqua-blue waters of the Caribbean.

Stink swam a few strokes in the exceptionally warm water of the ocean, until he became exhausted.

When he finally came up to the shore, he noticed Ambria lying on the beach comfortably.

Stink couldn't help but to admire her innocent beauty. She couldn't have been any more than twenty-one years old. Her sun tanned complexion, dark hair and voluptuous body made for the complete package.

As he exited the water, he desperately tried to pry his eyes away from the fat mound between Ambria's thighs. This proved to be even more trying once he noticed the fine black hairs that tried to escape the folds of her bikini bottom.

Just as Stink had peeled his eyes from the luscious sight, Ambria said, "Stink I think my mother wants to see you in the house." Spoken in her perfect English.

This instantly changed his course, as he was headed in the direction of the 'ducharse' [Shower].

When Stink entered the house, he thought maybe his eyes where playing tricks on him as he focused on the figure sitting beside Dr. Lopez.

"My friend, you look good as Nuevo [new], if not mejor [better]," Jose said standing to greet him.

Stink stood there in shock. For nearly two months, he hadn't heard anything from Jose, and now he just popped up.

Jose inspected Stink's wounds like a professional physician, then said," Yes, this is bueno. You heal real good, my friend." Once his inspection was complete, he turned to Dr. Lopez and said," Gracias, Juanna." Going into his pocket, he pulled out one single piece of paper and passed it to Dr. Lopez. Jose then turned toward Stink, and said, "Lets go home, my friend, your muchachas are getting worried about you."

As Jose led Stink out of the door, Dr. Lopez said, "Stink, hold, on. You're forgetting something," Catching up to them she placed the mangled slug that had extracted itself from Stink's chest." Be careful, she stated in warning, then closed the bullet into his palm.

Pepe was astounded at how much money was being made on the strip in Hampton. Had he known about the gold mine on Shell road before, none of their current troubles would exist.

Sitting in the living room of Clarissa's mother's house, Pepe counted stack after stack of money. Not only did he have Clarissa's older brother selling crack for him, he'd also befriended her mother. For the small amount of five thousand dollars, her mother took a vacation for an unspecified amount of time, giving Pepe full reign of the small house.

"Daddy, you ready to go home?" Clarissa inquired sexily, eyeing the neat stacks of money.

"Yeah, mami. Just wait for Chico and your brother to come back, then we out."

"Daddy, Jo-Jo might have Chico out their doing anything. That nigga crazy," she whined.

In response to Clarissa's statement, Pepe retrieved his phone and tapped in Chico's phone number. After a brief exchange, Pepe hung up.

In less than five minutes, the door swung open and in walked Chico and Clarissa's brother, Jo-Jo.

"So what's the deal, fam?" Chico asked.

"I need you to be here when Manny calls, so just lay," Pepe explained.

"Aight. I got you, fam."

Pepe gathered the back door, followed closely by Clarissa.

As he hopped into his brand new forest green Denali XL and pulled onto Shell road, he couldn't believe the traffic that he witnessed walking up and down the street. There was only one place that reminded him of the scene being played out before his eyes – New York City.

Soon as Manny returned with their third shipment of crack, he planned to turn the heat up on Pearl and his crew.

Thick clouds of smoke hung in the air, as the loud base reverberated throughout the small club. Pearl and Milk sat back and eyed the curvaceous sisters shaking their asses to the rhythm. There were three women on the stage in the 'Dew Drop Inn," each one attempting to garner the attention of Pearl. Without being said, every person in the club knew he was the man.

"Which one you want, my nucca?" Milk asked, hoping that it wasn't the redbone he had his eye on.

Licking his lips hungrily, Pearl said, "I'm feeling lil momma in the blue."

What are we waiting on my nucca?" Milk asked, then stood.

Quickly grabbing his sleeve, Pearl said, "Nucca, sit yo ass down. Let me handle this." He then turned his attention back to the stage. Motioning for the dancer that he wanted, he shot Milk a quick look, then said, "Watch this my nucca."

Mercedes sexily ambled her shapely figure in Pearls direction. As she squatted on the stage just above where he and Milk sat, Pearl eyed the plump flesh that struggled to escape the thin fabric between her legs.

"Look here lil momma, me and my nucca trying to holla at you and yo girl over 'dere," Pearl began, then reached in his pocket and pulled out a roll of money and tossed it onto the stage. "In five minutes, be out front. We in the yellow Navi." Coolly, Pearl stood and strolled out of the packed strip club, followed closely by Milk.

As Stink exited the car behind Jose, he eyed the sprawling estate before him in awe. After spending the last month at Dr. Lopez's small cottage on the beach, Jose's estate was the pinnacle of elegance.

Slowly ascending the winding stairs, Stink noticed the first doors to the house being flung open as Carmella and Melody exited in a haste headed straight for him.

Stink could see the bright smiles plastered on their faces as they approached.

"Papi!" Carmella yelled planting kisses on one side of Stink face.

"Daddy! I missed you sooo much!" Melody exclaimed kissing the other side of this face.

After they'd both drenched kisses, they quickly noticed the ragged gear that he sported.

"Come on daddy. We've got to get you cleaned up, and out of these clothes," Melody remarked.

"Yeah, Papi, we've got you a whole new wardrobe upstairs," Carmella stated, leading the way into the house.

Stink allowed the two women to guide him through the beautiful house and up a set of stairs to a large bedroom suite.

"Jose says this is your room, Papi," Carmella informed, as he walked through the suite astounded.

Easing up to Stink, Melody said," Daddy, let us get you out of this." Then pulled the worn tank top from his torso.

Instantly, both women converged on the spots where he'd been shot. Once their focus landed on his chest, both women inspected him through disbelieving eyes. There was only the slightest trace that there had been any trauma.

"Papi, how...I mean, didn't.... Carmella stuttered in amazement.

Melody simply rubbed the area gently with her forefinger, then looked up into Stink's eyes as a single tear rolled down her cheek. Refocusing her attention on the nonexistent wound, she began to place sensuous kisses down his chest to his stomach.

Quickly, Carmella joined in and began to assist Melody in the task she had embarked upon.

As Miguel pushed the big Benz through the tunnel, Bonnie laid her head back on the seat and thought of one thing; Stink. She could not get him off of her mind. The last few weeks she had been doing everything with him in mind. From choosing what to eat, to putting on make-up. She had put herself in a 'boot camp' of sorts for Stink.

She'd begun to diet and exercise vigorously, and although it had only been a short time, the changes were noticeable. She had even began to regulate her sleep in the cozy environment.

One thing was certain, when Stink did reappear he would have to take notice of Bonni's new appearance.

"Miguel, before you stop by my mother's house, please stop by my house, there's something I need to pick up," she instructed.

"Yes maam, Mrs. Bonita.

Pepe, Chico, and Manny strolled through the coliseum mall as if they were a platinum selling rap group. Not only did they actually feel as if they were a famous rap trio, they were also receiving the attention of one.

There were teenagers and adults alike following them through the mall. Each man sported the shiniest jewelry known to man, which only attracted that much more attention.

Pepe, walking in the middle of the trio, soaked the attention up like a sponge. This was how Pepe always knew he was supposed to live. In the limelight.

"Hey yo, Chic, the next trip uptown is yours; then mine; then Manny. That's how we doing it, fam, " Pepe explained as they walked through a group of onlookers.

"No question, fam," Chico replied in agreement.

Just as Pepe was about to say something else, a very familiar hulking figure approached them in the opposite direction.

Before Pepe could say anything, Chico said, "Ay yo, fam. That's one of Pearl's boys right there."

"I know. I know," Pepe replied, cutting his eye at the man.

Bear, who strolled hand in hand with a petite brown skinned girl, was oblivious to the three men who'd just passed. This would prove to be deadly.

Pepe quickly pulled out his cell phone and dialed Jo-Jo's number. Even though they'd only known Jo-Jo for a short time, he'd proven that if need be he wouldn't hesitate to pull his trigger.

"Hello," Jo-Jo answered.

"Yo, fam. This is Pep. I need you out here at the Coliseum Mall, ASAP."

"Give me five minutes and I'm there, baby, " Jo-Jo said, then hung up.

A broad smile covered Pepe's face once he placed his phone back on his hip. Everything was going just as he'd planned it.

Pearl laid back on the bed while Mercedes vigorously used her mouth to pleasure him. Although he was enjoying the warm friction her mouth was causing around his manhood, he desperately wanted to feel her moist center engulf him.

"Stop, lil ma. I'm trying to get in them guts," Pearl said prying her mouth away from his shaft.

"I hope you got a condom," Mercedes snapped as she wiggled out of her panties.

Eyeing her body hungrily, he retorted," Bitch, I gave yo ass a gee! If I want to fuck you raw, I will! You ain't got shit do you?"

Horror instantly showed on her face. She knew that things were going too good to be true.

"Answer me! Is you got something or not?" Pearl repeated.

"No! But do you have anything?" She asked in a quivering voice.

Chuckling at her question, Pearl shot her an incredulous look, then said, "Bitch please."

Quickly, he covered the short distance that separated them and began to roughly pinch her soft nipples.

Pearl mistook the soft whimpering coming from her as a pleasurable moan. Pinching her nipples harder, he began to grind his pelvis into her naked ass.

Mercedes closed her eyes tightly and said a silent prayer.

Suddenly Pearl pushed her to the bed roughly and kneeled down behind her. The submissive role she was playing in addition to the hairy lips that hung below, caused him to become defiantly hard.

Pearl pulled her waist to his pelvis while aiming his shaft directly at her womanhood.

As Mercedes braced herself on her knees, she felt a sharp pain shoot through her entire being once Pearl forcefully entered her unaroused. This caused a demented cry to escape her lips.

Once Pearl felt her warmth engulf him, he began to pound her furiously.

"Please!   You're hurting me!" She exclaimed.

This only incited Pearl even more, as he humped Mercedes' backside while gripping her firm ass cheeks.

All Mercedes could do was bite down on her lip to suppress her cries.

Pearl began to slow his stroke, while he continued to grip her ass.

Mercedes had begun to get into the slow stroke. "That's it daddy. You don't have to be rough with this pussy," she huffed sexily, looking back at Pearl. Before she could get her next comment out, she felt something at the opening of her anus. "Hold up daddy! I don't get down like that."

With a deranged smirk on his face, Pearl said," Tonight you do."

Melody mounted Stink carefully and instantly felt him fill her up. Carmella was laying beside him trying to put as much of her tongue down his throat as possible.

The look on Stink's face was pure ecstasy. Melody slowly moved up and down on his pole, savoring every inch.

"Mmmm, daddy, you feel so good in me," Melody crooned looking deep into his eyes.

Carmella had moved to Stink's nipples and was sucking them gently.

Melody began to pick her pace up as her orgasm mounted. "Oh, yess! Please daddy! Give it to me!" She exclaimed as she enjoyed the spasms of her orgasm.

Carmella moved up to Melody's jiggling titties and latched on to her nipples.

"Oh, my…..God! Carm…..Carmella, I love feeling your mouth on my nipples."

Stink laid back and watched them through lascivious eyes.

Carmella maneuvered herself between Melody's thighs, giving Stink a clear view of her womanhood.

Stink eased behind her and placed his dick at the entrance of her pussy and began to rub it into her juices.

"Ooh, papi! Please put it in me! Please! "She whimpered.

He tantalized her for just a little longer, then guided his shaft into her wanting center.

"Oh, papi! OH God! Yess, papi! More," she panted.

Melody passively rubbed Carmella's head as Stink pounded into her.

Sweat poured from Stink's face as he concentrated on the euphoric feeling that he was experiencing. Just as Carmella turned her head and glared at Stink through lust filled eyes, he felt his seed blast from his loins for the second time that afternoon.

"Oh, yess, papi! Cum for me papi! Yesss!" Carmella coaxed.

Pepe sat behind the wheel of his Denali with his phone glued to his ear. "Yeah, that's him with the little skinny bitch with the fat ass," he said into the phone. Turning toward Chico, Pepe asked, "Did that nigga have on a sweat shirt?"

Chico nodded his head affirmatively.

"Yeah, Chico said he had on a sweat shirt," Pepe said into the phone. After answering a few more questions, Pepe ended the call.

"So what he say?" Chico asked.

"He said that he's got 'em. But only time will tell," Pepe concluded with a sly grin on his face.

"Oh...my God! Why are you doing this!" Mercedes screeched as tears ran down her cheeks.

Pearl held on tight to her hips and drove his entire length deeper into her rectum.

Had Mercedes known that her screaming and crying was only motivating his assault, she would have kept silent through the tormenting experience.

"You like this dick, don't you?" Pearl spat as he gyrated his hips into her.

Unable to reply, Mercedes sobbed hysterically.

Pearl pumped into her one final time, then released himself deep into her rectum. Instantly, he collapsed on top of her breathlessly.

Once his heavy breathing subsided, the only sounds that could be heard were those of Mercedes sniffling.Pearl jumped up from the bed and looked down at her motionless figure, then said, "Come on lil ma, you know you like that shit."

Instead of using what little energy she had left in her body to reply, Mercedes allowed the burning muscles in her rectum to relax, which instantly caused a flow of feces and blood to run from her anus onto the bed. Pearl quickly dressed and exited the hotel room.

Chapter Thirteen

After Pepe had given him Bear's description, it didn't take Jo-Jo long to pinpoint the giant in the sea of shoppers. He was careful not to arouse any suspicion in the man, as he followed him at a safe distance out of the mall and to a crème colored Infinity Q45.

Bear casually hit the alarm on his car and helped Veronica put her purchases into the back seat. Once he hopped in the driver's seat and pulled off, he was completely oblivious to the car that followed him.

It wasn't until Jo-Jo had trailed them into a condominium complex in Hampton, did he cut his pursuit short. As a devilish smile spread across his face, he picked up his phone and began tapping numbers.

"Hello," a professional sounding woman answered.

"What up, Sheryl? This is Jo-Jo. What can I do for you?" She inquired in a seductive tone.

"Tag number 'YZF-36241,' I need an address?"

Giving an exasperated sigh, she said, "Hold on."

Jo-Jo had gotten Sheryl to give him countless addresses in the past. Some had ended up dead, some just robbed. Nevertheless, they all ended up experiencing some type of atrocity. There would be nothing different with Bear; Jo-Jo had his man.

Bonnie awoke feeling rejuvenated. Not only had her rigorous workouts began to show, she'd also received a call the day before from Carmella and Melody. They gave her a detailed update of Stink's miraculous recovery. From what they'd described, the scar that was sure to be evident on his chest was nothing more than a scratch.

The giddiness of the two women when they talked about Stink left Bonni perplexed. She desperately wanted to ask either of the women if they were involved with him. Somehow, she just couldn't find the words to do so. Bonni undressed in the mirror and eyed her physique. She had truly transformed her body into somewhat of a sculpture, in comparison to what it had been before.

In just a short time, she'd lost all of the fat that lined her midsection, leaving a perfect V shaped waist. Inwardly smiling, she couldn't wait until Stink saw her new look.

Stink exited the shower and began to meticulously pick through the expensive, conservative wardrobe that Carmella and Melody had picked out. Deciding on a pair of Dolce & Gabbana cream colored linen slacks, a Gucci button up, and a pair of Gucci loafers, his outfit was complete. Looking himself over on the wall mirror, he inwardly beamed at his immaculate reflection.

Exiting the room, Stink couldn't help but notice the debonair way he walked in the expensive loafers. Just as he reached the first floor landing, Jose stood there waiting.

"Stink, I see you've picked up on how we dress in my country," Jose teased eyeing Stink's outfit.

Holding his arms wide, Stink twirled on his toes in a model's pose.

"Well come along, there's somebody I want you to meet," Jose said leading the way out into the driveway, where a long Mercedes sedan waited.

A fashionably dressed Dominican man held the rear door open as Jose and Stink entered.

Once they were seated comfortably, Jose turned to Stink, and said, Stink, we are going to meet a very dear friend of mine."

Stink nodded his head and looked out the dark tinted window at the passing scenery. It seemed as if the longer they drove the more urban the scene became. It wasn't until the Mercedes entered an area that was extremely reminiscent of any ghetto in America, did Stink become alarmed.

Jose noticed Stink's expression as they came up on the bridge located inside of Gualey. This was Jose's true home. These slums had raised him into the drug mogul he was. It was rumored that none of the country's law enforcement would attempt to enter this downtrodden section of Santo Domingo. Yet here Stink and Jose were, cruising through the streets in a hundred thousand dollar automobile.

"Reminds you of Nuevo York Ciudad [New York City], eh?" Jose asked.

"Yeah, it does, "Stink replied eyeing the rough faces standing on each corner.

With a serious look suddenly covering his face, Jose said, "Stink, before your accident I promised to make your problems in the states disappear, and I will. However, I have taken it upon myself to make sure your nina's and their mother have been well taken care of. I did not know whether the problem would have harmed your familia. Therefore they have been living with my staff in Virginia."

Stink intently listened to everything Jose had said. At that very moment, he knew that Jose possessed a genuine love for him. As an emotional lump formed in his throat, Stink swallowed hard, then said, "Thanks for everything, Jose."

"No. Thank you, my friend," Jose quickly responded as the Mercedes came to a stop in front of an apartment building. The parking lot was full of the same hard faces that Stink had noticed on the way there.

Quickly the men surrounded the car, holding machetes and assault rifles.

Stink looked to Jose in panic, as they young men converged on the car.

With a calming look covering his face, Jose pat Stink on the shoulders." My friend, these people are our familia. Let's go, "he said, then stepped from the car.

Jo-Jo calmly squatted in the closet of the strange house. After a few days of surveillance he had the traffic at the condominium down to a science. Checking the time on his sports watch, he knew that Bear's girlfriend would be coming through the door any second with her teenage daughter. Like clockwork, Jo-Jo heard the door knob turn as they entered the condo. He smiled to himself, because everything was going according to plan.

He patiently waited for Veronica and her daughter to become engulfed in their everyday routine.

Once he heard the water from the shower, he casually exited the closet. Tiptoeing down the hall, he approached the young girl's room and eased inside. Before she could make a sound, Jo-Jo attacked her.

Quickly taping her mouth shut with duct tape and tying her up securely, he closed the door to her room and made his way to the partially opened bathroom door. As steam escaped the shower, Jo-Jo eased up to the curtain and snatched it open.

Instinctively, Veronica tried to cover her nakedness instead of yelling. Jo-Jo swiftly snatched her from the shower and attempted to stuff a rag into her mouth.

Fighting for her life, Veronica scratched, swung and kicked frantically. With his forearm around her throat, Jo-Jo chocked her until her violent actions subsided. He didn't want to kill the woman just yet, so he quickly loosened his grip.

Instantly an exasperated gasp escaped her mouth, as she attempted to say, "Please! Please! Whatever you want, just take it! Just don't rape me! Please!

Jo-Jo couldn't believe all this woman cared about at a time like this was her sex. In all actuality, pussy was the furthest thing from his mind. Yet, just as she mentioned it, Jo-Jo looked down at her naked body hungrily.

Stink cautiously exited the car behind Jose as every eye present was glued to them.

Suddenly the sea of men parted as a dark complexioned man approached with a broad smile on his face. "Como estas, Jose? What brings you to the gueto [ghetto]?"

"Mizi yah! My friend, you have such a sense of humor," Jose stated in a joyous tone, then added. "Now come meet Stink, our familia."

As Miziyah approached, Stink could see he was physically bigger than him, yet Miziyah carried a presence that made him seem as if he was a giant.

With his hand extended, he said, "Stink, I've heard tremendous things about you. Please call me, Miz."

Stink gripped the man's hand. "Nice to meet you, Miz."

There was something about Miziyah's character that Stink couldn't put his finger on at that moment, yet somehow he knew it would soon come to him.

What Stink didn't know was that he was in the company of a trained assassin. Miziyah was actually born in Port-au-Prince Haiti and defected to Dominican Republic during his country's second civil war. During those times, Jose was smuggling molta [marijuana] from the border town of Himani.

Once Jose met the young Miziyah, he instantly pulled him in and treated him as a son. In fact, Jose didn't have any biological kids. Therefore, throughout the years, Miziyah had actually become his son. However, now that Stink was in the picture, Jose looked at him as a son also.

"So, Miziyah, are you and Stink going to stand there all day, or are we going to go inside?" Jose inquired sarcastically.

After forcing Veronica to call Bear, and a number of other inhumane things, Jo-Jo sat in the living room window patiently waiting for the crème Q45 to pull into the parking lot.

Once the car pulled up and parked hastily, Jo-Jo knew that he couldn't play any games with the gigantic man. Quickly screwing the suppressor onto the Glock 40, Jo-Jo stood behind the door calmly.

Soon as the door swung open and Bear opened his mouth to yell for Veronica, Jo-Jo placed two well aimed shots into the back of both his thighs. He then quickly moved over to a grimacing Bear, while keeping his gun steadily aimed at his head.

"Well, Well, if it ain't big Bear. Looks like you in a trap now," Jo-Jo taunted while checking him for a gun.

"Come on man! Please! What you want, my nucca? Please, just don't kill me! Please! He begged.

"I'll tell you what, big boy. How much paper you got in this spot right now?"

"My nucca, please! Ahhh! I got fifty grand in the car! Please, Shit!" Bear grimaced in pain.

"Oh, yeah. Well I'm do you a favor then. I'm-a go in here and kill this non dick sucking bitch of yours. Then I'm-a kill her daughter, cause she ain't gonna be shit but a non dick sucking bitch like her mom. But first, I'm-a kill you," Jo-Jo stated tormenting him before firing two shots into Bears skull. "Pow! Pow!"

Standing over Bear admiring his work, he quickly went into each of the bedroom as if he was the angel of death.

Pepe pulled up behind Manny's Lexus and casually exited his truck. Their operation had been running smoothly. After being in Hampton for a little over a month, the money was rolling in by the barrel. The operation's initial investment had nearly quadrupled.

"What's the deal, fam?" Manny asked as Pepe approached.

"I'm supposed to be meeting Jo-Jo out here. You seen him?"

Before Manny could reply, the earth shattering base from Jo-Jo's Cadillac DTS could be heard approaching.

Jo-Jo parked across the street from Pepe and Manny, then hopped out and walked over to them in his customary gait.

"Yo, what's poppin, Pep?" Jo-Jo stated embracing Pepe. Turning his attention toward Manny, he asked, "What's up with you, Manny?" While giving him the same greeting.

"Just chilling," Manny replied.

Pepe cut the embrace short by saying "Hey yo, if you handled that 'B.I,' then why haven't we heard anything yet?" he asked incredulously.

"For real Pep, I'm just as confused as you. But the only thing I could think of is they laying up in that bitch stankin," Jo-Jo replied with a demented smirk, then added, "Cause I definitely left everything up in there sleep."

Pearl and Milk had begun to worry about Bear. It had been three days and there hadn't been a word from him. It wasn't like him to just up and disappear, that in itself heightened their concern.

As milk pulled beside Bear's Q45, he quickly noticed the way in which it was parked. It seemed as if he'd pulled in as if he wasn't staying long.

Once he and Pearl got out of the car and began to inspect the inside of Bear's car, it looked like someone had ransacked it.

Instantly, both men gripped their firearms and cautiously made their way to the entrance of the condo.

As Pearl grabbed the door knob and slowly turned it, the door creaked open. Instinctively, he felt a rush of fear as he eased the door open.

Once the door was completely open, the powerful stench of dead bodies quickly invaded their senses.

"What the fuck!" Milk gaped as the food he'd digested earlier that day came rushing to the surface.

Pearl was already doubled over extracting everything in his stomach. Milk, he said, "My nucca, they got my cuz, man! He's gone, my nucca! I know it!"

"Nah, my nucca, we going up in here, just wrap your shirt around your face. Come on," Milk explained pulling his shirt over his head.

Pearl followed suit. Once both their shirts were securely covering their mouths and noses, they entered the condo.

The first thing they saw knocked all hope from any other assumptions. There sprawled out on the floor, Bear's hulking figure was twice its normal size. The gaping holes in his head had oozed all the substances it had to offer, leaving behind purplish goo, stuck to his face.

Pearl's cries were muffled by his shirt as he looked down at his cousin's swollen body. Without venturing any further into the condo, they knew that the house held no survivors. They quickly retreated and slipped off as they'd come.

Bonni sat on the sofa wrapped in a terry-cloth robe sipping green tea. Her focus wasn't on the large screen in front of her, however, once the news reporter showed the three bodies being carried from an apartment, she tuned in.

"That's right, Ed, three bodies were found in this condominium this morning. Authorities aren't releasing any names at this time. However, they have said that one of the victims was a thirteen year old girl. Back to you, Ed."

Bonni cringed at just the mentioning of a child so young being murdered. Immediately, she thought of her own two girls. She couldn't bear the thought of losing either of them in such a manner.

Suddenly, Bonni felt the need to touch her babies. Exiting her room, she searched the gigantic house until she finally found them.

"Mommy! Mommy!" Rahsaanique yelled running towards her mother. "Hey, Mom," Tayvia said nonchalantly as she sat on a bar stool intently watching Consuella over the stove." Consuella's teaching us how to cook, mom," she offered over her shoulder. Bonni smiled at her daughter's regal demeanor, then said," I'm sorry Miss Tayvia, I just wanted a hug from my girls."

Tayvia quickly hopped off the stool she was sitting on, and made her way to her mother with her arms held wide.

Stink, Jose and Miziyah sat around a table in the immaculately decorated apartment. The interior of the apartment was a total opposite of the decrepit exterior. As Stink explained the situation back in the States to Jose and Miziyah, both intently listened to every word.

"So, it is possible that this Pearl was not responsible for your shooting and your familia's demise?" Miziyah asked.

Shrugging his shoulders, Stink said, "Possible."

"Do you know if your cousin may have had any enemies?" Jose added inquisitively.

"He may have, but I don't think so," Stink answered.

"Stink, what I am going to do is come to the United States and investigate these situations. Whoever has transgressed will be annihilated. Comprende?" Miziyah concluded.

"Now that we have gotten our business behind us, let us go and celebrate!" Jose announced leading the way out of the apartment.

Chapter Fourteen

Pearl lounged in the chair with a demonic glare plastered on his face and a bottle of Hennessy tightly gripped in his hand. Tears of rage flowed from his eyes as he thought of Bear's swollen body on the condominium's floor. Deep down, he knew that Bear's murder was done in retaliation for what he orchestrated against Stink.The only people who he could think of that would pull such a stunt, were the Latinos that Stink ran with, he thought.

There had been rumors about a crew of Puerto Ricans or Dominicans who were in Hampton selling big weight. Pearl hadn't thought anything of it until now. If the Latinos in Hampton bear any resemblance to the ones that once ran with Stink, Pearl vowed to kill them all.

"Milk, lets take a ride, my nucca," Pearl announced through his alcohol induced stupor.

"Let's roll, my nucca," Milk replied standing. With that said, they exited the house.

Stink and Jose sat opposite one another in the plane's luxurious cabin. Melody and Carmella were seated a few chairs out of earshot, enjoying a frivolous conversation.

Turning to Stink, with a stern face, Jose stated, "Stink, I may be out of place for what I am about to suggest. But please hear me out."

Stink nodded his head, and turned to Jose attentively.

"I'm not sure if you were aware of the tremendous presence that your children's mother presented during your distressing situation. I have seen a lot of things in my lifetime, but the look of genuine love is universal. And Stink, I can see that look in her eyes. Don't get me wrong, your two amantes [Lovers] do have a love for you, but neither has the look of your children's mother."

Stink sat in silence, allowing everything Jose had said to sink in. There was no question that he still loved Bonni; yet the hurt that she'd cast unto him was almost unbearable. If there was something she could say or do to make the pain disappear, Stink would surely welcome it.

As if he was reading Stink's mind, Jose added, "If there is some terrible thing she has done to you, give her a chance to explain why she's done such a thing. My friend, for me, give her a chance to explain. I propose to you the usage of my plane to take your family wherever you'd like. Just give her a chance," he concluded earnestly.

Stink's mind was reeling with questions, locations and even situations, until Jose broke into his thoughts.

"Beside, Miziyah won't be in the states for another couple of weeks. So go enjoy yourself with your kids. I'll take care of your chicas for you," he stated smiling.

The remainder of the ride, Stink thought about everything Jose had said. Before the plane landed, he wasn't sure if Jose was rushing him back out of the country to reunite with Bonnie or whether he was afraid for his life.

Once Stink pondered the situation, he knew that Jose was absolutely right about everything he said. However, forgiveness was very low on Stink's to do list.

Bonni's nerves were on edge as her and the kids were chauffeured to the airport to meet Stink. It had been nearly two months since she'd laid eyes on him. Although Bonni still loved him dearly, there was no way she'd solicit his forgiveness again.

"Mommy, does daddy know we're coming?" Rahsaanique asked, jarring her from her thoughts."

Uh, I would think so, Nique-Nique," she replied.

"Mom, is dad going to come stay with us at 'Casa Rojo'?" Tayvia inquired.

Bonni thought for a moment, then said," Tayvia, I don't think any of us will be staying at 'Casa Rojo.'"

Instantly, Tayvia and Rahsaanique's expression turned gloomy at the mentioning of them not returning to the lavish estate.

Bonni averted her attention from her daughters' sad faces and looked out of the window.

As they pulled into the airport, Bonni noticed that the other two Mercedes that were present on the day that they saw them off were parked beside one another. Once Miguel joined the convoy of Mercedes Benzes, he exited the car and joined the two Latin giants who just exited their cars.

Silently, Bonni looked on until she noticed them pointing upward. Getting the kids' attention, she announced, "I think they're getting ready to land."

"Mommy, we wanna see. Please. Pretty please," Rahsaanique begged.

Without a second thought, Bonni grabbed the door handle, then said, "Come on, let's see."

Quickly, they all exited the car and turned their gazes to where the men pointed in the sky.

Bonni could see the excitement on her daughters' faces as they followed the small plane from the sky, until it landed on the tarmac and taxied toward them.

Once the plane came to a complete stop, the two giants and Miguel rushed the plane as the steps were being lowered.

Bonnie eyed the passengers as they exited the plane one by one. As each person descended down the short steps, she held her breath in anticipation of the next person being Stink. However, once Melody, Carmella and Jose had exited the plane and she still hadn't seen Stink, Bonni's heart began to pound in her chest.Suddenly, Jose made his way toward her and the kids with a broad smile etched into his tanned features.

The closer he got, the more apprehensive she became of the message that he would bear.

Pepe steered his Denali behind Chico and Manny's matching Lexus', which were tailing Jo-Jo's DTS Cadillac. They were en route to one of the hottest clubs in the Tidewater area: The Mirage.

Ever since Bear's murder and the subsequent murders of Veronica and her daughter where plastered across the news, it had been a nonstop party for Pepe and his crew.

As they pulled into the packed parking lot of the Mirage nightclub, all eyes immediately turned to the line of luxury automobiles equipped with the shiniest and largest rims available.

As always, Pepe thrived on the attention he and his crew received. Drawing even more attention, Pepe turned the volume up on his system a few notches and allowed the growlin of 'DMX' to do the talking for him.

Once they'd parked and were preparing to enter the club, Pepe's phone began to vibrate. Noticing the strange number that had been calling him all day, Pepe decided to see whose voice was behind the strange number.

"Hola! Depate de quien? [Hello! Who's speaking]" Pepe answered.

"Hermanito! It's me, Carmella!"

"Damn Carm, I didn't know this was your number calling me all day," he offered apologetically, then asked, "where are you?"

"In Virginia, estupido, [stupid]" she snapped sarcastically.

"Oh, aight, but where's Stink?" Pepe inquired. Instantly, there was a tense silence on the other end.

Pearl and Milk were canvassing the streets like hunters. Each was strapped with an AK417 assault riffle loaded to the gills. They had driven every block numerous times, yet they hadn't seen anything that would arouse their murderous intentions. However, the drug activity on Shell road was beyond believable. This was inconsistent with the otherwise mediocre traffic that frequented the strip.

"You believe this shit, my nucca?" Milk asked eyeing the drug fiends incredulously.

"Naw, my nucca. But it's got to be something. I bet them suckers around here somewhere," Pearl stated, then added, "And we gonna find out tonight."

Stink sat on the plane and watched the interaction between Bonni and Jose through scrutinizing eyes. (His decision to make such a brash move could possibly backfire in his face.) However, once he saw how Tayvia and Rahsaanique's faces lit up, he felt his decision was a good one.

Once the kids sprinted in the direction of the plane, Stink made his way towards them.

"Daddy! Daddy!" Tayvia and Rahsaanique yelled in unison once they caught glimpse of him.

Kneeling to accept their embraces, Stink braced himself as they bolted towards him.

Once they reached him, they began to plant kisses all over his face.

"Daddy, we missed you!" Rahsaanique whined.

"Yeah, we were worried about you," Tayvia added.

As the kids and Stink continued to enjoy his homecoming, Bonnie watched on through sentimental eyes.

Abruptly, Stink looked up into her eyes. Instantly he noticed the physical changes in Bonnie. It was as if she'd turned the clock back on her decline. No longer did she look her age, she looked years younger. Her body's contour now held the curvaceous features that once made Stink's blood boil.

Standing from his kneeling position, he held his arms wide, and said, "Damn, can I get a hug?"

Bonnie stepped into his arms and allowed her body to mesh into his once familiar embrace.

Reluctantly releasing her body from his grasp, Stink turned to the kids, and asked," So where do ya'll want to go?"

Almost simultaneous, Tayvia yelled, "Walt Disney!" And Rahsaanique yelled, "Disney Land!"

Stink knew that both amusement parks were on opposite coast, nonetheless, he blurted, "We'll go to both of them, then!"

This garnered a round of 'Yippees' from the girls as they converged on his legs.

As he balanced himself while the girls hung on, Bonnie eyed the scene through tear filled eyes. At that moment, she was as happy as she'd been in years.

Carmella sat inside the confines of Casa Rojo and patiently waited for her brother to arrive. It had been over two months since she'd seen Pepe and she desperately wanted to see him.Carmella looked over to a sleeping Melody and instinctively thought back to the conversation they'd shared earlier that evening.

As they were leaving the airport, Carmella noticed the gloomy look that Melody sported, causing her to ask, "Melody, what's wrong?"

"Um…nothing," she replied in a startled manner.

"Come on, Mel. You should know me by now. I know when something is bothering you," Carmella stated eyeing Melody accusingly.

Turning her head from Carmella's piercing gaze, Melody mumbled, "I miss him already."

Sucking her teeth impatiently, Carmella said, "Melody, poppi is taking his kids on a vacation. He'll be back. Damn!"

Looking to Carmella evilly, Melody asked, "What about Bonni, Carmella? Did you not see her board the plane also?"

"Yeah, I saw her. And?"

"Carmella, maybe you don't understand. But I went through years of turmoil, while Stink went home to Bonni every night. I played second fiddle for years, and once she turned her back on him while he was locked up, I became number one," Melody explained on the verge of tears.

"So what's the problem?" Carmella inquired incredulously.

"Carmella, they're still in love. I can see it in their eyes," Melody concluded. Moving in close, Carmella huskily purred, "You know what they say. Love who loves you." Then she hungrily covered Melody's mouth with her own.

Just as Pearl and Milk had given up their search and were headed home, they came to a stop light near the Newport News/Hampton line. Sitting at the red light, patiently waiting for it to change, Pearl eyed the convoy of luxury vehicles that approached from the opposite direction, closely.

When the light changed, Pearl intently tried to identify the driver's of each vehicle. Every one of the cars were equipped with limousine tint, except for one of the black Lexus coupes.

As Pearl locked eyes with the driver, he quickly blurted, "Turn around! Follow them, fuck nuccas!"

For some odd reason, Pepe snatched the keys to Manny's Lexus once they'd exited the club. In all actuality, it didn't matter who drove what in their crew, all eyes were on them regardless. Pepe hopped in the Lexus and accelerated through the lot, closely followed by the rest of his crew.

As they exited the interstate in Hampton, Pepe quickly remembered his planned meeting with his sister. Once the stoplight turned green, Pepe pulled through the intersection, and then abruptly made a U-turn headed back toward the interstate.

Pulling his cell phone from his hip, he dialed Manny's number. "Yo fam! I'm-a go holla at Carma, I'm-a meet y'all at the spot later," he announced, then ended the call without waiting on a response. Once he had secured his phone on his waist, he stomped down on the accelerator urging the powerful V-8 to slice through the night air.

Stink sat in the hotel suite, located within a rock's throw of Disney World. After enjoying a much needed nap, he was completely rejuvenated. The problem was that it was nearly nine o'clock in the evening. Bonni and the kids had been out all afternoon and were due back any minute.

As Stink lounged on the couch in the living room area, watching the strange newscast, the front door opened.

In walked the kids carrying large stuffed animals, followed by Bonni.

"Hey, dad!" The girls yelled in unison, as they ran towards him.

"Hey!" Stink replied full of energy, as they hung around his neck. Turning his attention to Bonni, he said, "I know you're tired. Go ahead and get yourself some rest. I've got these two."

Bonni stepped over to the couch and planted a quick peck on both Rahsaanique and Tayvia's foreheads. Just as she turned to leave, she locked eyes with Stink. The short amount of time that they'd been tuned to one another seemed to be an eternity, until Bonni peeled her eyes from him and sauntered off.

Milk and Pearl stayed close to the Lexus coupe without arousing any suspicion to the driver. The high speed that the Lexus was traveling was nothing compared to what the Impala SS was capable of doing. Their entire plan of following the Lexus had nearly been blotched when the driver had abruptly made a U-turn. Had it not been for Milk's expert driving, their cover would have been blown.

"My nucca, you sho' that's one of them wetbacks?" Milk asked as he pushed the Chevy though the late night traffic.

"Nucca, what's my name?" Pearl questioned in a matter of fact tone.

"Aight. I'd hate it if we murdered the wrong square," Milk replied sarcastically.

Before Pearl could respond, the tail lights of the Lexus lit up as the brake lights blared to life.

Abruptly, Milk hit his brakes too. Nonetheless, it was too late once he saw why the Lexus' driver had hit his brakes. As the bright blue lights emerged from the side of the interstate and tracked the Impala down, Milk pulled over onto the shoulder.

"Damn!" Pearl exclaimed as the Lexus' tail lights disappeared into the night.

"Get up, Scott!" A Correction's Officer. yelled in the doorway.

Attempting to focus his eyes past the blinding light of the officer's flash light, Cross slowly rose from his sleeping position. "What's up, man?" he asked groggily.

"I said, get up!" The C.O. repeated, then added, "And get dressed! You're being transferred! Now let's go!" The officer concluded forcefully.

Cross knew exactly what was going on. He was being transferred in the middle of the night so he wouldn't be able to try anything funny. Little did they know, any funny business coming from him was surely to come after he learned his fate in court. However, no matter how early they got up for him, they could never sleep. The moment they did was the moment he'd make them pay.

"Scott! This is your last time! Let's go!" The C.O. yelled.

"Yo, Shy! I'm out, son. Hold me down, B," Cross said to his cellmate, then exited the cell.

Chapter Fifteen

Trina could feel the warmth of Stinks hand caress her body. She instinctively snuggled up to him making her soft ass press against his piercing bulge. His hands moved up to her breast and began to knead her erect nipples, causing a slight gasp to escape her mouth.

This seemed to encourage his busy hands as they traveled down to her moist center. As he pushed one finger inside of her, she eased her legs further apart giving him more access.

"Ummm, yes....ooh..," Trina moaned.

In his husky voice, Stink whispered into her ear, "Baby, you're sooo wet."

Put it in! please put it in!" she begged.

Quickly, he pushed her already raised leg higher and aimed the head of his shaft at her opening. He rubbed the head of his dick within her fold, completely coating it with her juices.

"Please! I can't wait any longer!" She exclaimed forcefully while gritting her teeth,

Unable to wait any longer himself, he pushed his entire girth into her depths. "Oh shit, I miss this pussy," he stated pumping in and out of her.

"I miss you too, daddy! Ooh, yes! Get yo pussy! Please," she yelled throwing her ass in motion with him.

"Baby, I ain't had none of his good pussy in so long. I'm ...about to nut!" he exclaimed.

Trina continued to throw her ass as she felt her own orgasm building from her depths." Come on daddy! Cum in your pussy, Stink! This pussy has always been yours!" She announced as spasms racked her body.

Suddenly the movement behind her ceased. As she opened her mouth to say something, her eyes shot open. There, sitting on the nightstand was a picture of her, Pearl and Rah-Rah.

"Bitch, what did you say!" Pearl inquired full of rage.

Trina couldn't say a word as a tense silence engulfed the sex smelling room.

Trina's eyes were clamped tight when the first blow rained down on her numb body. She laid there and took every punch Pearl launched, until she was asleep, once again. It was the worst time to have a wet dream about Stink.

Once the kids were tucked away, Stink and Bonni lounged in the living room area of the suite watching a movie. The entire time that they'd been there, Stink slept on the couch, while Bonni took the bed. However, tonight the atmosphere seemed somewhat relaxing.

"Rahsaan, do you want something to drink?" Bonni asked standing.

Turning his attention from the television, he looked to Bonni, and said, "Yeah. Get me some juice or something."

Bonni spun on her heels and began to walk off in the direction of the kitchenette.

For some reason, Stink was unable to avert his attention from her shapely backside that teasingly peep from underneath the T-shirt that she wore. It had been years since he'd sampled any of her lovin' and at that moment he felt himself being physically drawn to her.

Turning, Bonni said," No ice, right?" Catching him in the act of ogling her.

With his mouth gaped open and a look of lust lingering in his eyes, he stammered, "Uh….yea …. Yeah." Quickly averting his attention back to the television.

Bonni smiled broadly as a familiar tingling shot through her body and her face turned scarlet.

It was no secret that she still loved him dearly and since she wasn't able to have him, those feelings were magnified tenfold.

As Bonni made her way back to the living room area, she decided to throw caution to the wind and get her man back. Instantly, putting a little sensuality into her stop, she walked over to Stink and handed him the glass of juice. Instead of taking her seat on the tiny couch opposite Stink, she flopped down beside him.

This brought a slight glance from him, but he didn't say a word. As they both became engrossed in the movie, Bonni was purposely easing her T-shirt up her legs, revealing creamy thighs.

Out of the corner of his eye, he could see Bonni's beautifully toned thighs and her pretty pedicured toes, sporting blood red nail polish. As much as he didn't want to, there was something brewing inside of him and he didn't feel he could control it.

Abruptly turning to Bonni, Stink looked deep into her sincere eyes and asked, "Bonni, why did you leave me? Just answer that one question for me."

Bonni held his piercing glare for what seemed like eons, then took a deep breath and said, "Rahsaan, I never truly left you. I just…."

Melody and Carmella sat in the backseat of Pepe's Denali as Manny steered it through the gates of Stink's house. It had been nearly three months since they'd been there.

Once Manny brought the SUV to a stop, a famished looking Fire and Ice surrounded the truck, gritting their teeth. The food dispensers that where located inside their cage had gone dry weeks before. Up until then they'd been they'd been surviving on any live animal that attempted to make the ground a rest stop.

Initially, both Melody and Carmella were afraid to approach the beast. However, Melody, being the brave one rolled the window down and attempted to sweet talk the animals. "Fire, Ice! Come here boys! Come here! Yeah, that's right!" She sang, noticing the dogs tails began to wag joyously. Cautiously, she exited the truck and made it to the house without incident. The first thing she did was drag a large bag of dog food to their dog kennel and allow them to tear into it. Once she made it back to the front, Carmella, Pepe, and Manny all still sat inside the truck.

Pepe stuck his head out of the window, and asked, "You pet them fucking perros [Dogs]?"

Melody nodded her head then motioned for them to follow her.

Pearl continued to rain blow after blow upon Trina's lifeless body. When he finally came to his senses, Trina's face looked like a bloodied disfigured mess.

Abruptly, he stopped hitting her and began to shake her, as if he was attempting to awaken her from a light slumber. It wasn't until Pearl began to violently shake her that he realized what he had done.

In the midst of his rage, he had beaten Trina to death. There was not an inkling of life in her battered body.

Pearl quickly jumped up and called Milk. "My nucca, I 'dan fucked up! I need you to come out to my crib, ASAP!" He instructed on the verge of panicking.

"What'chu mean, my nucca? Tell me wasup," Milk replied cautiously.

"Just come on!" Pearl blurted then hung up.

As he looked around the room in dread, he began to wrap Trina's body up in the blood soaked bed linen. Once her body was securely wrapped in the sheets and blankets, he went downstairs to the kitchen and grabbed garbage bags. When he re-entered the bedroom, the smell of death invaded his senses. At that moment, the raw irony of the situation hit him as tears began to pour from his eyes.

"Rahsaan, I never truly left you. I just… didn't want to go through the pain of seeing you caged and not being able to do a thing about it. I didn't leave you to be with someone else. I didn't leave you because I didn't love you anymore, I simply removed myself from the pain…. It hurt…to …. Not be able …. To be with you," Bonni concluded through tears.

"But why didn't you just tell me, huh?" Stink asked reaching out to hold her chin up to face him.

"I….I did, Rahsaan. I did," she replied with tear filled eyes.

"What you mean?   You never told me that –"

Bonni abruptly cut him off by placing her forefinger to his lips, then she said, "Rahsaan, do you remember me telling you that 'without you I don't think I could make it'?"

Stink nodded his head.

"What else was I to say, Rahsaan? How much clearer could I have been?" She inquired rhetorically, then added, "But I know now in my heart that I made the wrong decision. No matter how much I hurt, I should've stuck it out, and I…am…sorry," she concluded as the sobs racked her body.

The sincerity of her words crashed into Stink like a ton of bricks. Reaching down for her, he pulled her limp frame into his arms and began to kiss her salty, tear stained cheeks.

Once Bonni felt his lips on her face, she pulled away and looked into his eyes. The veil in his eyes that had kept his heart from her was now gone. Leaning in close, Bonni sensuously placed her lips to his as the once familiar feelings in each of them came to life.

"Rahsaan, I missed you sooo much," she whispered sexily as Stink caressed dangerously close to her womanhood.

"I'm home, baby. Daddy's home," he announced huskily.

Bonni reached for his shaft through his shorts and began to stroke him. It had been years since she'd felt him and she instantly wanted to get a closer look at it. Suddenly, she pulled his manhood from its confines and placed it into her warm mouth.

"Hmmm…Hmm…oh…oh shit!" Stink moaned as he threw his head back in ecstasy.

Bonni continued to work her mouth as if her life depended on it.

Just when Stink couldn't take the sensations any longer and he felt himself on the verge of ejaculating, he heard, "Daddy, where's mommy?" Rahsaanique asked sleepily.

Instantly, Bonni froze with him in her mouth.

"Um, mommy…is, um….right here…um, sleep, baby," Stink stammered.

"Oh. I thought I heard somebody crying," she said looking at her mother's head buried in her father's lap.

"Oh, nah baby. That was…um…the TV," he offered, then added, "Why don't you go on back to bed and I'll come and tuck you in. OK."

"O.K." she replied, then waddled off toward the bedroom. Before she disappeared through the door, she turned around, and asked, "Dad, does this mean that you and mommy are back girlfriend and boyfriend?"

Stink's mouth nearly hit the floor, as he managed to say, "We'll talk about it tomorrow. OK."

After Trina's body was conveniently dumped into the dismal swamp, he focused on finding the people responsible for his cousin's death. However, before he fully directed his full interest on annihilating the crew of Domicans, he needed to insure that Trina's untimely death wouldn't come to haunt him.

The first action he took was to call Trina's mother and explain to her that Trina had apparently run off with some man, leaving her son behind. It was a hard pill to swallow as a mother, yet when Pearl expressed his interest in keeping Rah-Rah, her mother bought it, hook, line, and sinker.

His next order of business was to sit Rah-Rah down and explain the situation to him, man to man.

Pearl could see the hurt in the young boy's eyes, yet somehow he sucked it up and didn't shed a tear. Once Pearl saw that, he knew he had a trooper.

The final thing he did was allow Lashonda aka Mercedes to move in. He knew that the move was risqué, but the violent sexual acts that she'd now allow him to bestow upon her seemed to be therapeutic to his being.

Once everything was set, Pearl concentrated on the task at hand.

Cross was transferred to Rikers Island without incident and assigned to housing unit C-74.

Though tens of thousands visited the infamous prison, yet only a fraction of that number would actually survive without some inhumane act happening to them while they were there.

Cross was at the top of the small fraction. He had jailing down to a science. His demeanor depicted that he wasn't to be tested.

After being in the cell block for no more than 15 minutes, Cross had pinpointed the cell block bullies, bitches, and murderers. Only one of these groups was Cross worried about and due to him being one himself, he knew how to deal with murderers.

In his customary gait, he accosted what looked to be the biggest, boldest bully in the cell block, and said, "Yo, B, I'm-a use one of these jacks next, aight."

The big man turned his demented glare in Cross' direction, then opened his mouth to cast some type of belittling remark.

Without warning, Cross snapped a crisp left jab into the man's jaw, then instantly followed with a precisely launched right hand that landed directly on the man's chin, sending him straight to the floor in delirium.

Meanwhile, each category of men looked on with different expressions. The bullies eyed the spectacle in fear while the bitches reflected a look of awe, and finally the murders looked on with respect written across their faces.

Cross casually stepped over the unconscious man, walked over to the telephones on the wall and dialed his mother's phone number.

"Hello," his mother answered on the first ring.

"Mom, I'm here," he announced solemnly.

"Oh goody, Georgi," she replied in a festive manner, then added, "I'm going to get your sister to bring me out there this weekend."

"Aight that's cool, but don't forget to bring me some sneakers and clothes. Oh, and have ou heard from Stink?" He concluded inquisitively.

"No, I'm afraid I haven't. But do you want to call that girlfriend of his? She seems to know what's going on with him," she offered.

"Nah. He'll come around when he's ready. I know him," Cross replied then hung up. Nonchalantly, he walked through the spectacle that was taking place around the big bully and into his cell.

Against Jose's wishes, Carmella and Melody decided to stay at Stink's house instead of Casa Rojo. They felt that Pepe, Chico, and Manny were capable of protecting them from any impending danger, so they packed up their things and moved them into Stink's house.

Carmella was proud of the accomplishments that her younger brother had made in such a short time. It seemed as if he had taken over Stink's operations and wealth in one smooth motion. She had begun to have aspirations of life without Stink. Of course, she still had Melody and her glorious body as her playground.

Carmella had already made the decision to become more active in her brother's operations and subsequently build her own empire.

Turning to Melody, she announced, "Mami, we're about to take a trip to Nueva York [New York]."

As Stink, Bonni, and the kids boarded Jose's Lear jet at Orlando International Airport, Stink was sure that two things were destined to happen once they landed in sunny California. One was that he'd be sure to get a suite with two private bedrooms, and two was that he and Bonni consummate their new found union.

While Bonni ushered the kids into their seats, Stink was eyeing her hourglass figure from the back. He licked his lips lustfully as his mind previewed some of the lewd acts they would be experiencing in just a few hours.

As he passed her, bending over buckling Rahsaanique's seatbelt, he smoothly rubbed between her thighs, instantly feeling the fiery mound of her womanhood.

Bonni slowly turned and offered him a salacious smile, then said, "Keep playing boy and we won't make it to California."

Pearl and Milk camped outside of the small house on Shell road, eyeing the constant traffic come and go. What was intriguing to the pair was that every one of the people that made a quick stop at the house seemed to be hustlers, not smokers.

"Do you believe this shit, my nucca?" Milk asked incredulously.

"Nah, my nucca. I really don't," Pearl replied indifferently.

"So how you want to handle these green ass nuccas?" Milk asked.

"I don't know yet. But believe me, we gonna handle these bitch ass nuccas," Pearl concluded eyeing the line of luxury cars that came and went at the residence.

Melody calmly navigated the 330i BMW through the midnight traffic on the New Jersey Turnpike. Unbeknownst to her, there were 30 Kilos of crack cocaine hidden in a stash compartment located in the dash board of the car. Carmella sat poised in the passenger seat enjoying her new found status as a high level drug courier. Pepe had appointed her to make all the runs to New York for him. In return, he compensated his sister exceptionally.

In just two runs, Carmella had bought the car they were driving and managed to take herself and Melody on a mini shopping spree, walking away with two three quarter length Chinchillas in the process.

Looking over to Melody, Carmella said, "Mami, Im-a take a nap. Wake me up if you get tired, and watch your speed. I ain't ready for no tickets on my shit already," she stated in a joking manner, then laid back.

Melody turned the 'Lauryn Hill' CD up and concentrated on the road ahead.

After maybe an hour, Melody glanced over to an angelic looking Carmella deep asleep. Once she refocused back onto the highway, she was approaching the toll at the Delaware Memorial Bridge. She broke her speed down to a snails pace, then paid the toll and continued onto the bridge without disturbing Carmella from her sleep.

As she descended the high bridge, the car seemed to be picking up speed at a rapid pace. Once she cleared the bridge, she quickly glanced down at the speedometer and noticed she was going twenty miles per hour over the posted 55. She instinctively pressed the brakes and looked into the rearview mirror. Breathing a sigh of relief, she relaxed and continued on her way. Suddenly a set of blinding headlights appeared dangerously close to the bumper of the BMW, causing Melody to look into the rearview mirror suspiciously. However, once the blue lights of the Delaware State Troopers car came to life, she banged her fist against the steering wheel, and yelled, "Shit!"

This instantly woke Carmella from her slumber as she leaned up. "What? What's wrong?" she asked yawning.

"Looks like I'm going to be the first person to get a

ticket in your car," Melody concluded dryly.

"What!" Carmella exclaimed in a distraught tone.

Pulling the car onto the shoulder, Melody repeated, "I'm getting a ticket, Carma."

"Oh Shit! Melody just be cool! Act like everything's cool! A Dios Mio! [Oh my God]" Carmella blurted in a panic.

Melody shot Carmella a quick glance, then asked," What is wrong with you, Carmella? It's only a ticket for speeding. You act like we murdered somebody."

Looking back nervously, Carmella advised, "Just be cool, Melody."

After checking into the five star hotel suite, equipped with two private bedrooms, Stink went into his and Bonni's room and laid across the bed. In the last week, he'd flown from Santo Domingo to Florida and now California. His body was apparently experiencing its first bout with jet lag.

The kids and Bonni were seemingly unaffected by the plane ride, as they went straight to the amusement park as soon as they were unpacked.

Meanwhile, Stink tried to catch up on his rest. Before he drifted off to sleep, he desperately wanted to call home to see what was going on. Yet, the promise that he'd given Jose replayed in his mind.

As sleep engulfed him, he knew he had to get back home soon. There was some unseen force pulling at him, and only God knew.

Dressed in all black, Pearl and Milk eyed the house through the slits. They had been watching the residence for 48 hours straights. At that very moment, every person affiliated with Pepe's crew was inside the house. If Pearl and Milk were going to move, it was now or never.

Looking to his life long partner, Pearl pulled the ski mask over his face, hoisted this AK-47 onto his shoulder, then said," You ready to do this, my nucca."

Returning his partners glare, he replied, "I'm ready."

Pepe had been dialing Carmella's cell phone for the last twelve hours, and there was still no response. He was past worried as he paced back and forth inside the small house.

"Pepe, did you call your madre? [Mother]" Chico asked.

"Like veinte [twenty] times!" He snapped.

Jo-Jo casually entered the room, and said, "Man, if we don't get no coke soon, them motherfuckers gonna start killing each other out there."

"Fuck the muthafuckas! If I don't hear from my hermana [sister] in the next thirty minutes, Imma murder them muthafuckas myself!" Pepe announced furiously, as Clarissa rubbed his shoulders soothingly.

"Ms. Bonillia, you said that you just bought the automobile. Is that correct?" The dapperly dressed DEA agent asked.

Raising her head from the table, Carmella replied, "I've already told you that a hundred fucking times! Look, can I just use the phone?"

Calmly, the agent said, "Yes, of course. Ms. Bonillia. But first please help us figure out how an automobile in YOUR name in which you were a passenger was transporting over 60lbs of CRACK cocaine?"

"I told ya'll I don't know anything about no drugs!" She blurted.

"But you did purchase the automobile with 33 thousand dollars cash?" The agent slid in slyly.

"Yeas- "Carmella replied unthinkingly.

Without any further questions, the agent exited the room with a smirk on his face. Now it was time to break the other girl down.

"Hello Ms. Jordan," The agent asked, jarring Melody from her uncomfortable slumber." I'm sorry to have kept you waiting, but we just finished taking Ms. Carmella Bonilla's statement," he stated with a twinge of sarcasm. Giving Melody a minute to drag herself to the small table in the middle of the room, the agent pulled out a folder and threw it onto the table. "Now, Ms. Jordan, Ms. Bonillia has already informed us that you knew the crack cocaine was inside of the car. All-"

"I don't know what you're talking about!" Melody blurted, abruptly cutting the agent off.

Leaning in close, the agent said, "All you have to do is tell us who the drugs were going to and you're free."

Melody took a deep breath, then replied, "Sir, I don't know what you are talking bout, but I would really appreciate it if you bring me a phone so I can call my lawyer."

Once the agent heard the word 'lawyer', he knew his line of questioning had reached it's end. "O.K. Ms. Jordan, have it your way," he stated in a defeated tone, then exited.

Stink lay on the bed and listened to the sounds of Bonni inside the adjacent bathroom. Once the water stopped running, he turned onto his stomach and faked a light snore. He could feel Bonni's presence hovering over him, yet he continued to act as if he was asleep. When the bed began to move, from Bonni easing under the covers, a smile spread across Stink's face as he lifted his head.

"Oh, you was just gonna let me sleep, huh?" Stink asked.

"I…I thought… you was tired or something," Bonni replied.

Reaching over to her, Stink pulled her into his arms and inhaled deeply. Bonni's body held such a sweet natural scent that it seemed to be intoxicating. Looking into her eyes with a lascivious smile on his face, he asked, "Are the kids asleep?"

Nodding her head affirmatively, she grabbed the back of his head and pulled his mouth into hers hungrily.

As their tongues wrestled for position, Bonni maneuvered herself on top of Stink, then looked down at him as a hunter does when it has captured its prey. Rubbing her palms from his chest to his nether region, she grinned in a passionate manner. "Rahsaan, you don't know how much I've missed you," she stated sexily as her hands ventured inside of his boxers, causing a slight gasp to escape his lips.

"Baby, your hands cold!" he gasped.

"Don't worry, you'll warm them up," she said, then pulled the nighty over her head, revealing her perfect 36 C's with a large areola surrounding her erect nipples.

Stink wasted no time attacking her breast. He sucked and nibbled on her nipples as if he was a baby.

"Rah….saan, I love the way your mouth feels on my nipples," Bonni hissed, rubbing the back of his head encouragingly.

Stink went back and forth tantalizing each breast. He could feel the warmth from her vagina through the thin fabric of her panties. Suddenly Stink began to struggle to release his rock hard manhood from its confines.

Bonni quickly assisted with releasing his shaft and discarding her panties in what seemed like one motion.

Once their bodies reunited after the brief separation, the heat of the bodies seemed to be scorching.

As Bonni leaned down and placed a toe curling kiss on his lips, Stink could feel the juices from her center oozing onto his shaft.

Unable to hold out any longer, Stink reached down and aimed his defiantly hard dick at the entrance of her opening. Teasing her, he allowed the head to rest just inside the folds of her lips. He could feel the hot juices run from her pussy onto his dick.

Biting down on her bottom lip, she whimpered, "Please daddy! Please fuck me!"

In a voice that caused her insides to melt, Stink said, "Baby, I miss you and I love you." With that said, he drove his stiff dick into her quivering pussy.

"Oh! Oh, yess! Mmmm, daddy! Give it to me!" Bonni moaned as she rode his shaft into oblivion.

Stink could feel every crevice of her insides as she bounced on his manhood. Looking deep into her eyes, he could see trace's of tears rolling down her cheeks. Instinctively, he grabbed her on both sides of her face and pulled her to him. As he planted soft kisses on her tear stained cheeks, he could feel her body abruptly becoming stiff.

"Rah...Oh, my ....God! I'm cum....ming!" She gasped enjoying the spasms of an intense orgasm.

Stink could instantly feel her juices escape her pussy and run down between his thighs. Once her orgasm subsided, Stink said, "Turn over, baby."

Just as Pepe's cell phone rang, there was a knock at the door. Manny eased over to the door and peaked through the peep hole. Turning back, he looked to Jo-Jo and said, "Its some of your people."

Giving a sigh of frustration, Jo-Jo hopped up and casually sauntered over to the door. Releasing the chain and turning the lock, Jo-Jo snatched the door open and opened his mouth to speak but was halted by the long barrel on the assault riffle.

Without warning, Milk opened fire on the unsuspecting man, instantly turning the domicile into a bloody murder scene. Quickly entering the house closely followed by Pearl, Milk opened fire on every live target with the fully automatic riffle. Pearl followed suit and squeezed off numerous shots at the helpless victims inside the house. Moving stealth like through every room, Pearl fired at empty beds and closets, just in case.

Milk's bullets had literally disfigured all of the bodies in the front room, making it hard to identify which body belonged to whom.

However, once the two men exited, there wasn't a living soul inside of the house, just the faint sound of a vibrating cell phone inside one of their victim's pants' pockets.

Carmella held the phone to her ear, as Pepe's voice mail picked up. Quickly hanging up, she dialed the number again only to be met with the same outcome.

She repeated this act until the agent stepped over to her, and said, "Ms. Bonillia, I'm giving you one more attempt to call whomever it is you're trying to call, then it's back to the bullpen for you. So you'd better make it good."

As Carmella's face depicted the frustration that she was experiencing at that moment, she decided to call her mother and allow her to contact Pepe.

Unbeknownst to Carmella, there wasn't a person in the world who would be able to contact Pepe, for Pepe was dead.

As the morning sun beamed rays through the partially cracked curtains, Stink and Bonni laid tangled in the sheets. Their bout of love making left them both in a euphoric state, which ultimately placed them into a comatose condition.

Suddenly, the loud ringing of the bedside phone jolted them from their sleep.

Stink abruptly snatched the receiver up. "Hello."

"My friend, how has your vacation been?" Jose inquired cheerfully on the other end.

Somewhat surprised, Stink replied, "Damn, Jose. How'd you find me?"

Chuckling, Jose said," Oye Stink, you're my friend. I not only keep up with my friends, but also my friends' friends. Which is part of the reason I'm disturbing you." Allowing his words to soak into Stink's sleep induced hazed mind, he continued, "It seems as if your constituents have gotten into something in Virginia. However, I think it would be best if you would come to New York first, then you could travel abroad from there and take care of your affairs," he advised.

Stink held the phone in silence, wanting to ask a million questions; yet, he knew that enough had been said. Releasing an exasperated sigh, he said," I'm on my way, Jose." He then hung up.

Turning toward a visibly worried Bonni, Stink said, "Get the kids together. We're going home."

Cross sat opposite his mother and sister, in a crispy gray jumpsuit, and a pair of fresh, white on white Air Force 1's. They had been sharing a pleasant visit, reminiscing about some of their happier family memories, when Cross eased a piece of paper from the lining of his jumpsuit. Smoothly leaning toward his mother, he slid the paper into her hand, then said, "Ma, if anything were to happen to me, would you please make sure Stink gets this."

Mrs. Scott shot Cross an incredulous glare, and said, "Georgi, don't talk crazy, you hear? God has seen you through this much and he'll see you to the end."

Cross smiled at his mother's blinding religious faith, then replied, "Yeah Ma, I know. But just in case God's trying to get a look at me up close and personal, make sure Stink gets that." He concluded receiving a short round of laughter from his sister and mother.

Melody lay curled up in the cold cell wondering how she'd allowed herself to get caught up in such a tangling situation. All of the years that she'd been with Stink, not once did he ever ask her to place herself in such a compromising position.

Melody may have acted 'dingy' role, yet, in all actuality there was nothing slow about her. She knew that Carmella was transporting drugs for Pepe, she just hoped if something like what they were experiencing did happen, Carmella would be woman enough to admit her part. Nevertheless, the longer she laid there, the more it became evident that Carmella had no intentions of fessing up.

Quickly coming to her feet, Melody stepped to the big door with the tiny window and began to violently bang on the door. She knew exactly who to call, and they would know exactly what to do.

Pearl laid back and allowed Mercedes to work his shaft with her mouth.   Once again, he was feeling invincible. The more vocal Mercedes' mouth became, the further Pearl delved into his thoughts. He had thought past the murders, he was now thinking about business.

From the looks of things, the New Yorkers had the long strip in Hampton doing good numbers. Pearl knew he would have to wait until the investigation from the quadruple murder subsided, then he would seize the opportunity.

Gripping the back of Mercedes' head, Pearl violently forced his manhood down her throat, causing her to gag. Ignoring her silent pleas, he ground her face into his pelvis, as his seed escaped his loins and shot down her throat." Ahh…yea….yeah! Swallow that shit, bitch! Drink it!" He exclaimed in a vulgar tone.

Chapter Seventeen

As the sleek Lear jet descended the puffy white clouds, New York's crowded skyline could instantly be seen. Stink eyed the buildings in deep contemplation. He knew that it was something of extreme importance for Jose to call him. Once the planes tires skidded on the tarmac, Stink's immediately prepared himself for any possible situation. In comparison to some of the atrocious things life had thrown his way, Stink was prepared for just about anything.

"Baby, do you know where we're going to be staying, or how long?" Bonni asked snapping him out of his thoughts.

"Huh?" Stink asked unaware of what Bonni had said.

"I said, do you know how long we're going to be here, or where we're staying, because I've got to at least still call the girls school and -." Bonni began before Stink cut her off.

"Don't worry about nothing. I've got everything," Stink announced with a hint of finality in his voice.

Quickly shooting him an askance glance, Bonni chose to suppress any further comment.

As the plane taxied toward a long black limousine, Stink could only smile. He and Jose's relationship had surpassed the realms of business; it was now personal.

Melody held the phone patiently as she was put through a series of questions, before being put on hold.

Suddenly, a familiar voice came onto the line. "Hello."

"Jose, this is Melody. I'm in Wilmington Delaware. Apparently there was some..." She went on explaining the situation to Jose as best as she could.

The entire conversation, Jose held the phone in silence. Once Melody was finished, he said, "A lawyer will be to see you this afternoon. However, do not attempt to reach me again, tu comprende? [you understand]" Without waiting on a response, Jose hung the phone up.

Once Bonni and the kids were settled into Jose's newly acquired three bedroom apartment, overlooking the Hudson on the Jersey side, Stink was whisked off in the limousine to an unknown location.

As they traveled across the George Washington Bridge, Stink tuned the radio to HOT 97 and increased the volume as the disc jockey played a mix of DMX and the LOX.

Stink bobbed his head to the music as that familiar feeling overcame him whenever he entered the confines of NYC. To his surprise, the driver hopped onto the West Side Hwy., then quickly exited on 159th Street. Once they stopped at the light at 159th and Broadway, Stink eyed the fast paced traffic of Washington Heights through the tinted limousine windows.

A short ride up the block, and the driver pulled in front of one of Jose's buildings on 155th. It had been years since Stink had been to the residence.

He casually hopped out and made his way to the entrance. Pressing the buzzer as if he was a customer coming to buy drugs, the door quickly popped open.

Trekking the two flights of stairs, Stink approached the familiar door and raised his arm to knock, when the door was abruptly snatched open.

Standing there with a broad smile, Miziyah held his arms wide. "Stink, Como estas? [How are you?]" He said pulling Stink into a brotherly embrace.

Pearl pulled the yellow Navigator in front of the W&W market on Shell road, as all the hustlers milling about eyed the bright SUV in awe. Pearl and Milk exited the truck with their crispy new outfits, and their blinging jewels, garnering all attention.

One of the hustlers in particular eyed the pair in admiration as they passed. Quickly following them into the store, he prepared to approach the two.

This game of subliminal seduction was nothing new to Pearl or Milk. They were professionals at this act, and at that moment it was working to perfection. Eyeing the young man as he walked up, Pearl could only inwardly smile.

"Wazup, cuz? My name is Bam-Bam," the young man said extending his hand toward Pearl.

"What up, my nucca? I'm 'P', this my nucca Milk. What ya'll round here hitting fo'?"

"Shit dry round here, cuz. About a week ago, some mufuckas murdered a whole house full of people down the street. But make it so bad, the Spanish niggas they murdered was supplying the block," he revealed.

Pearl looked him up and down, then said," Oh yeah. Who they say did it, my nucca?

"They said it was the Puerto Rican's connect or something. Them mufuckas went through that bitch with AK's," he explained shaking his head in skepticism.

Flashing a gold toothed smile, Pearl reached into his 'Avirex' pocket and pulled out a piece of paper. Handing it to Bam-Bam, he said, "Give me a call, my nucca. I just might have something for you."

Cross walked around the cellblock in deep contemplation. He'd just come from a visit with his attorney, Mr.Cotler. From what he'd divulged to Cross, there was actually a good chance that the court would overturn his conviction. Nonetheless, Cross wasn't taking any chances. At that very moment, as he paced the floor, his mind was devising and revising a plan to free himself if any stages of his litigations began to look unpromising.

However the courts decided, didn't matter to Cross, he was walking out of prison regardless.

Melody entered the small room and quickly noticed the frail looking white man rise to his feet.

"Ms. Jordan, my name is Charles Sletzinger and I've been retained to represent you on these, um…matters shall we say," he said ruffling through some papers. Looking up to Melody he continued," You and Ms. Bonillia are in quite a bit of warm water. It seems as if the Drug Enforcement Administration has already presented these allegations to a grand jury. Now, from this point forward, I'm going to advise you not speak with anyone about this case. I am aware that agent…um," he paused to look down at his papers, then pressed onward," Mahoney talked with you. If you can recall, what exactly did you say to him?"

Taking only a brief second to think, Melody replied, "Nothing. Only that I wanted to use the phone to call my attorney."

As a broad smile appeared across the lawyer's face, he said, "Good, Ms. Jordan. Good."

Unbeknownst to Melody, Mr. Sletzinger had already filed a motion with the courts to relinquish any statements that his client had made and any evidence that was seized. However, his next client wouldn't be as easy to deal with.

Carmella had been calling her brother and her mother continuously to no avail. When the jailer called her name, she immediately thought that she was being released. She quickly jumped up and grabbed her belongings.

"There's no need for that, Ms. Bonillia, you're coming back," the female deputy remarked with a twinge of sarcasm.

This statement seemed to knock the color from Carmella's face. "But…. What…who is it?" She stammered in a confused state.

"Your lawyer," the jailer snapped.

Slowly exiting the cell, Carmella was led to the same room that Melody had just been removed from.

Carmella eyed the old man contemptuously as he extended his hand. "Ms. Bonillia, I'm Mr. Sletzinger. I've been retained to represent you, "he revealed.

"By who?!" Carmella snapped.

"Um, Mrs. Bonillia, that's something we should discuss later. Just know I have been retained on your behalf. Now if we may-."

"No! Who sent you? Did Pepe send you? Because if he did, tell him that he'd better get me outta here. NOW!"

Trying to hide his dismay, Mr. Sletzinger said, "Ms. Bonillia, please allow me to do my job. As for your brother, Pepe Bonillia, he was murdered yesterday in Virginia."

Carmella shook her head in disbelief, then whispered, "No, that can't be true. You must be mistaken."

"Ms. Bonillia, I'm sorry to have to reveal this to you under these circumstances, But yes, Pepe Bonillia, Manuel Villareal, and Antonio Martinez, were all murdered in Hampton Virginia yesterday," Mr. Sletzinger revealed in a somber tone.

In a voice that cracked with emotion, Carmella hysterically declared, "No! Please No!"

Mr. Sletzinger sat patiently while Carmella endured an array of emotions.

With a coldness in her voice, she violently barked, "It was Stink's fault, I know it! A Dios Mio! [Oh my God!]" Banging her fist against the table, she cried out, "No! Mi hermano Pepe! [My brother Pepe!]"

The scene had become too much for the attorney to handle. Standing, he muttered his condolences, then exited the room.

"So, oye Stink, you see what type of situation we are dealing with," José said, summing up the information that he'd received in the last 48 hours. Turning his attention to Miziyah, he added, "I'll let Miziyah explain to you what he has gathered."

With a devilish grin plastered on his face, Miziyah stated, "Before I began, Stink, do you know a Latrina Jamison?" He inquired casually.

In a perplexed state of mind, Stink eyed Miziyah in a grouchy manner.

Miziyah quickly picked up on Stink's change in demeanor, then added, "The reason I asked was because, from my investigations it seemed as if Latrina was the mother of your son, a Rahsaan A. Jamison," he explained.

"Nah, nah. I know Trina, but her son turned out not to be mine. But what's this got to do with anything?" Stink asked suspiciously.

"I was simply checking, because this punta [Spanish expletive], murdered Trina and dumped her body in a swamp. The fucking policia still haven't figured out what has happened," Miziyah concluded chuckling.

"So are you saying Pearl murdered her because of me?" Stink asked confused.

"Well, I'm not sure if it was because of you or not. But I do know that she lived with him." Digging through his pocket, extracting a tiny device in the shape of a cell phone, Miziyah continued, "Now, let's get to business. Oye Stink, this guy did attempt to murder you and ultimately killed your cousin. He was also one of two gunmen who entered the residencia at," pausing to eye the tiny electronic gadget, he concluded," 3704 Shell road, leaving behind the bodies of your bandilla [gang]."

Stink sat there allowing what had just been divulged to soak into his mind. The more he grasped the raw irony of the situation, the more his blood began to boil. Of course, he was upset about P.J., Pepe, Manny, and Chico and even Trina; yet none of that compared to the anger he felt about nearly being murdered himself. As he sat there seething in his anger, Miziyah interrupted his murderous thoughts.

"Oye Stink, I might add, you would've been proud of the job that your Padilla [gang] put on this Maricon [faggot], Pearls cousin," Once again looking down to the tiny device, Miziyah finished, "Bear." Smiling, he added," The scene was even more gruesome than some of my more maldad [evil] jobs. Nonetheless, I had to clean things for the amateur [AMAH-Che-ur]," he concluded cockily.

Stink looked to him and knew that he was truly a killer, which brought him to his next question." Why didn't you just murder him if you knew all this?"

Miziyah broke out into a fit of laughter, then said," My friend, I save that for you."

Bonni strolled from room to room in the spacious apartment. Eyeing the sprawling skyline just across the river filled Bonni with a sense of exhilaration. Although she still hadn't formally been to the 'Big Apple,' she was so close she could taste it.

"Mommy! Mommy! Tayvia won't stay out of my room," Rahsaanique whined. Turning toward her daughter, Bonni said, "Nique-Nique, none of these rooms is ours. We're just staying here until your father handles some business."

Rahsaanique looked to her mother confused, and asked, well how did all of my clothes get in the room if its not mine?"

Slightly startled by her daughter's remark, Bonni quickly remembered who they were dealing with. Allowing a smile to form on her face, she said, "Nique-Nique, I guess you're right about that. It must be your room."

Carmella lay curled up in a ball as a torrent of tears continuously ran from her eyes. She couldn't accept the fact that Pepe was gone. Her mind continued to replay their final interaction together. He seemed so happy living the life of a kingpin. Just the thought of her brother's smiling face caused her body to spasm with sobs.

Suddenly, the sound of the jailers keys could be heard opening the door. "Ms. Bonillia, you have a visitor."

"Go away, I don't want to see anybody!" Carmella yelled.

"It's your mother, Ms. Bonillia," the deputy stated, instantly garnering Carmella's attention.

Pearl leaned against his gleaming white S-class Mercedes Benz, as the music thumped from within the confines of the expensive automobile. In a short time, Pearl and Milk had flooded Shell road with their signature 'fishscale' cocaine. The fiends and Hustlers that ran back and forth from Bam-Bam's house had never experienced the potency of the drug that Pearl was offering.

"My nucca, we got these mufuckin squares out here going bananas," Milk stated smiling broadly.

"Yeah, my nucca, I'm feelin this spot out here. This shit like a whole new city compared to green ass 'Bad News'," Pearl added returning Milk's smile with a blinding gold-toothed one of his own. Instantly, his smile turned into a somber frown, once he added, "I just wish my big nucca, Bear, was here wit us, my nucca."

Just the mentioning of Bear cast a gloomy cloud over both men.

Turning to Milk, Pearl said, "Let's be out, my nucca." Then grabbed the door handle on his Benz instantly releasing the thunderous base from within.

As the black Suburban cut through the wintry night air, Stink eyed the bright lights from the numerous electronic devices that lined the dashboard of the SUV.

Turning toward Miziyah, behind the wheel of the SUV, Stink asked, "Hey yo, Miz. What is all this computer shit?"

Without taking his eyes from the highway, he explained," The 8 inch monitor is a P.C. equipped with internet access. There's also an electronic scanner."

Stink instantly thought of the small phone-like

apparatus that Miziyah produced while they were in Jose's spot." So, what was the little thing you had in the house, that looked like a phone," he inquired.

Going into his pocket, Miziyah pulled out the electronic device. "You talking about his?" He said handing the device to Stink.

Taking the phone-like object, Stink eyed the bright 'indigo' screen suspiciously. What is it?" he asked.

"It's a number of things. First of all, it's a phone. Secondly, it's internet capable. It's also a palm pilot that holds enough information to write a book," he explained.

Stink played with the device, until it abruptly rang in his hand. Quickly passing it to Miziyah, Stink laid back while Miziyah answered the phone. He still hadn't given the information that had been divulged to him that day, his proper contemplation. Stink was more affected by Carmella and Melody's situation than the death of Pepe, Chico and Manny.

An important rule in the drug game was never to become attached to your cohorts, and Stink obeyed that rule. Yet somehow he felt partly responsible for Melody and Carmella's plight.

Once Miziyah ended his call, he turned to Stink, and said, "Looks like one of your novias [girlfriends] is blaming you for her hermano's [brothers] demise.

Chapter Eighteen

Mr. Sletzinger replaced the receiver from just having a short conversation with agent Mahoney. He knew that he had to call Jose immediately and relay the information he'd just received.

Dialing the familiar number, Mr.Sletzinger laid back in a comfortable office recliner and listened to the phone ring.

"Hello," Jose answered.

"Como estas, Jose? [How are you Jose?]"

"Estoy bien, Frank," Jose replied, then added, "So what do I owe the pleasure of this call?"

Releasing a frustrating sigh, Sletzinger said, "Jose, we have somewhat of a problem down here. One of these young women have attempted to contact a DEA agent. Now I can -."

Cutting Sletzinger off, Jose blurted, "Frank, handle it immediatamenta! [Immediately]" Then abruptly slammed the phone down.

Mr. Sletzinger sat there in deep contemplation, then picked the phone up again and punched in a local number.

Stink grabbed the phone nestled between the seats in the SUV and dialed the number that Miziyah had just given him.

"Hello," Bonni answered sleepily.

"Wazup, baby? Did I wake you up?" Stink inquired

in a tender tone.

"Mmm-mm. I was just -."

"Girl stop lyin! You know you was sleep," Stink blurted in a joking manner. Bonni responded by chuckling.

"Its 5 o'clock in the morning, I know you're knocked out."

"Yeah, I was sleeping good in this big ole bed," she confessed, then added, "when are you coming to warm me up?"

Sighing heavily, Stink replied, "Baby it might be a few days before I make it back that way."

"What you mean, "back this way?" Bonni snapped.

Eyeing the highway sign that read, 'Newport News next 7 exits', Stink said, "Baby I'm going to handle some business, o.k." he stated with a sense of finality in his tone.

After a brief silence, Bonni said, "Alright baby, I understand. But please just be careful."

"I will, Ma, but while I'm away, I want you to take the kids out and have some fun."

"But, how?"

"Jose said something about the driver and maid from 'Casa Roho', or some shit are supposed to be there today," Stink explained.

"Oh! He's talking about Consuella and Miguel, or maybe Pedro, or…"

"Yeah, yeah, yeah. Consuello, Cumacho, Pedro, whatever. Just make sure ya'll have some fun, aight," Stink concluded.

"We will, baby. Oh! Rahsaan, I love you daddy," Bonni stated, then replaced the receiver without waiting on a response from him.

Stink held the phone in his hand, with a smile the size of Uranus plastered across his face.

Cross sat on the edge of the tiny bunk with his head

resting in the palms of his hands. He had become somewhat accustomed to being awakened in the middle of the night to be whisked off to unknown locations and court appearances. Unbeknownst to the jail staff, Cross had been aware of his court appearance for a few days. Had he wanted to plan some type of hoax, his lawyer had given him ample time to plan one.

"Scott! You read?" the C.O. asked appearing at Cross' cell door. Without a response, Cross stood and walked over to the cell's door.

Bonni was awakened by the bud chimes from the doorbell. She jumped up and wrapped her Kimono around her body, then made her way to the door. Peaking through the thin floor to ceiling window, Bonni's features broke into a broad smile once she noticed, Consuella, Pedro, and Miguel standing on the small porch.

Snatching the door open, Bonni threw her arms wide and released a joyous screetch at the familiar faces. "It's so good to see y'all!" She announced, hugging Consuella.

"It's nice to see you, too, Ms. Bonita," Miguel said in his deep baritone voice.

Bonni quickly invited them inside and led the way to the living room. Consuella and Pedro quickly exited to different parts of the house to begin their work, while Miguel sat opposite Bonni attempting to plan a day in New York City for her and the kids.

Bonni sat intently listening to Miguel ramble on about New York's featured attractions. Once he was finished, she excused herself to go and get dressed. Stink had instructed her and the kids to have a nice time, and that's what she planned to do.

Stink punched the familiar digits into the keypad and watched the wrought-iron gate slide its opening position. It seemed as if an eternity had passed since the last time he'd been home.

He hopped into the passenger seat of Miziyahs SUV and directed him to pull behind Melody's Mercedes. He wasn't sure, but it seemed as though the positioning of his Porsche had been rearranged since he'd last been there.

Shrugging it off, Stink hopped out of the SUV, closely followed by Miziyah. As they rounded the corner of the garage, toward the rear door, Fire and Ice were in full stride headed their way.

With the command to halt the dogs, lost somewhere between the night of his shooting and that very moment, Stink stood still. Miziyah, as if he was some modern day super being, hopped in front of Stink's frozen figure, in what appeared to be a Karate stance.

Stink looked on in awe as the dogs neared and the command to stop the vicious animals was lost in his consciousness. In his incredibly calm stance, Miziyah waited for the animals to attack.

Just as the dogs were in Miziyah grasp, Stink yelled, "Galla-Goolla!" Both animals skidded on their paws attempting to stop, then sat on their hind legs as if nothing happened.

To Stink's surprise, Miziyah exhaled slowly, stood to his regular standing position, then said, "Stink you saved your perros' [dog's] life."

Allowing a slight snicker to escape him, Stink instantly wished that he could take it back once he saw Miziyah slide the razor sharp stiletto back into its compartment along his leg.

Pearl rode through the streets of 'Bad News' in his newly purchased Benz coupe, feeling a sense of invincibility run through his veins. It had only been a few weeks since he and Milk had gotten things in Hampton rolling. In fact, things were going so well, he'd brought in a new member from Miami into their fold.

Blue wasn't family like Bear and Milk, but he was just as close to Pearl. Pearl would have brought Blue to Virginia years ago, had he not been somewhat fearful of his murderous demeanor. There was no way blue would have played the fourth man without imposing his demented rage on somebody. Nevertheless, Bear's abrupt demise led the way for the acquisition of Blue.

Blue's chiseled body and plum complexion was all one needed to see in order to understand why he was nicknamed blue. Yet it was his sadistic acts of murder that solidified the true meaning behind the name. The cold acts that he'd displayed in his fits of rage left even the coldest killers in awe.

Turning his attention toward Blue, whose dark 'Gucci' frames covered any trace of his squinty eyes, Pearl said, "So my nucca, you bout ready to show dees nucca's how a nucca from da 'swamps' get dat paper?"

Allowing a slow smile to spread across his face, revealing his shinning gold teeth, Blue replied cockily, "And you know 'dis, my nucca."

Pearl smiled at his man's fearlessness, then pulled his cellphone out and began dialing. Once the phone began to ring, Pearl returned his man's unwavering grit and spoke into the phone. "Yo! What up!"

Little did Pearl know, not only were they being followed closely, but every word he was about to say was being listened to as well.

'Ain't shit! What's up with you?'

" I just scooped Blue up from the airport and we cruising the hood."

"So my nucca finally made it, huh?"

"Yeah. But we about to go up to the crib, meet me

out there in about an hour. Cool?"

"Alright my nucca, I'll be there"

Stink looked astounded as the conversation played through an invisible speaker in the dash of Miziyah's SUV.

"They're on their way to this guy Pearl's casa in the Northern section of the city," Miziyah explained.

Instantly Stink remembered the information that Pepe and his crew had given him before he was shot. "Yeah, I do remember Pepe telling me something about Pearl living in Williamsburg," Stink revealed.

"Si, si, [yes, yes] Williamsburg is the name of the place, Miziyah agreed, then added, "I have been to the residence plenty of times. It is a beautiful estate, yet it lacks the proper security."

Looking to Miziyah dumbfounded, Stink asked, "So how do you propose we slump this nigga?"

Returning Stink's look with an inquisitive look of his own, Miziyah said, "Slump?"

"Yeah, slump! Murder! Kill," he quickly explained.

"Oh, OK. I understand. Well first of all, I think we should eliminate his comaradas [comrades], then we focus on dealing with him any way you like."

With an evil smirk forming on his face, Stink nodded his head in confirmation. The manner in which Miziyah had explained his plan was right up Stink's alley. However, in all actuality, Stink was nowhere near ready for Miziyahs atrocious style of slaughter. "There's one thing though, Miz, I want all of his money. I've got somebody to look out for," Stink concluded, thinking of the wife and two kids that were left without their caretaker when PJ was murdered.

"No problem."

Chapter Nineteen

Melody patiently sat at the defense table while Mr. Sletzinger ambled around the courtroom carefree. At that very moment, he was saying something to the court stenographer that caused light snickers to escape her mouth.

The entire court was being held up for Carmella's arrival. The Federal courtroom, located directly across the street from the jail, seemed to only be a short walk. However, the lengthy wait that they were enduring had begun to raise eyebrows.

Suddenly, a bailiff rushed into the courtroom and whispered something into the U.S. Attorney's ear, who relayed the information to Mr. Sletzinger.

Mr. Sletzinger's face instantly contorted into a look of dismay. Dropping his head for a few minutes, he made his way over to Melody.

Melody witnessed the entire scene through suspicious eyes. As the lawyer approached her, she braced herself for some atrocious news.

Mr. Sletzinger stood over Melody for a minute, then said, "Ms. Jordan, it seems to be some kind of mix-up. We're going to have to reschedule this hearing."

A court marshal instantly appeared behind Melody, urging her to a standing position. She quickly stood and allowed the cold steel to be wrapped around her wrist.

As the court marshal led her out of the courtroom, Mr. Sletzinger stopped her, and said, "Don't worry young lady. Just keep your mouth closed and I promise I'll have you out of here in a month."

Melody nodded her head in reply, yet the icy tone in which he stated it caused a chill to run up her spine. Taking one last look at her lawyer, he gave her a sneaky wink of the eye, along with a sly smile.

Stink and Miziyah kept a safe distance behind the 7 series BMW driven by Milk. Stink didn't have a clue as to how they were going to actually murder the man.

As if he was reading Stink's mind, Miziyah advised, "Get just a little closer."

Pressing the pedal on the big SUV, Stink glanced over to Miziyah, who was tinkering with a small 'bow' type of mechanism. As Stink steered the Suburban dangerously close to the BMW, Miziyah rolled the window down and aimed his machinery at the rear of the car.

In response to the soft 'thud' that Stink heard as the 'bow' released whatever it had fired, there was a blinding explosion seen coming from the BMW.

Suddenly the car began to weave across the interstate erratically, until it ended up spinning out of control on the shoulder of the interstate.

Miziyah quickly turned to Stink, and said, "Pull over behind him."

Stink pulled the SUV behind the smoking BMW. To his surprise, Milk was exiting the automobile.

Calmly, Miziyah turned to Stink, and said, "Stay here, I shouldn't be long." With a evil smirk on his face, he smoothly exited the truck and met Milk at the rear of his car.

Stink eyed the exchange between the two through disbelieving eyes. Miziyah was actually on the ground inspecting the damage to Milk's car. Once he stood, there was a brief exchange, then Milk kneeled to take a look at the damage. Unbeknownst to him, that would be his last movement as a living being.

Stink watched in awe as Miziyah extracted his stiletto and nearly severed Milks head from his shoulders in one quick motion. As the rush of blood sprayed from his crumpled body, Miziyah casually walked back to the truck and hopped in.

The female jailer struggled to open the door of Carmella's cell for the third time that morning. She had already attempted to open the door twice before. She was now trying the third set of keys.

Eyeing the figure through the small, battered, and scratched fiberglass window, the jailer jiggled the key until it turned. Pushing the door open, she looked down at the lock, inspecting it, then announced, "Ms. Bonilla! Get ready for court!"

Receiving no response, she looked up and noticed the hideous spectacle before her. It was at that moment that her hysterical screams erupted throughout the jail.

Carmella's purplish, swollen body was strung up by what looked like a shoe string around her neck. Her once beautiful face was now a grotesque sight for human eyes.

Rushing from the cell, the deputy held her hands over her mouth as vomit spewed onto the floor.

Bonni eyed the passing buildings of New York City, as Miguel navigated the Mercedes Benz through the streets. Even though New York was a very festive city, Bonni couldn't totally enjoy herself while constantly worrying about Stink. It had been 48 hours since he'd called. Nobody seemed to know where either he or Jose were located.

Bonni had even attempted to run game, just to get in contact with Jose, yet nothing worked.

As before, she and the kids were treated as if they were royalty. Bonni looked around the cabin of the Benz at all of the bags that they had accumulated from their day of shopping.

Allowing a long exasperated sigh to escape her, Bonni silently said a prayer for the man she planned to be with for the remainder of her life.

After choosing twelve people, and two alternatives who were supposedly responsible for his future, Cross was led to an awaiting van, handcuffed and shackled.

As he was being led out of the courtroom, Cross was mentally taking pictures of as many angles of the courthouse, on 100 Center Street, as his mind could store.

He had already made up his mind that if he was going to make any moves, it would have to be at the courthouse.

Once he was securely in the dark tinted van, he still scanned the perimeter for anything that would assist in his escape.

"See, this the shit I'm talking 'bout, my nucca!" Pearl stated slamming the phone down. Turning to Blue, he continued, "This nucca 'sposed to been here a fucking hour ago, my nucca! I bet anything 'dis nucca out there fucking one of them skank ass hoes!" He concluded, then picked the phone up and dialed Milk's number again.

After three rings, someone picked the phone up. Before they could speak, Pearl barked, "Nucca, you on that square shit! I told yo ass an hour! It's been 3-4 fucking hours! Where the fuck you at, nucca?"

After a brief silence, someone said, "Sir, I'm detective Barnes of the Newport News homicide squad! Apparently you were unaware that Mr. Milton Jeffries was found slain an hour ago. If you would give me your n-."

Pearl quietly hung the phone up stunned. he couldn't say a word, all he knew was that his lifelong partner was gone.

Turning to an attentive Blue, Pearl whispered, "Milk's dead, my nucca."

Stink and Miziyah had ditched Miziyah's Suburban for an off white utility van, equipped with all of the mechanics. There was even a hydraulic boom lift atop the van.

At that very moment, they were parked around the corner from Pearl's estate listening to every call he made from the residence or his cellular phone. Every so often, either Stink or Miziyah would exit the van dressed in their overalls and tinker with the telephone pole.

It had been nearly 24 hours since the brutal butchering of Milk had taken place, and Miziyah was already devising a perfect scheme to bring Pearl to his own demise.

Stink looked over to Miziyah who intently listened to one of Pearl's many phone calls that morning. Stink instinctively thought back to the act that played out before him that night.

The coolness that Miziyah demonstrated during such a violent attack was something that Stink had never endured. Miziyah's calmness was almost frightening. Stink knew that if Jose ever wanted him dead, there was absolutely nothing that would stop the man beside him from making that happen.

Tuning in a CB type of devise, Miziyah looked to Stink, and said, "Tonight, we go pay our friend a little visit." With a chilling smile etched into his feature, he gave Stink a conspiratorial wink.

Cross eased the small capsules that his sister had slid him into the cuffed sleeve of his jumpsuit. His mother sat there witnessing the exchange through disapproving eyes.

"Georgi, what are you going to do with that stuff?" Mrs. Scott asked in a troubled tone.

"Ma, don't worry about me. I got everything under control," Cross replied assuredly, then asked, "Have you heard from Stink yet?"

Shaking her head in disappointment, she said, "No. Not yet."

Cross didn't allow his frustration to show, instead he formed his face into a wide smile. "Yeah, my lil nigga probably handling his B.I.," he offered half heartedly. Deep down, the seeds of deceit had begun to take root.

Melody sat on the tiny bunk bed with her head buried in her hands. As the raw irony of her situation crashed into her reality, she felt that she was at her lowest point at that very moment.

The apparent suicide of Carmella didn't affect her one bit. It was Carmella who Melody had attributed all of the negativity that she had endured.

According to what her attorney, Mr. Sletzinger, had explained to her, Carmella's death was actually good news for her case. They were due in court in a week and Mr. Sletzinger had so much as promised her freedom.

Stink and Miziyah exited their vehicle around the corner from Pearl's estate, and began to trek their way through some shallow woods. They were each armed with high caliber firearm; however, Miziyah also carried an array of body mangling explosives in a duffel bag thrown over his shoulder.

Unbeknownst to Stink, the route that they were taking had been studied by Miziyah weeks before. After his investigations pointed to Pearl as the culprit of Stink's shooting, Miziyah instantly devised a scheme for his demise. Now it was time to enact those plans.

Stink followed close behind Miziyah as they approached a tall wooden gate at the wood's edge.

Turning to Stink, Miziyah placed his forefinger to his lips, then went into the bag he carried and pulled out a plastic bag containing what looked to be meat inside.

Extracting the meat from the bag, Miziyah tossed it over the tall fence, then listened intently. The sounds of trampling hoofs could be heard approaching the gate.

Miziyah instantly looked to his watch as if he was setting the timer. Once whatever specified time he'd prescribed ran out, he looked in Stink's eyes, and said, "Let's go."

Without warning, Miziyah threw his bag over the fence, causing a thud as it landed, then hopped the fence himself.

Stink hesitantly jumped onto the fence and peaked over. What he saw nearly caused a slight chuckle to escape his lips. There on the ground were four gigantic Rotweilers in different stages of what looked to be sleep.

Once Stink pulled himself over the fence, and readjusted the jumpsuit he wore, Miziyah tossed him a smirk. "Carnivores should never be relied on to protect," he stated, then began to make his way towards the house.

Pearl and Blue lounged around the large room with bottles of Hennessy glued in each of their hands. The death of Milk affected him even more than the death of his own cousin had.

"Blue, my nucca was like my brother, man," Pearl stated on the verge of tears." That nucca been through too much wit me, my nucca. Whoever killed my nucca gots to pay in a big way," he concluded as the tears of frustration began to flow freely from his eyes.

Blue laid back and analyzed the entire situation in his mind. The truth of the matter was that Milk's demise was actually his come up. Looking to his longtime friend, he said, "Don't even sweat that shit, my nucca. I'm-a handle these square nuccas."

Pearl looked to Blue as if he was seeing him for the first time. He was actually tired of avenging the deaths of his longtime friends. Wiping the tears from his eyes, he said, "My nucca, I'm 'bout ready to hang this ship up and just take my shit back down to 'tha bottom'."

This was music to Blue's ears, as he sat stone face, trying extremely hard not to crack a smile.

Continuing, Pearl said, "My nucca, I still got like 10 birds of soft. You can have that shit if you want, I'm bouncing," he concluded.

Pearl sat up attentively nodding his head affirmatively. All he could see was his new celebrity status being born in the foreign city. However, what Blue didn't know was that he'd never get a chance to enjoy an inkling of his new position in life, for death was lurking just outside the window.

Bonni laid in bed with her eyes shut tight. She was psychically attempting to send Stink a message. She desperately needed to talk to him, just to hear his voice and be reassured that he was alright.

Bonni had spent the last two days smiling broadly, perpetrating the happy spouse face. Yet, at night, the turmoil she endured was beginning to wear on her heavily.

Just as Bonni had opened her eyes from mentally calling Stink, the bedside phone rang. "Hello!" She blurted hastily.

"Como esta, Bonita?" Jose announced jovially.

"Uh….uh, hello Jose," Bonni replied somewhat shocked.

"How are you and the kids enjoying New York City?"

"Oh, well it's been fun, but I can't wait to get home."

"Bueno, bueno [Good, good]. Well you'll be happy to hear that 'Stinkito' should be back from his business trip tomorrow, then maybe you all could finish your vacation," Jose offered.

"I surely hope so. I have been so worried about him, that I – "

Cutting her off, Jose said, "Never worry mi nina [my child]. It only brings upon stress." He concluded in a fatherly fashion.

Bonni took a deep breath, then said, "Thank you, Jose."

"De nada [Your welcome]" Without saying anything further, Jose hung the phone up.

As Bonni continued to lay there, a small portion of the anxiety that she was previously feeling had been lifted. Yet, she couldn't help but wonder, had her message somehow miraculously reached Stink and been relayed through Jose. Allowing a smile to form on her precious features, she slowly drifted off to oblivion.

Stink and Miziyah eyed the two figures in the room downstairs, and the one in the upstairs bedroom. At that moment they didn't know whether the person upstairs was man, woman, or child. As far as they were concerned, everybody in the house had to die.

Miziyah leaned in close to the garage door and began to insert some type of thin key-like utensil, which easily unlocked the door. Turning the knob very slowly, Miziyah opened the door, then beckoned Stink to follow.

Once they were inside of the spacious garage, Stink eyed the luxurious automobiles present. There was a gleaming white S-class Mercedes sitting on twentys; a bright yellow Lincoln Navigator also on dubs; and a Mercedes SL.

While Stink had been appraising their victim's automobiles, Miziyah had maneuvered his way to the door leading into the house. There was only a small window on the door, partially covered by a decorative curtain. Miziyah peered through the window intently; until he'd seen what it was he wanted to see. Turning to Stink, he whispered, "There is a motion alarm on this door. Once the doors cracked, it makes a beeping sound. Now we can do one of two things. One, wait until someone come through that door, or two cut the power off inside the entire house."

Instantly, an evil smirk appeared on Stink's face, as his mind quickly narrowed the options down to the one, more to his liking.

Returning Stink's smile with one of his own, Miziyah said, "You're thinking like me: 'The lights.'"

Cross sat in his cell, mentally trying to prepare himself for the enormity of what he was once again facing. Although it had been years since he had actually been convicted of the double homicide, the first day of his trail had brought back a lot of memories.

One thing that had caught Cross off guard, was the warm smile that Mesha's mother greeted him with as he was being led into the courtroom. In his first trial, she seemed to be a bundle of hate, even going as far as to lie on the stand.

Cross quickly pushed the now aging mother of his one time girlfriend out of his mind. What ever her itinerary held was not his concern. His only concern was his freedom, by any means necessary.

Checking his sleeve for the tiny pills, Cross was just waiting for the opportune time.

Pearl was now stretched out on the couch, with the Hennessy bottle still nestled in his grip. He was filling Blue in on all the 'do's' and 'don'ts' of the drug trade in Virginia. He'd even cleared the table off to draw Blue a makeshift map of the city.

After Pearl had covered quantities, location, and even his views on drug etiquette, Blue felt like he was ready to roll that night. However, Pearl wasn't ready for his last and only friend to part.

Yelling for Mercedes to come down the stairs, Blue looked to Pearl suspiciously.

Once Mercedes made her way into the large den, wrapped in a Kimono that revealed her every curve, Pearl said, "Cedes, this my nucca, Blue. He's going to be handling shit around here from now on so....." his voice trailed off as he picked up on Mercedes' 'I could care less' attitude.

Quickly standing to his feet, Pearl covered the distance between himself and Mercedes in 'warp speed,' then gripped her around the throat. Speaking through clenched teeth, he hissed, "Bitch, this my muthafuckin nucca, and when I roll out, you gone be his bitch!"

Mercedes' eyes instantly showed fear. Pearl had done just about every degrading thing possible to her, and now he was throwing her to his friend.

Blue sat on the couch, eyeing the spectacle through lust filled eyes. The tighter Pearl's grip became on her neck, the higher her gown rose up her thighs. Blue could clearly see her pubic hairs peeking through the sides of her panties.

Once he'd seen enough to give him a raging hard on, he jumped to his feet and intervened. "Cool out, my nucca.

The lady understands. Don't you, baby?" Blue said turning his attention to a visibly horrified Mercedes. Looking back to a staggering drunk Pearl, he said, "As a matter of fact, my new lady getting ready to show me what you mean right now. Ain't you, baby?"

One look at Pearl, and Mercedes began to nod her head feverishly. Leading her by the hand, Blue exited the room, leaving Pearl alone, in his drunken stupor.

Stink and Miziyah eyed the scene as it played out before them. Miziyah was in the act of disconnecting the power, when Pearl began to yell. Once the girl came into view, the question of who was the other person in the house was immediately answered. However, once she was led away by Pearl's companion, the plan of cutting the power off was quickly ditched.

Turning to Stink, Miziyah said, "Did I mention plan C?"

Blue stood at the foot of the bed eyeing Mercedes deliciously curvaceous figure. Once she dropped the Kimono from her shoulders, revealing her athletically pert breast, Blue's manhood strained against the fabric of his jeans.

Quickly shedding his clothes, he climbed onto the bed between Mercedes' thighs.

Looking into his eyes nervously, Mercedes asked, "Do you ….um have a condom?"

As a slight smirk spread across his face, Blue said, "I 'ont need one. You my woman now." Reaching between her legs, he gently rubbed her lips. The tenderness that he displayed startled Mercedes, causing her to slightly spread her thighs further apart. His hands seemed to be magical as they caused short jolts of pleasure to shoot through her center.

Blue could feel her center become moist under his touch. Leaning in close, he popped her nipple in his mouth and began to work his tongue expertly. He instantly felt her began to gyrate her hips onto his expert finger.

Without warning, Mercedes reached for Blue's throbbing manhood. To her surprise his shaft was by far the biggest she'd ever encountered. Immediately, her heart began to pound in anticipation. She didn't know if she could handle the massive tool, but she was willing to try.

In the mist of all of the panting, neither of them paid attention to the loud beep, signaling one of the house's doors was being opened.

Deep in his alcohol induced coma, Pearl heard the motion sensor beep its customary one time, yet he was unable to open his eyes to see.

In what seemed like hours since his mind had registered any activity, there was the feel of something cold being pressed against his temple. Instinctively swatting at the object, Pearl was abruptly brought to reality by a crashing blow to his head.

"Argh!" Pearl yelled jumping to his feet.

Instantly, a second blow landed on the side of his head sending him reeling back into his slumber.

Once Stink and Miziyah had made their way into the house, they quickly split up. Stink moved stealth like up the winding staircase, while Miziyah made his way into the large den.

Once Stink ascended the stairs with his gun aimed high, he methodically checked every door, until he came upon a room where loud moans could be heard through the door.

Suddenly, a door at the end of the hall creaked open. Exuding the speed of a cheetah, Stink swiveled the barrel in the direction of the opening door.

Eyeing the tiny figure exiting the room, Stink lowered his aim, then placed his forefinger over his lips conspiratorially, urging the child not to scream.

The little boy backed into his room wide eyed and closed the door.

Turning his attention back toward the door, where the moans had become even louder, he took a deep breath and turned the knob.

Soon as the light from the hallway entered the dark bedroom, the male between the brown skinned girl's thighs, began to say, "Come on, my nucca! I know you gon – "

"Whack!" The blow sounded off against his skull, knocking him out cold.

Stink pointed the gun at the girl, and said, "Move real slow, "then directed her closer to him. "Who's he?"

"I don't know. Pearl made me have sex with him. Please don't kill me! Please!"

"Is that little boy down the hall your son?"

Shaking her head vigorously, she said, "No. But since I've been here I take care of him."

Stink pointed the mountain of clothes on the floor, then said, "Put some clothes on."

Standing there patiently while she pulled a nightgown tightly around her body, Stink noticed the figure on the bed stir. Quickly grabbing a belt from the rumpled pile of clothes, he wrapped it around the girl's wrist securing her.

"Sir, please don't kill me. I swear I don't want to be here. Please! Pearl made me, please!"

Ignoring the woman's pleas, Stink walked over to the naked man and pointed his gun at his head and fired two shots into his skull. As silence engulfed the room, Stink led the girl out of the door, but not before hearing the sounds of the dead man's final bowel movement.

Just as Miziyah had secured Pearl in the chair, bound and gagged, he heard two shots fired upstairs. He wanted to climb the stairs to make sure that Stink was alright, but quickly thought against it. Nonetheless, once Stink rounded the corner behind the girl, he breathed a sigh of relief."

Turning toward the girl, Miziyah said, "You must be the stripper, Mercedes?"

Nodding her head as tears flowed from her eyes, Mercedes eyed Pearl's bound figure with extreme contempt.

"Come on, Miz, put me on to how you know this broad?" Stink asked with a smug look on his face.

"I do my homework, Stink. I always do my homework."

Stink smiled sarcastically, than shifted his attention to Pearl. "So is our friend ready to talk or what?"

Smiling devilishly, Miziyah went over to Pearl, pulled the cloth from his mouth, and said, "Lets see."

"Bitch! You set me up! "Pearl yelled at Mercedes accusingly.

Before she could launch a reply, Miziyah said, "No, she didn't set you up. You set yourself up. Now we can handle this situation one of two ways. The first –"

"Fuck you, Motherfucker! I ain't making no deals!" Pearl spat, cutting Miziyah off in mid-sentence.

Allowing a mischievous grin to spread across his face, Miziyah tossed Stink a look giving him the green light.

Slowly, Stink made his way over to Pearl and kneeled in front of him, so they were eye to eye. "You remember me?" He asked inquisitively.

Pearl allowed his gaze to settle on Stink's features. As recognition began to set in, a befuddled look appeared on Pearl's face as he realized what was taking place.

Stink instantly picked up on the change in Pearl's features. "Yeah nigga, it's me," he revealed, then added, "You killed my cousin, nigga, but you getting ready to die a death ten times worse," he concluded, then rose to his feet and threw his head in Miziyah's direction.

One cue, Miziyah pulled the razor sharp stiletto out, and methodically made his way over to Pearl.

"A Stink, man! Come on, my nucca! We can work something out, man! I'm out, my nucca! Please, man!" Pearl begged as Miziyah slowly made his way toward him with a demented smirk on his face.

Stink bent on his heels to face Pearl, then asked, "Something like what, Pearl?"

"Look, my nucca, I'm out the game. I got some bird put up and a nice piece of money."

"Like how much money?"

"Two hundred and fifty grand," Pearl divulged.

Stink giggled at his response, then waved his hand at Pearl dismissively.

Miziyah quickly stepped over to Pearl and smoothly placed the stiletto against the side of his head. Without warning, he sliced Pearls entire ear off in one quick motion.

Once Pearl saw his own ear fall to the floor, he yelled frantically, "My ear! My ear! please man you cut my ear off!"

Stink eyed Miziyah barbaric act through disbelieving eyes, then offered, "You'd better tell me where all the money is, or my friend's gonna have a ball cutting the rest of your um.....extremities off."

Blood was freely flowing from Pearl's head as he tried to pull himself together.

"You'd better get to talking if you're planning to save that ear," Stink added with a tinge of sarcasm.

"Up....upstairs....in the ... master ...suite," Pearl said through sobs. Inwardly smiling, Stink said, "Now, I'm-a go check this out. If I think that you're holding back in any way..." Stink swung his hand through the air as if it was a knife, then turned to leave.

"17-31-17!" Pearl yelled at Stink's back.

It only took Stink a few minutes to find the huge safe nestled in the closet. However, once he opened it, his eyes nearly popped out of his head. There were stacks and stacks of money inside the safe. As he did a quick calculation of the many ten thousand dollar stacks, he guessed it to be anywhere near ten million. For what he was trying to do, it would be more than enough.

Dumping the clothes from two duffle bags on the floor, Stink began to load the bags with the money.

After filling the bags with the stacks, and stuffing the rest into his pockets, Stink made his way down the hallway to the room that he'd seen the kid emerge from earlier.

Pushing the door open, Stink didn't see anything in the room designed in a boy's décor. As he stepped inside the room, eyeing every corner intently, a movement at the foot of the bed caught his attention.

Stink moved in closer and grabbed the tiny foot. One he pulled the little boy from under the bed, the fear that registered on his face immediately softened Stink." Don't be scared, nobody's gonna hurt you," he stated attempting to calm the boy.

"I want my, mommy. Please!" The little boy cried.

"Where's your mommy at?"

"I ...don't know."

"What's your mommy's name?"

"Trina ... Latrina Jamison."

Stink dropped his head. He was aware that Pearl had murdered Trina; however, he wasn't aware that he'd kept her son in the wake of her death.

Stink immediately became furious, placing his hand on the little boys shoulder, he said, "Don't worry, Rah-Rah, you gonna be alright...I promise."

The little boy's features instantly showed shock at Stink mentioning his name.

"I promise," Stink repeated in a reassuring tone, then stood and exited the room.

Once Stink made his way down the stairs with the heavy duffle bags, spewing stacks of money thrown over his shoulder, he walked straight up to a visibly grimacing Pearl, and said, "Man, it looks like we might have a little problem."

Pearl looked up to him dreadfully, then said, "My nucca, please! I gave you all the money, I swear!"

"Where's the coke at?"

"In the garage, my nucca. In the trunk of the white Benz," he explained in agony.

Stink walked over to Mercedes and loosend the belt from her wrist.   Eyeing Miziyah for any signs of disapproval, he turned back to Mercedes after not receiving any.

"Here. Get in that car and drive the fuck off, and don't look back," he said, handing her two of the stacks from his pockets.

Mercedes scurried to her feet and headed out of the room. Before she was out of earshot, he added, "Don't forget you got at least 10 kilos in the trunk. Oh, and if you ever say anything to anybody about tonight, I promise that you and everything you love will be murdered." Raising his glock 40 in Pearl's direction, he said, "See you in hell, 'my nucca', Pop! Pop! Pop! Pop! Pop! Pop!" once the final slug entered into Pearl's floundering body, Stink and Miziyah cleaned up and quietly exited the estate as they'd come.

Chapter Twenty

Cross sat through the numerous testimonies, detailing how he murdered two supposedly innocent people. At one point he wanted to actually break out laughing when Kamesha's mother detailed how she witnessed him verbally threatening her daughter's life the night before her murder.

Cross specifically remembered putting on a show of love as he and Stink exited the apartment. Just the thought of Stink cast a saddened expression on Cross' face. It had been nearly three months and he hadn't heard a thing from his friend.

From the looks of things, the trial wasn't looking too promising for him. That was why Cross had already made the choice to put his plan into affect, once the state called its final witness.

Cross eyed the jury with an indifferent demeanor, and allowed his boyish grin to speak for itself. In his own language, Cross was saying 'With or without you Muthafuckers, I'm free.'

"Baby, it's getting so bad here. I just don't know what to say, "Bonni's mother explained.

"Ma, you just be careful. I should be home soon," Bonni said.

"Chile, you take yo' time. I'm alright here. Sides, deem folks is killin each other bout dem drugs," her mother offered.

"Yeah, I know, Ma, but soon as Rahsaan comes back, we're coming home."

"Baby, I'm so happy you and Ray-shawn got y'alls act together. Now I just hope y'all keep it together.

"We will, Ma.   We will," Bonni surmised in an earnest tone.

"I hope so, baby.   Cause 'dese niggas is killin now-a-days."

Melody calmly sat at the defense table, while Mr. Sletzinger went through an array of motions in an attempt to get the drug trafficking offense that she was being charged with thrown out of court.

"Your honor, sir, if you would check the record, you will see that the owner of the car in which the drugs were found has committed suicide.   That in itself should reflect her guilt."

Quickly standing to his feet, the U.S. Attorney said, "Your honor, what Mr. Sletzinger has said is true, however, Ms. Jordan was the driver of this vehicle, and according to the arresting officer, she is the one who acted strange, prompting him to search in the first place."

"Your honor, this is insane.   The owner of his vehicle has committed suicide, and here the government is still trying to prosecute a 'ghost case.'   I'd like to petition to the court for a dismissal of all charges, beside that of...," looking down to his pad, Mr. Sletzinger concluded, "Sixty-nine, in a fifty-five."

The judge looked over to the U.S. Attorney, then removed his glasses and rubbed his eyes restlessly.   "If the government cannot come up with any more evidence than the defendant was driving the car in question, I will be forced to dismiss the complaint," the judge advised.

As a defeated sigh escaped the U.S. Attorney, he rose to his feet and said," the government moves to dismiss!"

Once Stink fluttered his eyes open, Miziyah was navigating the SUV through the Holland tunnel into lower

Manhattan. Stink quickly replayed the last 24 hours in his head.

Not only had they succeeded in eliminating Pearl, they'd also turned over half of the money they'd taken from Pearl to PJ's children's mother, Sharon.

Turning around, Stink eyed the tiny figure balled up on the back seat. It was ironic that years ago, that was the same life he tried so desperately to denounce. Yet, nearly eight years later, he had gladly taken the responsibility on.

"Are you alright?" Miziyah asked stealing a quick glance at Stink.

"Yeah. I'm good," Stink replied readjusting the setting on his seat. Laying his head against the soft leather seat, he glanced out the window at the bustling morning New York commuters.

As Miziyah pulled up to a stop light, Stink peered at the caption on the front page of the newspaper on a corner stand. Looking closer, the bold print seemed to draw Stink in. *'Seven year murder of two goes to deliberation for the second time.'* As he eyed the newspaper intently, Miziyah pulled from the light. "Hold up, Miz! Pull over!" Stink yelled.

Miziyah jammed the brakes abruptly. "What's the problem, oye?" he asked looking to Stink quizzically.

"I need to get a newspaper real quick," he said hopping from the truck. Once Stink had approached the Newspaper stand and read the caption in it's entirety, his eyes nearly popped out of his head. Snatching one of the paper, he tossed the stand owner a bill that caused a wide smile to cover his face, and an array of colorful greetings to come from his mouth.

Stink then hopped back into the truck with his eyes glued to the newspaper. He could not believe what he was reading was true.

'Today, a jury will begin deliberations in a seven year old murder. George Scott was convicted in 1994 without much fanfare. However, after retaining the highly respected, and sought after attorney, Bruce Cotler the tables may be about to turn…'

Once Stink finished reading the article, he turned to Miziyah, and said, "116th and 7th, quick!"

Cross sat in the small holding cell of the courthouse, contemplating exactly when he should enact his plan. Even with Mr. Cotler promising him a mistrial if the jury found him guilty, Cross had long ago made up his mind.

Digging into the sleeve of his jumpsuit, he pulled out the two tiny capsules his sister had given him weeks before. He popped both of them into his mouth, but failed to swallow. He then hopped on the floor and began to do push-ups. His body was already accustomed to doing high repetitions of the exercise, yet that wasn't his goal today. As his heart rate began to rise rapidly, he continued to pump, while watching for anybody passing the small cell.

Once his heart rate became abnormally high and sweat popped off of his head, he turned on his back and allowed a stream of crimson colored saliva to run from his mouth. The tiny pills that he'd smuggled from his sister, would now assist in obtaining his ultimate goal. Freedom.

Stink pumped his legs furiously up the four flights of stairs. Once he ascended the stairs, he quickly made his way to Cross' mother's door. After excessively ringing the doorbell, the door was abruptly snatched opened by a modestly dressed woman who closely resembled Cross.

As she looked Stink up and down in obvious contempt, a familiar voice broke the tense silence. "My goodness, it's Stink!" Cross' mother yelled, then added,

"Come on in, baby! We were just getting ready to go down to the courthouse."

"Mrs. Scott, I um.. "Stink began, then trailed off after noticing the evil glare she cast in his direction." I mean, Ma. I'm sorry for not calling or getting in touch. It's just been so much going on. I got -."

"Shot," she said cutting him off." I know all about it. I'm just glad you're alright," she stated in an earnest tone, then turned to the woman who answered the door." This is my daughter, Josetta. Josetta, this is Stink," Mrs. Scott introduced.

Josetta's features softened at the mentioning of his name. "So, I finally get to meet the infamous, Stink. My brother seems to think the world of you. Every time he calls, you're the first name out of his mouth," she stated sarcastically.

Stink smiled at her quip, then turned his attention back to Cross' mother. "So what does that trail look like? Does it look like he can beat it?" he inquired.

"I don't know, baby, but he gave me an envelope to give to you once the trial was over. And I guess it's just about over," she stated somberly, then walked off to retrieve the letter.

The deputies rushed into the tiny holding cell, appalled at the scene that laid before them.

There on the floor, Cross' body jerked convulsively as a stream of blood ran from his nose and mouth.

Instantly, there was absolute pandemonium as the officers scrambled to contact E.M.T. staff.

As one deputy, who was also trained in the medical field, leaned over Cross' body to take his pulse, he looked back with a gloomy expression covering his face, and said, "He's alive, but it doesn't look good. His pulse is racing as if he's going into cardiac arrest."

This in turn only caused more panic stricken faces to appear. A few of the court reporters and clerks even appeared, then assembled off to the side holding a small vigil.

Unbeknownst to any of them, Cross' plan was going accordingly.

Stink read the short letter through disbelieving eyes. He read its words over and over trying to make some sort of sense of the letter.

'Lil bro, if you're reading this, I'm either dead or somewhere chilling on a foreign island sippin' on Pina Coladas. Whatever the case, hold ya head and hold my love even stronger.

One Love,

Cross!

Looking over his shoulder, where Cross' mother and sister looked on inquiringly, Stink said, "I gotta get to the courthouse.

Stink hopped in Miziyah's SUV and quickly filled him in on what he felt was going on, therefore encouraging him to get to the courthouse as fast as possible.

As Miziyah quizzed Stink on the situation, he pushed the big SUV through the streets of NYC like a bat out of hell.

Stink braced himself as they flew through crowded intersections as if they were the police. Taking a look back at Rah-Rah, Stink was surprised to see that the boy was sitting up with a big smile plastered across his face.

it didn't take Miziyah long to get to the Westside highway, which would in turn take them downtown where the courthouse was located.

All Stink could do was sit back and hope his man hadn't done anything crazy yet. If he could get to him before he had, then stink knew he could talk him out of doing anything. However, if he couldn't reach him, Stink knew Cross would surely attempt to escape his captors.

Once they arrived at the courthouse, there were emergency vehicles blocking every point of entrance.

Stink turned to Miziyah, and said, "Stay here. I'm going to see what's up." He quickly jumped from the SUV and made his way through the crowd to the entrance. Just as he was entering the courthouse, emergency medical technicians, police, and even courtroom officials all surrounded a gurney being ushered out of the courtroom.

Standing to one side, Stink eyed the spectacle closely as they passed, but was unable to get a view of the injured person.

Once they were down the courthouse steps, Stink rushed into the courthouse, and approached the information desk.

"Uh, yes maam, I'm looking for the courtroom containing the trial for George Scott?" Stink asked breathlessly.

The woman behind the desk put her forefinger to her temple as if she was in deep contemplation, then said, "Scott? I think that's the person that was just rushed out of here, if I'm not mistaken."

Stink stood there willing the woman to be precise. Finally, the woman looked up to Stink, and said, "Yeah, I'm sure. Scott was the defendant that was just rushed out of here."

Stink quickly turned on his heels and rushed from the courthouse.

Cross calmly lay on the gurney, as the medical technicians frantically worked on him. Through tiny slits, he noticed that there were three E.M.T. employees and an armed officer in the rear of the ambulance. He could also hear a much different sounding siren than the one from the ambulance he was in. Making it clear that there was also an NYPD following closely.

The leg restraints that were tightly clasped around his ankles made it nearly impossible to maneuver. However, his hands were free, besides the intravenous needles that were inserted into his wrist.

Cross still knew he had one thing on his side, the element of surprise.

Stink exited the courthouse in search of Miziyah's SUV. After scanning the area where he'd last seen it, and still unable to locate it, Stink rushed over to a line of yellow cabs.

Hopping into the cab, Stink blurted, "Take me to the hospital!"

The driver of the cab turned and look at a visibly irate Stink, then asked, "Which host-peatal do you want, sir?"

Stink struggled to understand the cabbies foreign accent, then said, "the closet one!" And threw a fresh 'Benjamin' in the money tray.

Cross observed everyone's position in the ambulance, then abruptly opened his eyes wide. To his surprise, nobody present had their eyes on him. Quickly, he bolted up to a sitting position and landed a crashing blow to the head of the officer, sending him sprawling to the floor.

Moving cat-like, Cross jumped on him and relieved him of his weapon.

"Please! Please don't shoot! Please!" the officer pleaded as tears began to cascade down his cheeks.

"Shut the fuck up before I give yo' bitch ass something to cry for!" Cross spat taunting the officer.

The three E.M.T. employees looked on in shock as Cross relieved the officer of his gun, then pulled the large ring of keys from his hip.

Turning toward the employees, Cross asked, "How do you open the door?" Each of the three looked to the other for a response, causing Cross to remark, "Don't you all speak at the same time now."

"Um... it can only...um, be opened from the outside," One of them finally said.

Thinking quickly, Cross asked, "So how do y'all talk to them?"

Slowly, one of the E.M.T. workers pointed to a two-way type CB apparatus on the wall.

Pointing the gun at the worker who hadn't said a thing, Cross said, "Looks like it's your turn. Grab that C.B. and tell these muthafuckas to stop and open the door. I don't care what you tell them, just make sure they stop this muthafuka and pop that door," he concluded in a chilling tone.

Hesitantly the worker made her way to the C.B. and picked it up.

Stink stared through the window of the cab in disbelief. The traffic jam reached as far as the eyes could see. At that very moment he felt totally helpless.

Not only did he not know where the hospital was located, he wasn't even sure if Cross would be taken to that hospital.

In a fit of frustration, Stink slammed his fist against the Plexiglas, and yelled, "Where the fuck is the hospital, Muthafucka!"

"Please! No get violent, sir. The host-peatal is seven or eight blocks away."

Stink jumped out of the cab and began to walk in the direction the cab driver had pointed.

Cross stood braced against the inside of the ambulance. He could see the E.M.T. drivers as they were in the act of opening the door.

Soon as the doors swung open, Cross sprung from the rear of the ambulance. To his surprise, the NYPD had the entire scene blocked off.

Instantly, bullets began to fly near Cross' head.

Ducking behind a parked car, Cross' heartbeat seemed to be coming out of his chest.

Suddenly, a bullhorn blared to life, "Come out with your hands up! If you don't surrender immediately we will move in with full force!"

Cross knew it was useless to fire his weapon, which only held six rounds, so he looked around for an escape. The police had cleared the block completely, which ruled out the hostage route.

Cross dropped his head in frustration; the situation he now found himself in wasn't part of his plan.

As if on que, all of the officers in attendance began to simultaneously fire their weapons.

Cross crouched behind the car as bullets mangled the vehicle. Closing his eyes to say a quick prayer, he darted off towards another parked car.

The closer Stink got to the hospital, the more law enforcement he noticed were present.

Once he reached a certain point, there was a police barricade, detouring all pedestrians.

Curiously, Stink asked one of the police officers, "What's happening up there? I've gotta get back to work."

The officer looked at Stink blankly, then said, "Some crazy fool has just broke out of jail and he's got a gun. You still wanna get to work?" he asked sarcastically.

If Stink's expression had been correctly read by the officer, he wouldn't have been sharing the hearty laugh with his partner. Looking to his left, Stink noticed a NYPD detective walk straight through the barricade, with just a wallet on a chain, around his neck. Instantly, Stink had a bright idea, but not before hearing a barrage of gun shots that sent the crowd into an uproar.

Cross crouched behind the second car, as police snipers fired aimlessly at the vehicle. Up until that point, Cross hadn't been hit by a bullet, however, the glass and medal from the car was cutting into him fiercely.

Suddenly the gunshots stopped and the bullhorn blared to life once again, "Mr. Scott! This is your last and final warning to drop your weapon and come out with your hands up!"

Inside, Cross wanted badly to laugh at their assumptions. He hadn't fired a shot at them, yet they were insisting that he drop his gun. He was also aware that the moment he stood, the entire NYPD would use his body for target practice.

Caught between a rock and a hard place, literally, Cross racked his brain for some type of plan that would assist in his getaway.

One the gunshots rang out, Stink was able to slip past the barricade without resorting to impersonating a police officer. As he slowly made his way up the block toward the action, Stink's heart raced frantically.

Just as he approached a group of NYPD police officers huddled in deep conference, a second wave of gun fire erupted.

Initially, Stink made a quick move for shelter, until he noticed none of the officers made a move. He knew then that all of the gun fire were those of the police.

As Stink continued to trek forward, a sense of dread suddenly overcame him. He witnessed a massive number of police officers kneeling behind their cruiser's doors with their guns cocked and aimed. From the looks of things, it was going to be impossible for Cross to get out of the situation. 'If it is Cross?' Stink thought to himself.

As if the officers were reading his mind, a bullhorn blared to life, "Mr. Scott! This is your last and final warning to drop your weapon and come out with your hands up!"

This immediately caused Stink to drop is head in defeat. His question had been answered it was Cross on the opposite end of the police officer's guns.

Chapter Twenty-One

Miziyah calmly sat behind the wheel of the SUV and watched Stink go into the courthouse. Once Stink had disappeared inside of the courthouse, emergency medical personal and police exited, ushering a patient on a gurney.

Miziyah eyed the scene intently, until he got a clear view of the person being loaded into the ambulance. Instantly, his skills in warfare kicked in as he furiously punched up the location for the nearest hospital into the truck's computerized navigation system.

Once the information was displayed on the tiny screen, Miziyah had already maneuvered the SUV in front of the convoy. There was no way that he would be thwarted from what he was trained to do.

Stink stood off to the side as NYPD's SWAT team made their way through the crowd.   Their costumes instantly caused fear to arise in the average civilian.

Stink eyed the robotic looking officers with contempt. If there was absolutely anything he could do at that moment, he would surely have attempted. Nonetheless, he knew he was faced with a no-win situation.

Looking on helplessly, Stink could only stand there and witness his friend get murdered.

Looking into the rearview mirror, Miziyah noticed the ambulance coming to a stop. Pulling over less than a block ahead, he sat there patiently until he was absolutely sure that this was the spot that the showdown would be held.

Tapping a few buttons on the dashboard, all of the monitors switched to a colorful game. Turning to the young boy in the backseat, with a bright smile on his face, he said, "You want to play a game?"

Rah-Rah nodded his head and returned the smile.

"You play the game while I go to get you a soda. OK?" Miziyah waited for the boy's animated smile to be become engulfed in the game that played on the monitor in the headrest, then smoothly slid from the truck.

Cross looked around like a caged animal for an escape. He was totally surrounded by the NYPD. He knew it was only a matter of time before snipers moved in and plucked him off like a sitting duck. However he went out, suicide was not an option for him. He still had six bullets in the revolver that he clutched in his hand. If he was going out, then six police officers were going with him.

In a matter of seconds, Cross' focus had shifted from escaping unscathed, to a kamikaze.

Slowly rising to a kneeling position, Cross leveled the .38 across the hood of the bullet riddled car and squeezed off one well placed shot that caught everyone off guard. However, once the shot was heard an unsuspecting officer's head exploded like a blood filled pumpkin.

This act alone caused every officer present to unload their weapons.

Cross felt slugs tear into his right shoulder, knocking the gun from his grip. Grimacing in deep pain, he reached out and retrieved the gun as his shoulder burned incessantly.

Stink looked on in awe as the police officer's head exploded into mid air. Ducking for cover, he inwardly praised Cross' protagonistic act. However, the number of shots they fired in his direction made Stink wonder whether his partner was still alive.

Suddenly the bullhorn screeched, "Mr. Scott, you are completely surrounded. SWAT has you in their crosshairs as we speak! Put your gun down immediately and come out!"

"Fuck you Motherfuckas! I ain't going back!" Cross retorted from behind the parked car.

Stink instantly felt a sense of pride at his man's act of bravery.

Miziyah removed the manhole top then casually climbed into the sewer as if he was a city worker. From his calculations all he would have travel was a couple of blocks until he was right in the middle of Cross' crusade.

After traveling the short distance, Miziyah climbed a short ladder ascending from the murky conditions. Inconspicuously sliding the manhole top from its position, he peeked out. Judging his location from the action, Miziyah slid the sewer top back into its original position and trekked on.

Just as he was about to open the next manhole top, there was one gunshot followed by a succession of others.

Calmly waiting for the gunshots to cease, Miziyah checked the detonator on his bomb.

Once the shots stopped, he eased the sewer top off as he'd done before. To his surprise, he'd popped up right behind a visibly distraught Cross. 'This will even be easier than I thought,' he surmised.

Cross jerked his head in the direction of the blurring figure behind him. In a fraction of a second the dark figure had subdued him. The gun that he'd possessed was now laying in the gutter. With his back pinned against the concrete, Cross witnessed his entire life replay through the evil eyes of his attacker.

Unable to mount a defense, Cross allowed his body to relax and for the angel of death to take him away.

Once he closed his eyes, there was no reason to attempt to reopen them, for he was dead.

Stink stood tentatively amongst the other onlookers as the SWAT team methodically enclosed on the automobile that Cross was hiding behind.

The closer they got, the more intense Stink's heart rate became. He just knew his man was going out in a 'blaze of glory' and there was absolutely nothing he could do. There was something he could do, but it wouldn't change the outcome of the current situation. Instead of the one body bag that would be needed for Cross, another would be needed for his own bullet riddled body.

Just as the heavily armored SWAT converged on the parked car, they began to look back toward the ranking police officers confused.

One of the tactical members pulled his helmet up, and yelled, "He's not Her-."

Before he could finish his statement a deafening blast exploded, sending bodies flying in all directions.

The force from the blast sent Stink and the rest of the dangerously close onlookers reeling.

After struggling to pull himself together, Stink stood up and eyed the seen through disbelieving eyes. The car that Cross once used as a shield was now a burning shell. The SWAT team that had approached the car were scattered into chunks of human flesh.

Eyeing the scene as if he was memorializing it, Stink turned and slowly staggered away from the chaotic scene.

EPILOGUE

Stink gunned the engine in the 360 Modena Ferrari as he made his way down George Washington Avenue. Looking into his rearview, he noticed the 911 Porsche Carrera Turbo tailing close behind.

Allowing a wicked grin to cover his face, Stink down shifted the powerful car, then braced himself as it darted in and out of traffic on the busy street.

It wasn't until he was entering Boca Chica did the black Porsche reappear. Smiling to himself, he pulled into the driveway of the luxurious estate and hopped out.

Shortly thereafter, the deep roar of the Porsche could be heard pulling up. Stink approached the car with a victorious grin on his face. "You could never drive better than me," he announced in an egotistical manner.

"Oh yeah. What makes you so sure of that, B?" Cross asked in a mocking tone.

Stink threw his arms up, as if to say 'DUHH,' then burst out in a hearty laugh. AS he and Cross made their way into the house, Stink could tell that everybody was out near the beach.

Going straight through the wide glass patio doors, he and Cross walked – out onto the beach located at the rear of the house.

The first person to notice them was Rahsaanique as she yelled, "Daddy! Uncle Cross!" and then bolted through the white sand into Stink's arms.

As the three of them made their way further toward the water, Stink saw Bonni and Tayvia lounging in their beach chairs dressed in their Baby Phat swimwear soaking up rays. With their dark tinted Gucci frames covering their eyes, they each mumbled their greetings, then returned to their diva mode.

Looking around for the final member of their bunch, Stink asked, "Where's Rah-Rah?"

Rahsaanique quickly pointed out to the beautiful blue waters of the Carribean sea.

Stink squinted his eyes against the blinding sun, and instantly saw him deep in the ocean, jumping waves on the high powered jet ski that Miziyah had given him.

Allowing a short sigh to escape him Stink turned to Cross who was dumping the contents of a Cuban Cigar onto the beach and refilling it with marijuana. "You trying to get some get-back on that earlier race?"

"No question, nigga. Just let me spark this up first."

Shooting Cross an incredulous look, Stink replied, "What! You can't smoke and drive at the same time?" Grinning, he chuckled as he strolled off enjoying his sarcastic humor...

The End

Find out what happens in part 3. Coming in March 2012.

Sample Chapters

From Hoodfellas

By
Richard Jeanty

Chapter 1

The Natural Course

"Mr. Brown, we're not really here to negotiate with you. It's more like a demand, or whatever you wanna call it," said Crazy D.

"What makes you think I'm gonna do what you're telling me to do?" Mr. Brown asked. "Yo, Short Dawg, bring her out," Crazy D ordered.

Short Dawg appeared from behind Mr. Brown's storage area with a knife to Mr. Brown's wife's neck while her left hand is covered in blood. "She still has nine good fingers left, but next time we won't be cutting off fingers, oh no, we ain't interested in the same body part twice. Next time it might be one of her eyeballs hanging out the socket," Crazy D said as he signaled for Short Dawg to bring the knife to Mrs. Brown's eyes. "Tell me what you want and I'll do it, just don't hurt her," said Mr. Brown. "We've been watching you for a while now and my guesstimation is that you make about fifty to a hundred thousand dollars a month. Forty percent of that is ours and we're gonna collect it on every first of the month," he said. "How we supposed to survive? The shop doesn't even make that kind of money," Mr. Brown pleaded. "Do you need motivation to make that kind of money?" Crazy D asked as he raised his hand to Short Dawg, ordering him to start taking out one of Mrs. Brown's eyes. Before he could stick the knife in, Mr. Brown chimed in and said, "Okay, I'll do it. I'll give you forty percent of what we make." Crazy D smiled and said, "No, you'll give me forty percent of a hundred thousand dollars every month. He ordered Short Dawg to drop the knife with a swift movement of his head.

As Crazy D and Short Dawg were making their way out of the shop, Mr. Brown reached for his shotgun. However, before he could cock it back, Crazy D had his .45 Lugar in his face saying, "It's your choice, old man, you can die a hero or you can become a zero." Mr. Brown wisely placed his shotgun down, and then apologized to Crazy D. What Crazy D did to the Browns was routine since he came out of the State Pen. Crazy D walked out of jail wearing some donated clothes that were twenty years out of style and fit a little too snug around his six foot-plus frame. The difference this time was the tightness of the fit. He had gained a considerable amount of weight in muscle. The shirt was tight around his arms and his pants barely made it past his thighs. He was ridiculed as he rode the bus back to his old neighborhood. The kids were pointing at him, adults shook their heads at him and women just laughed at him. Crazy D was fed up with the treatment he received his first day out of jail. He looked like a buff homo. With no money and no skills to get a job, Crazy D had no choice but to turn back to a life of crime. After serving a twenty-year sentence for robbery and second-degree murder, the system failed him miserably, but even worse, they failed the rest of society by letting a loose canon out of jail without the proper rehabilitation.

While in jail, Crazy D's mom only visited him the first few months. She soon fell victim to the crack epidemic and ultimately had to turn her back on her son at his request. There came a time when she could hardly remember that she had a son. While constantly under the influence of crack cocaine, his mother did her own stint in prison for prostitution and other petty crimes only to get out and start using again.

Crazy D went to jail at the young age of seventeen and it was there that he learned his survival tactics. Wreaking havoc on people before they got to him was what he learned when he was in prison. The attempted rape on him the first week after he arrived at the Walpole facility in Massachusetts brought his awareness to a level he never knew existed. He was lucky that one of the toughest inmates in that prison was a friend of his father's. Word had gotten out that Crazy D was being shipped to Walpole and his father's best friend made a promise to his mother to look after him. Crazy D's dad, Deon Sr., and Mean T were best friends before his dad got killed, and Mean T was sent to prison for thirty years after a botched armed robbery against a store owner.

Chapter 2

Mean T and Sticky Fingers

Mean T and Sticky Fingers aka Deon Campbell Sr. were best friends throughout their entire lives. They were more like vagrants from the time their mother decided to allow them to walk to school by themselves. In fact, the very first day that they walked to school without any supervision, they decided to make a detour to the corner store. Mean T was the lookout while Sticky Fingers robbed the store of candy, potato chips, juices and other valuables that matter to kids. It was a little distance from Evans Street to Morton Street in Dorchester, Massachusetts, but their parents trusted that they would walk directly to school everyday. The Taylor Elementary School was where most of the kids who lived on the Dorchester side of Morton Street went to school. Stealing became a fun habit for the duo and every morning they found themselves down the block at the corner store stealing more items than their pockets could afford. Mean T was the bigger of the two, but Sticky Fingers was the conniving thief. He could steal the bible from a preacher, and Mean T would knock the daylights out of a pregnant woman.

Over the years, the duo broaden their horizons from stealing candy to stealing sneakers and clothes out of a store called 42nd Street located in Mattapan Square. By then, they were in high school being promoted because of their age and not the work that they did. The two were dumb as a doorknob, but one was an expert thief and the other an enforcer. The two friends were the best young hustlers from their block. The Korean owner of the store was forced to install cameras because Sticky Fingers and Mean T kept robbing the store and there was never any proof to prosecute them. Usually, the cops didn't respond on time and by then the two had made it home safely with their stolen goods. The shop owner was growing tired of this and decided to arm himself in order to keep from getting robbed.

Mean T and Sticky Fingers wore the freshest gear to school. Everything was brand name because they stole the best of everything from the different stores downtown Boston. Their favorite stores were Filene's, Jordan Marsh, Filene's Basement and of course, 42nd Street in Mattapan Square. On top of that, the two of them sold some of the stolen merchandise to some of the kids at the high school when they needed money. Their bad habit became an enterprise. The two thieves outfitted their bedrooms with stolen goods from stores all over the Boston area. They had enough merchandise to supply a whole high school of kids with clothes, shoes and other clothing items such as socks, t-shirts, underwear and long johns needed for at least a month. However, Mean T and Sticky Fingers would run into some difficulty when they decided to rob the 42nd Street store once more. The Korean owner had had enough and he felt he needed to protect his livelihood, so he bought a gun.

By this time, Mean T and Sticky Fingers were pretty known to the entire Korean family who worked as a unit in the store. While Sticky Fingers walked around and stuffed his bag with stolen items, so he could dash out of the store using the same tactics they had used in the past with Mean T knocking out the father who stood guard at the entrance, the father looked on. However, on this day, they would meet their fate. As Sticky Fingers rushed towards the exit, all he felt was a hot bullet piercing through his heart. Mean T didn't even have time to react as the small Korean man raised his gun and stuck it in Mean T's mouth. Pandemonium rang out in the store as everyone tried to make it to the exit. Meanwhile, Sticky Finger's lifeless body lay on the ground with his hands clutched around a duffle bag filled with stolen items. The cops arrived in no time. Someone's life had to be taken in order for the cops to respond in a timely manner.

Mr. Chang, as the community later found out the store owner's name, had to defend himself against the whole community. No one came to his defense when he was being robbed blindly, but everyone was angry because another young black life had been taken. Sticky Finger's mom came out shedding tears as if she didn't know what her son was doing in the street. A search of the victim's home revealed about fifty thousand dollars worth of stolen items from different stores, including Mr. Chang's 42nd Street. Sticky Finger's mom had to have known that her son was hawking stolen merchandise because the officers could barely take a step into his room without stepping over stolen clothes while serving the search warrant. The whole place was cluttered with clothes scattered all over the room.

To top off an already insane situation, the cops found a loaded gun on Mean T after searching him at the scene. Mean T aka Tony Gonsalves, an American born Cape Verde heritage young man was handcuffed and taken to jail where he faced aggravated robbery, illegal possession of a handgun, first degree armed robbery and a list of other charges concocted by the district attorney to ensure his proper place away from society for the next thirty years. It didn't help that Tony and Deon weren't in good standing at school. No teachers, counselor or principal would vouch for them as good people. The media smeared their names even further and there was no way that Tony was going to walk even though his friend was killed.

A few months after Deon's murder, the media revealed that he had left behind a pregnant woman with an unborn child. That child would be named Deon after his father. Mean T would receive a thirty-year sentence, the maximum allowed under

Massachusetts law. He was transferred from the correctional facility in Concord to the facility in Walpole after his sentence. As a young man, Mean T didn't really understand the extent of his sentence, so he chose to act in a machismo way and accepted his fate. On the van ride from Concord to Walpole, while shackled to other hardcore criminals, reality started to set in for Mean T and he understood clearly that his life had taken a drastic turn for the worst and he had better start thinking about his survival tactics. Mean T rose to prominence very quickly at the prison as he engaged some of the tougher inmates in fights and defeated quite a few of them while earning their respect.

Mean T was tested the very day he was headed to Walpole to start his sentence. One repeated offender wanted to impress all the impressionable first timers in the van, and he made the unthinkable mistake of picking on Meant T.

"You're gonna be my bitch when we touch down," he said to Mean T with a tempted grin. The whole van was laughing except Meant T. He was sitting in the row in front of Mean T and had to turn his neck around to talk to him. Before he could turn around to say something else, Mean T threw his handcuffed hands around his neck and choked him until he passed out. Words had gotten around about the incident and Mean T was given his props for almost killing a man who was known as Nutty Harold in prison. Nutty Harold was released on a technicality and he unfortunately had a confrontation with Mean T on his way back to prison after killing a man six months out of prison.

It was almost eighteen years later, a few months short of his eighteenth birthday, when Crazy D aka Deon Campbell Jr. would walk into the prison in Walpole to meet the guardian angel known to him as Abdul Mustafa Muhammad. Mean T had converted to Islam while serving his sentence. He had gotten into many fights after arriving at the prison, including one that involved sending a prison guard to the emergency room, which earned him an additional ten years to his sentence. Mean T was casually walking to his cell after code red was called. This one particular guard, who hated him for garnering the respect of his fellow inmates, felt Mean T was not walking fast enough. He used his stick to rush Mean T back to his cell thinking that the other two guards behind him provided a safe haven from an asswhip. Mean T was much too quick and strong for the guard as he found his neck wrapped inside Mean T's massive biceps. The two guards stood back as Mean T threatened to choke the life out of the guard who unjustly pushed and hit him with the stick. The white guard started turning pink and his eyes bulging out of their sockets as he fainted from the chokehold feeling that life itself was about to end. The other two guards could only watch in horror before stepping in to provide some relief for the guard using their night stick. He became a lifer. Abdul, formerly known as Tony Gonsalves also formerly known as Mean T on the streets, was a highly respected man in prison. As a lifer, he had earned the reputation of a tough, intelligent and manipulating leader. He protected those close to him and destroyed those who went against him.

Serosa becomes the subject to information that could financially ruin and possibly destroy the lives and careers of many prominent people involved in the government if this data is exposed. As this intricate plot thickens, speculations start mounting and a whirlwind of death, deceit, and betrayal finds its way into the ranks of a once impenetrable core of the government. Will Serosa fall victim to the genetic structure that indirectly binds her to her parents causing her to realize there s NO WAY OUT!

In Stores!!!

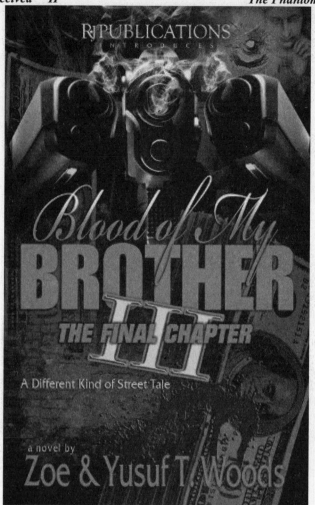

Retiring is no longer an option for Roc, who is now forced to restudy Philly's vicious streets through blood filled eyes. He realizes that his brother's killer is none other than his mentor, Mr. Holmes. With this knowledge, the strategic game of chess that began with the pushing of a pawn in the Blood of My Brother series, symbolizes one of love, loyalty, blood, mayhem, and death. In the end, the streets of Philadelphia will never be the same...

In Storess!!!

After Chasin' Satisfaction, Julius finds that satisfaction is not all that it's cracked up to be. It left nothing but death in its aftermath. Now living the glamorous life in Miami while putting the finishing touches on his hybrid condo hotel, he realizes with newfound success he's now become the hunted. Julian's success is threatened as someone from his past vows revenge on him.

In Stores!!!

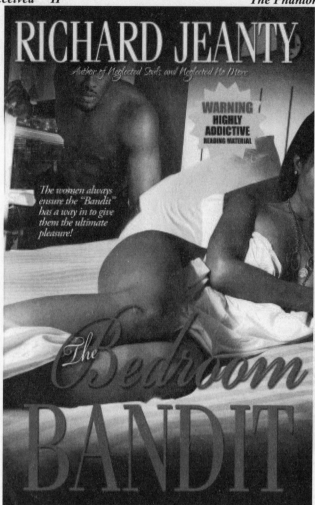

It may not be Histeria Lane, but these desperate housewives are fed up with their neglecting husbands. Their sexual needs take precedence over the millions of dollars their husbands bring home every year to keep them happy in their affluent neighborhood. While their husbands claim to be hard at work, these wives are doing a little work of their own with the bedroom bandit. Is the bandit swift enough to evade these angry husbands?

In Stores!!

NEGLECTED SOULS

Motherhood and the trials of loving too hard and not enough frame this story...The realism of these characters will bring tears to your spirit as you discover the hero in the villain you never saw coming...

In Stores!!!

Jimmy and Nina continue to feel a void in their lives because they
haven't a clue about their genealogical make-up. Jimmy falls victims to
a life threatening illness and only the right organ donor can save his life.
Will the donor be the bridge to reconnect Jimmy and Nina to their
biological family? Will Nina be the strength for her brother in his time
of need? Will they ever find out what really happened to their mother?

In Stores!!!

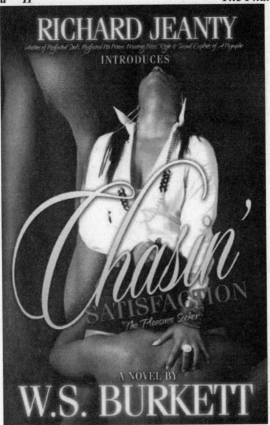

Betrayal, lust, lies, murder, deception, sex and tainted love frame this story... Julian Stevens lacks the ambition and freak ability that Miko looks for in a man, but she married him despite his flaws to spite an ex-boyfriend. When Miko least expects it, the old boyfriend shows up and ready to sweep her off her feet again. She wants to have her cake and eat it too. While Miko's doing her own thing, Julian is determined to become everything Miko ever wanted in a man and more, but will he go to extreme lengths to prove he's worthy of Miko's love? Julian Stevens soon finds out that he's capable of being more than he could ever imagine as he embarks on a journey that will change his life forever.

In Stores!!!

The police in New York and other major cities around the country are increasingly victimizing black men. The violence has escalated to deadly force, most of the time without justification. In this controversial book, noted author Richard Jeanty, tackles the problem of police brutality and the unfair treatment of Black men at the hands of police in New York City and the rest of the country.

In Stores!!!

Just when Darren thinks his relationship with Tina is flourishing, there
is yet another hurdle on the road hindering their bliss. Tina saw a
therapist for months to deal with her sexual addiction, but now Darren is
wondering if she was ever treated completely. Darren has not been
taking care of home and Tina's frustrated and agrees to a break-up with
Darren. Will Darren lose Tina for good? Will Tina ever realize that
Darren is the best man for her?

In Stores!!

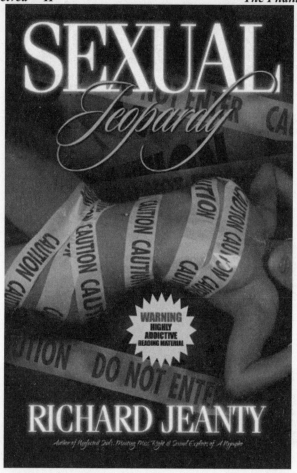

Ronald Murphy was a player all his life until he and his best friend,
Myles, met the women of their dreams during a brief vacation in South
Beach, Florida. Sexual Jeopardy is story of trust, betrayal, forgiveness,
friendship and hope.

In Stores!!!

Tina develops an insatiable sexual appetite very early in life. She only loves her boyfriend, Darren, but he's too far away in college to satisfy her sexual needs.

Tina decides to get buck wild away in college

Will her sexual trysts jeopardize the lives of the men in her life?

In Stores!!!

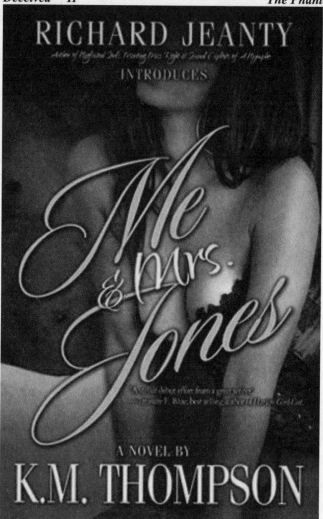

Faith Jones, a woman in her mid-thirties, has given up on ever finding love again until she met her son's best friend, Darius. Faith Jones is walking a thin line of betrayal against her son for the love of Darius. Will Faith allow her emotions to outweigh her common sense?

In Stores!!!

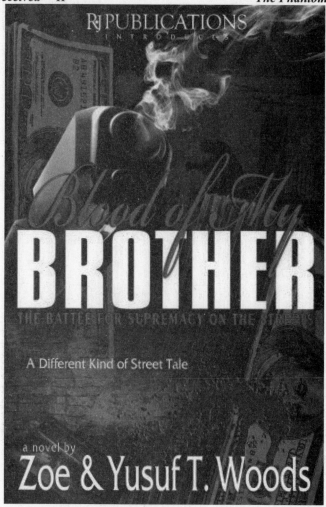

Roc was the man on the streets of Philadelphia, until his younger brother decided it was time to become his own man by wreaking havoc on Roc's crew without any regards for the blood relation they share. Drug, murder, mayhem and the pursuit of happiness can lead to deadly consequences. This story can only be told by a person who has lived it.

In Stores!!!

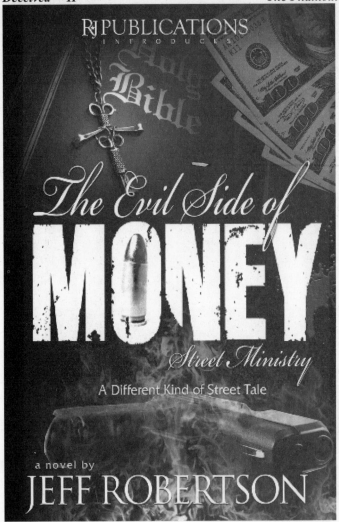

Violence, Intimidation and carnage are the order as Nathan and his brother set out to build the most powerful drug empires in Chicago. However, when God comes knocking, Nathan's conscience starts to surface. Will his haunted criminal past get the best of him?

In Stores!!

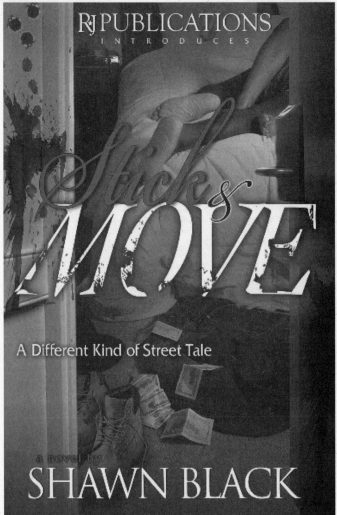

RJ PUBLICATIONS
INTRODUCES

Stick & MOVE

A Different Kind of Street Tale

a novel by
SHAWN BLACK

Yasmina witnessed the brutal murder of her parents at a young age at the hand of a drug dealer. This event stained her mind and upbringing as a result. Will Yamina's life come full circle with her past? Find out as Yasmina's crew, The Platinum Chicks, set out to make a name for themselves on the street.

In stores!!

RICHARD JEANTY

Author of Neglected Souls, Meeting Mrs. Right & Sexual Exploits of A Nympho

INTRODUCES

Too Many
SECRETS
& Too Many Lies

WARNING
HIGHLY
ADDICTIVE
READING MATERIAL

A NOVEL BY

SONYA SPARKS

Ashland's mother, Bianca, fights hard to suppress the truth from her daughter because she doesn't want her to marry Jordan, the grandson of an ex-lover she loathes. Ashland soon finds out how cruel and vengeful her mother can be, but what price will Bianca pay for redemption?

In stores!!

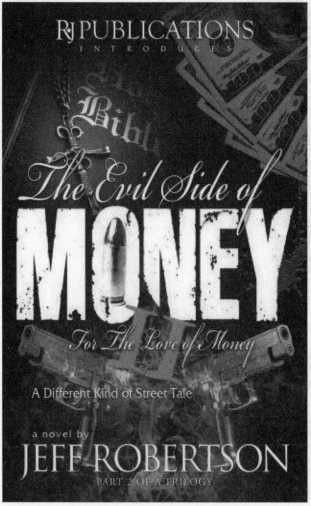

A beautigul woman from Bolivia threatens the existence of the drug empire that Nate and G have built. While Nate is head over heels for her, G can see right through her. As she brings on more conflict between the crew, G sets out to show Nate exactly who she is before she brings about their demise.

In Stores!!!

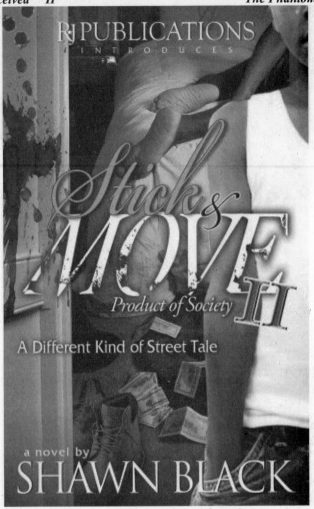

RJ PUBLICATIONS
INTRODUCES

Stick &
MOVE
II

Product of Society

A Different Kind of Street Tale

a novel by
SHAWN BLACK

Scorcher and Yasmina's low key lifestyle was interrupted when they were taken down by the Feds, but their daughter, Serosa, was left to be raised by the foster care system. Will Serosa become a product of her environment or will she rise above it all? Her bloodline is undeniable, but will she be able to control it?

In Stores!!

An ex-drug dealer finds himself in a bind after he's caught by the Feds. He has to decide which is more important, his family or his loyalty to the game. As he fights hard to make a decision, those who helped him to the top fear the worse from him. Will he get the chance to tell the govt. whole story, or will someone get to him before he becomes a snitch?

In Stores!!!

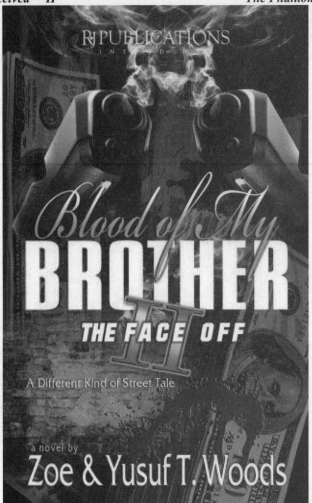

What will Roc do when he finds out the true identity of Solo? Will the blood shed come from his own brother Lil Mac? Will Roc and Solo take their beef to an explosive height on the street? Find out as Zoe and Yusuf bring the second installment to their hot street joint, Blood of My Brother.

In Stores!!!

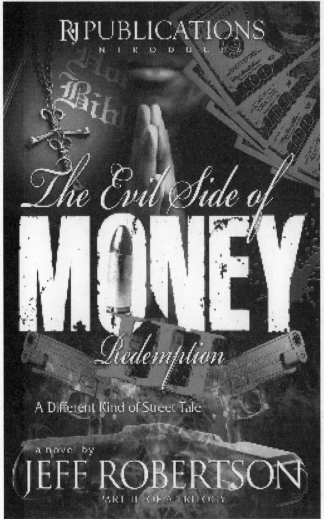

Forced to abandon the drug world for good, Nathan and G
attempt to change their lives and move forward, but will
their past come back to haunt them? This final installment
will leave you speechless.

In Stores!!!

Nafiys Muhammad managed to beat the charges in court and was found innocent as a result. However, his criminal involvement is far from over. While Jerry Class Classon is feeling safe in the witness protection program, his family continues to endure even more pain. There will be many revelations as betrayal, sex scandal, corruption, and murder shape this story. No one will be left unscathed and everyone will pay the price for his/her involvement. Get ready for a rough ride as we revisit the Black Top Crew.

In Stores!!

Dave Richardson is enjoying success as his second book became a New York Times best-seller. He left the life of The Bedroom behind to settle with his family, but an obsessed fan has not had enough of Dave and she will go to great length to get a piece of him. How far will a woman go to get a man that doesn't belong to her?

In Stores!!!

Deon is at the mercy of a ruthless gang that kidnapped him. In a foreign land where he knows nothing about the culture, he has to use his survival instincts and his wit to outsmart his captors. Will the Hoodfellas show up in time to rescue Deon, or will Crazy D take over once again and fight an all out war by himself?

In Stores!!!

The drama continues as Deshun is hunted by Angela who still feels that ex-girlfriend Kayla is still trying to win his heart, though he brutally raped her. Angela will kill anyone who gets in her way, but is DeShun worth all the aggravation?

In Stores!!!

Buck Johnson was forced to make the best out of worst situation. He has witnessed the most cruel events in his life and it is those events who the man that he has become. Was the Johnson family ignorant souls through no fault of their own?

In Stores!!!

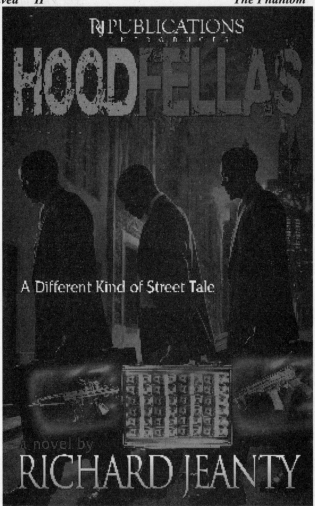

When an Ex-con finds himself destitute and in dire need of the basic necessities after he's released from prison, he turns to what he knows best, crime, but at what cost? Extortion, murder and mayhem drives him back to the top, but will he stay there?

In Stores !!!

What happens when someone falls insanely in love? Stalking is just the beginning.

In Stores!!!

Pharaoh decides that his fate would not be settled in court by twelve jurors. His fate would be decided in blood, as he sets out to kill Tez, and those who snitched on him. Pharaoh s definition of Going All Out is either death or freedom. Prison is not an option. Will Pharoah impose his will on those snitches?

In Stores 10/30/2011

RJ PUBLICATIONS
INTRODUCES

KWAME
AN AMERICAN HERO

A Different Kind of Street Tale

a novel by

RICHARD JEANTY

Kwame never thought he would come home to find his mother and sister strung out on drugs after his second tour of duty in Iraq. The Gulf war made him tougher, more tenacious, and most of all, turned him to a Navy Seal. Now a veteran, Kwame wanted to come back home to lead a normal life. However, Dirty cops and politicians alike refuse to clean the streets of Newark, New Jersey because the drug industry is big business that keeps their pockets fat. Kwame is determined to rid his neighborhood of all the bad elements, including the dirty cops, dirty politicians and the drug dealers. Will his one-man army be enough for the job?

In Stores December 15, 2011

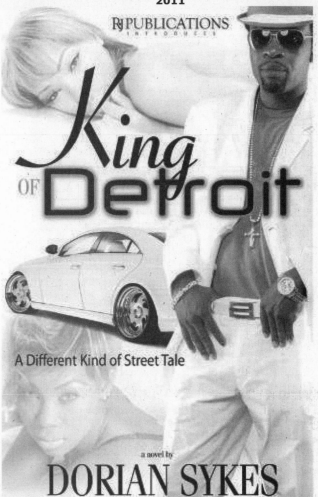

The blood-thirsty streets of Detroit have never seen a King like Corey Coach Townsend. The Legacy of Corey Coach Townsend, the Real King of Detroit, will live on forever. Coach was crowned King after avenging his father s murder, and after going to war with his best friend over the top spot. He always keeps his friends close. Coach s reign as king will forever be stained in the streets of Detroit, as the best who had ever done it, but how will he rise to the top? This is a story of betrayal, revenge and honor. There can only be one king!

In Stores February 15, 2012

PUBLICATIONS
BRINGING EXCITEMENT, FUN AND JOY TO READING

Use this coupon to order by mail

1. Neglected Souls, Richard Jeanty $14.95 Available
2. Neglected No More, Richard Jeanty $14.95 Available
3. Ignorant Souls, Richard Jeanty $15.00, Available
4. Sexual Exploits of Nympho, Richard Jeanty $14.95 Available
5. Meeting Ms. Right's Whip Appeal, Richard Jeanty $14.95 Available
6. Me and Mrs. Jones, K.M Thompson $14.95 Available
7. Chasin' Satisfaction, W.S Burkett $14.95 Available
8. Extreme Circumstances, Cereka Cook $14.95 Available
9. The Most Dangerous Gang In America, R. Jeanty $15.00 Available
10. Sexual Exploits of a Nympho II, Richard Jeanty $15.00 Available
11. Sexual Jeopardy, Richard Jeanty $14.95 Available
12. Too Many Secrets, Too Many Lies, Sonya Sparks $15.00 Available
13. Stick And Move, Shawn Black $15.00 Available
14. Evil Side Of Money, Jeff Robertson $15.00 Available
15. Evil Side Of Money II, Jeff Robertson $15.00 Available
16. Evil Side Of Money III, Jeff Robertson $15.00 Available
17. Flippin' The Game, Alethea and M. Ramzee, $15.00 Available
18. Flippin' The Game II, Alethea and M. Ramzee, $15.00 Available
19. Cater To Her, W.S Burkett $15.00 Available
20. Blood of My Brother I, Zoe & Yusuf Woods $15.00 Available
21. Blood of my Brother II, Zoe & Ysuf Woods $15.00 Available
22. Hoodfellas, Richard Jeanty $15.00 available
23. Hoodfellas II, Richard Jeanty, $15.00 03/30/2010
24. The Bedroom Bandit, Richard Jeanty $15.00 Available
25. Mr. Erotica, Richard Jeanty, $15.00, Sept 2010
26. Stick N Move II, Shawn Black $15.00 Available
27. Stick N Move III, Shawn Black $15.00 Available
28. Miami Noire, W.S. Burkett $15.00 Available
29. Insanely In Love, Cereka Cook $15.00 Available
30. Blood of My Brother III, Zoe & Yusuf Woods Available
31. Mr. Erotica
32. My Partner's Wife
33. Deceived I
34. Deceived II
35. Going All Out I
36. Going All Out II 10/30/2011
37. Kwame 12/15/2011
38. King of Detroit 2/15/2012

Name_____

Address_____

City_____State_____Zip Code_____

Please send the novels that I have circled above.

Shipping and Handling: Free

Total Number of Books_____Total Amount Due_____

Buy 3 books and get 1 free. Send institution check or money order (no cash or CODs) to: RJ Publication: PO Box 300771, Jamaica, NY 11434

For info. call 718-471-2926, or www.rjpublications.com allow 2-3 weeks for delivery.